Lloyd John Ogilvie

AUTOBIOGRAPHY
OF
GOD

GL
Regal
Books

A Division of G/L Publications
Glendale, California, U.S.A.

The foreign language publishing of all Regal books is under the direction of GLINT. GLINT provides financial and technical help for the adaptation, translation and publishing of books in more than 85 languages for millions of people worldwide.

For more information write: GLINT, 110 W. Broadway, Glendale, CA 91204.

Scripture quotations, unless otherwise indicated, are from the *New American Standard Bible*. © The Lockman Foundation 1960, 1962, 1963, 1968, 1971. Used by permission. Other versions quoted are:
RSV Revised Standard Version of the Bible, copyrighted 1946 and 1952 by the Division of Christian Education of the NCCC, U.S.A., and used by permission.
TLB From *The Living Bible*, Copyright © 1971 by Tyndale House Publishers, Wheaton, Illinois. Used by permission.
Phillips The New Testament in Modern English, Revised Edition, J.B. Phillips, Translator. © J.B. Phillips 1958, 1960, 1972. Used by permission of Macmillan Publishing Co., Inc.
KJV Authorized King James Version

Third Printing, 1979

Published by Regal Books Division, G/L Publications
Glendale, California 91209
Printed in U.S.A.

Library of Congress Catalog Card No. 78-53355
Hardcover edition: ISBN 0-8307-0683-6

51 081 01

To Richard Sholl

Son by my daughter's choice;
Friend by my choice;
Fellow disciple by the Lord's choice.

Contents

Preface 6

1. **The Prodigal God** 9
   Luke 15:11-24: Parable of Extravagant Love

2. **The Far Country at Home** 21
   Luke 15:25-32: Parable of the Elder Brother

3. **God Knows and Cares About You!** 27
   Luke 15:1-10: Parables of the Lost Sheep and Lost Coin

4. **The Tenant Who Owns the House** 40
   Matthew 12:22-47: Parable of the Empty House

5. **The Hearing Heart** 51
   Matthew 13:1-23: Parable of the Soils

6. **How to Live Without Anxiety** 66
   Mark 4:26-29: Parable of the Growth of the Seed

7. **The Most Dangerous People in the Church** 76
   Matthew 13:24-30,36-42:
   Parable of the Wheat and Tares

8. **Before You Give Up!** 88
   Matthew 13:31,32: Parable of the Mustard Seed

9. **God Can Change Your Personality!** 95
   Matthew 13:33-35: Parable of the Leaven

10. **The Treasure Is You!** 107
    Matthew 13:44-46:
    Parables of the Treasure and the Pearls

11. **The Virtue of Viability** 117
    Luke 5:17-39: Parables of the New Patch and New Wine

12. **Knowing What You Want and
    Wanting What You Know** 127
    Luke 7:31-35: Parable of the Children at Play

13. **While at the Banquet, Come to the Banquet!** 138
    Luke 14:1-24: Parable of the Great Feast

14. **The God of the Successful** 147
    Luke 12:13-21: Parable of the Rich Fool

15. **Christians with a Tang** 156
    Luke 14:25-35: Parable of the Uncompleted Tower
16. **Beyond Duty to Delight** 166
    Luke 17:1-10: Parable of the Unworthy Servants
17. **God Wants to Give You a Gift** 178
    Luke 11:1-13; 18:1-8: Parables of Importunity
18. **The Prayer God Won't Answer** 190
    Luke 18:9-14: Parable of the Pharisee and the Publican
19. **Shrewd Saints** 199
    Luke 16:1-17: Parable of the Unjust Steward
20. **How to Be a Lover** 209
    Luke 7:40-49: Parable of the Two Debtors
21. **The One Thing God Won't Do** 220
    Matthew 18:21-35: Parable of the Unmerciful Servant
22. **Spontaneous Love** 230
    Luke 10:25-39: Parable of the Good Samaritan
23. **The One Test of a Great Church** 242
    Luke 13:1-9; Mark 11:12-14,19-22:
    Parable of the Fig Tree
24. **How to Know the Will of God** 252
    Matthew 21:28-32: Parable of the Two Sons
25. **Unmerited Favor** 264
    Matthew 20:1-16:
    Parable of the Laborers in the Vineyard
26. **God's Love Knows No Limits** 273
    Matthew 21:33-41: Parable of the Cruel Vinedresser
27. **Ready, Aye, Ready!** 281
    Matthew 25:1-13:
    Parable of the Wise and Foolish Bridesmaids
28. **The Secret Source of Joy** 294
    Matthew 25:14-30: Parable of the Talents
29. **A Voice from the Dead** 308
    Luke 16:19-31: Parable of the Rich Man and Lazarus

Preface

The past two years have been the most exciting period of my life in my adventure with Jesus Christ. I should not be surprised. During this time I have been studying the parables of Jesus. The first year I utilized the parables for my own devotional reading. Each one challenged my thinking and reoriented my living. Every day was maximized because I had returned to the essential teaching of the Master as a basis of my quiet time. It was a year of unprecedented challenge and opportunity in my personal life and professional responsibilities. The Lord led the way daily through reteaching me about the demands and delights of seeking first the kingdom of God. So many of the parables of the Kingdom brought me back to my basic purpose: to discover and do the will of God. The gems of the Lord's wisdom taught me to trust the reign of God within, in my responsibilities and my relationships.

At the end of that first year, I took a study leave on

the island of Cozumel, Mexico. There in solitude for several weeks, I was blessed with the opportunity of a more comprehensive exposition of the parables. What had happened to me personally through my daily devotions was then deepened by the prolonged meditation. I became convinced that the greatest need in our time is to return to the essential message of the Master as revealed in His "earthly stories with a heavenly meaning."

As I worked, a profound conviction evolved. The parables were all aspects of the autobiography of God being written through His Son, Immanuel, God with us. Jesus came to reveal who God is and what we were meant to be. Each parable, I discovered, contained a basic element of the nature of God and how He works in our lives. Thus, the title of this book. The parables are God's own story about Himself.

A strategy of study evolved. I found that each parable had one central truth. They are not allegories in which each detail is significant. My questions which guided my research unfolded after concentrated thought.

1. What is the main point of each parable?
2. What does that tell us about God?
3. If I believed that truth, what would I do?
4. What was the context that motivated the parable?
5. How can I live the parable as a part of my citizenship in the Kingdom of God?

I found that interpreting the parables was like getting to know a person. They yield their inner secrets only after consistent and faithful relationship. Or, to shift the metaphor, they are like an island around which you have to row until you know where to land. Or, to illustrate further, the parables are like a ball of yarn with one single strand protruding. Get hold of that, and you can unravel the whole ball.

7

My study leave was followed by preaching a series of messages on the parables to my Hollywood congregation which intensified the time of study. The sermons prompted dialogue with my friends and the hours of conversation about many of the parables made my final writing of these chapters much more personal and practical.

It has been difficult to select which parables to include as the basis of the chapters. Some have been left out with great reluctance. My final decision was to choose those which would help you, the reader, move into a fresh experience of God's grace and be able to discover His unlimited resources for daily living.

In a world that is confused about God and is beguiled by distorted images of His nature, it's time to return to His own autobiography and learn what He has said about Himself and the amazing, abundant life He offers to each of us. That's what happened to me. I long for the same for you.

I want to express my profound gratitude to the officers and members of the First Presbyterian Church of Hollywood for the gift of time to think, pray and write as a part of my calling as their pastor. This book could not have been written, typed and retyped without the encouragement and help of my assistant, Gwen Waggoner. Stephanie Edwards MacLeod, noted television personality, typed several of the chapters and offered incisive suggestions as a gift of friendship. I am also indebted to Nancy McDonnell, Kathy Guzman and Bruni Sablan for their help in typing the manuscript.

Lloyd John Ogilvie

1
The Prodigal God

Luke 15:11-24: Parable of Extravagant Love

Rivet your attention on him. Don't take your eyes off him. Observe his actions and reactions. Listen to him, feel his heart break, sense the depth of his relentless love. He is the central character of Jesus' greatest parable.

The father. The spotlight is never off him. He is at center stage the moment the curtain goes up. He dominates every scene even when he's offstage. The two sons are but supporting characters, vivid contrasts to the father. Change the scenery and his gracious love still thunders through. He speaks both when delivering his eloquent lines and when he silently waits. Who is the father? Jesus hoped we'd ask. The father is God; and God is the real prodigal. This is the parable of the prodigal God!

Shocking? Perhaps. But read Jesus' amazing drama again. Then check the definition of prodigal. It means extravagant, lavish, unrestrained, and copious. That describes the father more than the sons. Their negative prodigality is set in bold relief to the creative prodigality of the father. And in the shadows: God.

Prodigal! Let the word stand. Take any of the alternative definitions, it still holds true. Tradition assigned it to the lost son. It belongs to the father. His love knew no limits, his forgiveness no boundaries, his joy no restraint—prodigal love for the lost. Jesus' parable was in response to the Pharisees' criticism of His involvement with sinners. It is the story line of the whole autobiography of God, lived and told by Immanuel, God with us.

What is God like? Look at the father. Behold what God was doing and would do through the Parablizer Himself. It would mean Golgotha, but would never end there. Wasteful? Lavish, extravagant, excessive? Yes! Especially when you consider the disastrous defection and the ultra-violence of man. Why track him in the corridors of conscience in the far country? Why this in-spite-of love? What did we do to deserve that? Nothing. That's the mystery and wonder of it all. But we need love, forgiveness, and reconciliation more than breathing, food, or sleep. That's what He offers because that's what He is. The Prodigal God.

The parable will have its full, intended impact on us if we dare to live in the skin of one or both of the lost sons. Some of us may be in a far country of rebellion. Others of us may never have left the father, but the far country is in our minds and hearts. In either case, Jesus wants us to meet our Father Almighty.

The tender word "Father" soars above all other designations in the autobiography of God. More than a projection of the qualities of earthly fathers, it is a name

10

that demands its own definition, by the Father Himself, through His Son. He taught His disciples to pray "Our Father"; punctuated His message about God with the sublime word; and articulated ultimate trust with His last breath on the cross, "Father!" The parable of the prodigal God was taught by one who was the Word of God saying, "This is what I am like. This is how much I love you."

The prodigality of the father in Jesus' parable is focused in several startling ways. The drama has barely begun when we are aware of the first: benevolent approachableness.

"A certain man had two sons" (Luke 15:11). The sibling substance of that catches the attention of everyone who has lived in a family. But what must this father have been like that the younger of the sons could go to him and ask for his share of the inheritance? He would never have asked if he had been uncertain about the response. "Father, give me the share of the estate that falls to me" (v. 12). But he kept his real agenda hidden. Notice he did not say, "So that I can get out of here and run my own life!" Did the father know? Of course. Yet his magnanimous response was immediate. He was true to what must have been an oft-repeated affirmation of his sons, "All that I have is yours!"

Why would the younger son want to leave a father like that? There's no hint of harshness. No rigid dictator, this father. He longed only for his sons to enjoy the fruit of his labors and careful accumulation dependant on him.

Linger for a moment on the meaning of our inheritance from our heavenly Father: the resources of life; intellect, emotion, will; healthy bodies and a beautiful world filled with the delights of existence. Enjoy! But with one qualification: that we acknowledge that they are gifts and praise the Giver. There's the problem. We want to claim them as our own, without Him, and live the lie that what we have and are is the result of our own clever creativity. A problem as old as Adam and Eve. The stupidity of independence. But then, none of us does very well with the realization that one could not breathe a breath, think a thought, or earn a dime without His momentary blessing. But we try! Like the younger son, we have to prove ourselves to ourselves. We all want to be the one thing we can never be: god over our own lives.

But there's a deeper reason why the impetuous son wanted to get out on his own. What he could not emulate he had to eliminate. The son wanted to reproduce the quality he saw in the father. He wanted to be like him, but on his own terms. The assertiveness he felt in leaving his father was mistaken for happiness. His basic error was that he thought self-gratifying indulgence would make him happy. He had to prove that he was as good as, or better than, his father. The "I'd rather do it myself" syndrome had begun to eat at him. Soon it would nearly devour him.

There's a word for that. It has lots of synonyms, but at root it's sin. But the younger son committed sins. There was the one taproot sin of willful rebellion. Independence. The desire to be great on his own. Sow a thought and you reap an act. The seed of defection was sown long before the act of desertion.

The father let him go, the second evidence of prodigal love. The father loved the son too much to restrain him. He knew that love only possesses what it releases. We only have what we give away. Our hearts beat at one with the father. We feel the wrenching agony of the separation, the good-byes with so much unsaid. Did the son know that he broke his father's heart?

Be careful how you answer. The question implies a deeper one. Do we know when we break God's heart? We do just that every time we turn our backs on Him, resist His control, refuse His guidance, and renounce His goodness as the source of our lives. Some of us have packed up our share of the inheritance and have left the Father as if never to come back. Others of us leave in a thousand little ways that result in a life fractured from God.

The far country is the realm of rebellion. More than geography, it is a condition of the soul. It may be a total rejection of a faith that was once warm and dynamic. Or it may be relationships, priorities, or involvements which focus our self-indulgence or aggrandizement. These are aspects of everyone of us who has left the Father and dwells in the land of self-will. Those are the things we leave out when we are reminded that all that we have and are is His gift for faithfulness and obedience. What is your far country?

The younger son left for the far country in a decisive departure. He renounced his dependent sonship. Most of us drift into the same condition. Little things at first. Then our plans. Soon our money. Before long our deepest relationships. Finally our hearts. We are too pretentious to admit that to others—often even to ourselves. But we are no longer at home with God. Prayer becomes difficult and then exists hardly at all. God's guidance for life's decisions begins to seem irrelevant. We say, "After all, how can God be concerned with the personal lives of millions of people? He expects us to do *some* things for ourselves." Soon it's everything! An uneasy embarrassment flushes through us when we meet people who talk about "knowing" God. Too emotional. We are intimidated by any intimacy with the Father. Things we permitted ourselves in either fantasy or action become

13

part of the equivocation, "Well, why not? Everybody's doing it!" But most of all, the Father is not very important to us. We live our lives. He's "up there," if at all. What's down here becomes our far country.

The lost son of the parable is too often the easy characterization of the offscouring of humanity—drunks, dope addicts, sexual indulgents, criminals. These people are easy to identify as those who squander their inheritance of life. Many of us are not squanderers with problems, but just wanderers from our potential. Whether we are sleeping it off on a park bench or working it out in an executive suite, the plight is the same. Worship in a rescue mission for a bowl of soup is the same at base as worshiping in the "right" church for an image. Both reach a god far below God. There are many forms of destitution. A mother whose children have become her only reason for being is no better than a prostitute whose men without meaning are a way to a meal. There's a sloth of inactivity and a sloth of overactivity; a brokenness of financial bankruptcy and a bankruptcy of financial success as an end in itself. The haves and have-nots share a lot in common beneath the surface: both can miss the reason they were born.

The hero in Winston Churchill's *The Far Country* is guilty not of wanton dissipation of appetite, but of the rejection of his inbred, inherited ideals and dreams. He gradually lowers his values and his conviction of right and wrong in the practice of his profession. There are many ways of squandering our inheritance. We can dissipate our true worth as quickly as our wealth. In fact, many of us are tempted more by the former than the latter in our far country.

One Sunday evening after worship, two people arrested my concern. One was a street person whose life had hit zero below bottom. The other was a man who could not appropriate the gift of grace because he said he was living a full and satisfying life and had no needs! Both were lost sons in the far country.

And so are we when anything or anyone is used to fill the emptiness. There are no nostrums for the incurable homesickness for the Father, but we try. Success, position, recognition, accumulation—like the lost son, we use good things inordinately for the wrong reason. The people and things he misused in the far country were not bad. It's what he did with them and the substitutionary satisfaction they provided. His values were loosened and a frantic lust for expression dominated his impulses.

What would we do in a strange city where anything was permissible because nothing mattered? Now add to that a strong intoxicant of seemingly limitless wealth to buy any person or pleasure you want. Remember: no rules, regulations, restrictions! What would you do?

I know a man who, when he travels in Europe and arrives in a city where he is absolutely sure no one knows him or cares, and with a fat wallet filled with unaccountable local currency, he gets an attack of gluttony, lust, and carelessness. There are always plenty of people to help him. Until the money runs out!

The lost son was not on the town for a lost weekend fling. He thought he had left home for good. His inheritance was tender for a new way of life. One thing mattered: what he wanted when he wanted it. After all, wasn't the money his? Wasn't he in charge of his own life now? Nobody could tell him what to do! No one dared, as long as he could pay for what he demanded.

We could leave that as an impersonal exposition of the parable if it were not for the fact that it's painfully true of life, our life. What have we done with the gift of life? Most of us are living in a frantic search for meaning, purpose, and significance. We stuff our lives with what

15

we can taste and touch, save or sell. The question is not, "What will we do when the money runs out?" but "What can we squeeze into life and acquire before the undertaker arrives?"

This far country will take all it can get. The only thing it has to offer is stark reality apart from the Father. The defecting son found that when his resources were depleted. A famine hit the land of his evasion. But the trouble gave him tread. The famine around him eventually forced him to realize the famine in his soul without his father. His descent into despair was rapid. Jesus describes that descent in vivid words which would make any Jew's teeth rattle: the rebellious son lost all of his money; then he lost hope. Hunger finally drove him to become a hired servant of a citizen of the far country—a lowly *misthios*, a day laborer, the bottom of the three ranks of servants. A *doulos* was at the top—he was responsible for the men and maidservants, the *paides* and *paidiskas*. The son was hungry enough to be willing to surrender his dignity and freedom, and attach himself (the Greek means "pinned himself") to his new master as a *misthios*. A pitiful end to his search for autocracy! He had left his father because he wanted to be free to be himself. Now, under a new master, he was to find out how shallow that self was. Look at him! A Hebrew feeding swine, which his ancient religion abhorred; so hungry he was willing to eat the carob pods the forbidden beasts refused. What ignominy!

It was then he came to himself. This means he saw himself as he was. It's not easy to take an honest look at oneself. We all resist it as long as we can. To face the complicated complex of attitudes, reactions, thought patterns and personality traits which are the real ME is frightening. Often it takes a tragedy, or the loss of a cherished relationship, or a disintegration of our carefully erected defense mechanisms. Coming to ourselves implies just that: seeing ourselves for what we are, what we could have been, and what we may become. It's the strangely-wrapped gift of the far country. A gift that enables us to see what we have done with the gift of life without moment by moment dependence on the Father. Then we can call it all by the right name: Sin. Unblemished reality that frees the liberating realization, Why am I living this way? "I will get up and go to my father, and will say to him, 'Father, I have sinned against heaven, and in your sight!' " (v. 18).

Note that the father of the parable did not step in to save his son from reality in the far country. There were no dispatched guardians standing by to soften the blows of coming to himself. The father allowed the shame and the degradation. Prodigal love again!

So often I hear people ask if God sends difficulties. He doesn't have to. Life offers more than enough. We cry out, "What's the meaning of this, God?!" He patiently waits until we can humbly ask, "What's the meaning *in* this, God?"

It's then, like the son, that we come to ourselves. Why do we insist on trying? A terrible loneliness sets in. It pervades our whole being. We want to go home. Thomas Wolfe was wrong, you can go home again! The motive doesn't matter. Hunger drove the son. A hunger no food can satisfy drives us. Our problems are only a focus of our deepest plight. What has happened around us drives us to realize what has happened in us. Life without the Father is no life at all!

Now the parable tells us what kind of prodigal love awaits us each time, every time, we return to the Father. He has been waiting, watching, longing for us. Behold your God! This is our God who sees His son a long way off and runs to meet Him. Jesus' picture of the father running down the hill to greet his son implies more than meets first glance. It was considered very undignified for a senior man to run. Aristotle expressed the same shibboleth: "Great men never run in public." But look at prodigal love give wings to the father's feet. He can't run fast enough; his legs won't respond quickly enough to express the expectant longing of his heart to welcome his son home.

Whatever else you believe about God, don't miss this. He runs to us. Our least response unleashes His immense, uncalculable responsiveness. Right now your God and mine is running to us to meet us and enfold us in His arms!

What a progression of lavish love! "But while he was still a long way off, his father saw him, and felt compassion for him, and ran and embraced him, and kissed him" (Luke 15:20). The son had not yet given his well-rehearsed confession. The father did not reserve his love for a period of restitution. He did not keep him at arm's length until he measured up. This is the gospel in miniature: unmerited favor and love. Forgiveness is offered before we ask. We dare to ask to be forgiven because we are forgiven already. The invitation is for all the lost sons and daughters reading this, and for all the lost or wandering dimensions of our lives. The invitation is to come home. The simple decision to respond sets the prodigal Father running toward us.

Have you ever been embraced and kissed by God? I have. Often. When I deserved it least and needed it most, He held me with tender, strong arms. It's happened not only after times of failure or resistance to His will, but also after seeking to handle life's complexities and problems on my own.

Recently, I was in a bind of frustration trying to pull off a miracle on my own strength. I believed it was

18

God's will and something I should do for His glory. But God's work done with our strength never succeeds. I was cornered on every side by impossibilities. A dear friend was concerned about me and the project. She felt compelled to pray for the Lord's wisdom for me. In her quiet, an answer came: "Tell Lloyd to get rid of the shackles." When she told me I was alarmed. What shackles? I searched my life for some area out of His will; some secret, unconfessed sin or attitude.

Then one night when I was all alone in prayer, the membrane of assertiveness broke, and I was able to confess my sin of determination which was blocking His power. A willingness to let go replaced the stubborn compulsion. I discovered the shackle—fear of failure. The Lord seemed to say, "My son, I love you whether you succeed in this venture or not. Give it to me. Only then can I give it back to you as a gift." Then I knew what to confess. All the Lord wants from us is complete dependence and daring faith. Then He can bless us.

Look at the extravagant blessing the father gave the son to welcome him home. Prodigality! The embrace and the kiss of reconciliation were followed by lavish, symbolic assurances of love. The father's astonished servants must have run after him to meet the son, trying to keep pace with the old man's burst of energy. They were there to take the sublime commands. "Quickly, bring out the best robe and put it on him ... " (Luke 15:22). The words "best robe" can mean either the father's own robe, the robe kept for the honored guest, or the son's former robe. Any, or all, are implied by the father's love-drenched command. It was his way of expressing delight and unrestrained excitement. After all he had done, the son was still an honored guest not only in his father's home, but in his heart.

Then a ring was placed on the son's calloused, dirty

hand. The signet ring was symbolic of filial bonds no failure could break. It was the father's way of saying, "You have been, and always will be, my son and recipient of my love." Then he noticed his son's bare feet. A telltale sign of the slavery to which his son had fallen. "Put sandals on my son's feet. He's no slave. He's my cherished and beloved flesh and blood!"

What more need the father say or do? He's already done so much more than was deserved or expected. But the whole household and the countryside must share the father's joy. "Bring the fattened calf, kill it, and let us eat and be merry; for this son of mine was dead, and has come to life again; he was lost, and has been found" (vv. 23,24). No wonder he wanted a celebration. He thought his son was lost forever. "He's alive! Spare nothing. I want the whole world to know my son is home and to celebrate with me."

That's what happens with God and all the company of heaven when you and I come home by faith. The heavenly celebration is repeated each time we come back after a time of trying to live without Him in ventures or relationships of our lives. The realization that we have the capacity to bring our heavenly Father joy is the liberating nature of the Christian life. Can it be true? Yes! His Son knows and He told us in a parable we can't forget. Jesus has caught our attention, indeed.

2
The Far Country at Home

Luke 15:25-32: Parable of the Elder Brother

The plot intensifies. Most of Jesus' listeners could not allow themselves to identify with any aspect of the lost son, but the account of the elder brother's response left them little room for escape.

"Now his older son was in the field." Not surprising. He is responsibility and industriousness personified. Life is a serious business. There's work to be done, duties to be accomplished. All the time the younger son was off squandering his portion of the inheritance, the older son was keeping the farm. With good reason: When the wealth was divided, as the firstborn, he received a double portion, two-thirds of the property. Deuteronomy 21:17 made that very clear. The elder son was not working those fields out of love and faithfulness to his father. They belonged to him! That's why he was working so hard. But like his brother he, too, forgot that what he had was a trust from the father to be enjoyed with thankfulness.

The elder brother is a look in the mirror for most of us. We are forced to see more than we want to acknowledge. The lines of pride, judgmentalism and self-sufficiency have been cut, like the plowman's furrows, in our brow. Our jaws are set with serious determination. Most frightening of all, there's no joy in our eyes. Little wonder. There's no experience of grace in our hearts.

Empathy and identification flow together as we watch the elder brother. He was so right, accurate and incisive. Why shouldn't he be indignant when he returned from his hard work to find a party in full swing. What's all the celebration about? Why weren't those servants and friends out in the field working with him?

Indignation became rage when he learned the reason for the celebration. His brother was back! Why celebrate that? That squanderer, loose-liver, irresponsible spender deserved no party. The elder brother would have no part of that. He would not dignify the celebration with his presence. He turned on his heel in consternation, white-hot anger flowing through his veins.

And there's the running, prodigal father again on center stage pursuing him as he had run toward the other lost son. "Come to the party!" Love's entreaty. The father took it for granted that his older son would be ecstatic over his brother's safe return. If not that, surely he would share the joy of his father's heart. "Your brother has come home!"

So much of the elder brother's attitude is focused in his response. "Look! For so many years I have been serving you, and I have never neglected a command of yours; and yet you have never given me a kid, that I might be merry with my friends; but when this son of yours came, who has devoured your wealth with harlots,

22

you killed the fattened calf for him" (Luke 15:29,30). In almost every word he exposed his self-justifying relationship to the father.

But more than that, did he not expose what was hidden in his own mind's far country? His indignant blast of anger includes accusations of sins not enumerated elsewhere in the parable. Harlots? Riotous living? Were these the elder brother's own sins of fantasy? He read into the record his own imagination of what his brother had done. Projection. His vitriolic tirade tells us more about him than about his brother. We become what we hide. The surface has to be kept carefully polished so no one will suspect.

The elder brother was self-righteous. His status with the father, he thought, was dependent on his service and obedience. He had never missed a move in his carefully plotted game plan. Completely missing his father's gracious heart, he was determined to be impeccable and flawless. All so that he could maintain his status on the basis of his own adequacy. He wanted to be loved for his perfection.

That made him proud. If our goodness is our status, what's left but to extol and worship our accomplishment? We soon build our whole life around an arrogant self-satisfaction. At the core we are no different than the lost son. We really believe that what we have and can produce are our own. Our rebellion is the same as the younger brother. "What's mine is mine! I worked for it, preserved it, multiplied it, perfected it."

That leads to bitter judgmentalism. The lost and broken are the way they are because they didn't work as hard as we have. It's their own fault. The older brother sounds so righteous, doesn't he?

But the raw nerve in him was his need for his father's approval and esteem. How could it be that a celebration would be given for a son who was so profligate? Had the world gone mad? Were there no standards? Had his father lost all his senses in sentimentality? What the elder brother was really saying was, "What about me? Don't you admire my faithfulness? Have I worked all these years for nothing? You've never given me an appreciation banquet!"

The pain in the father's voice expresses his dawning realization that his elder son did not share his heart of love. Competition and rivalry with his younger brother had been brewing for a long time. The old insecurity and fears of childhood returned in full force. Did the father love the younger son more than him? What the son could not accept was that his father loved them equally. If he had known that, he wouldn't have had to work so hard for the approval he had all along.

"My child [*teknon*—a word of tender endearment], you have always been with me, and all that is mine is yours. But we had to be merry and rejoice, for this brother of yours was dead and has begun to live, and was lost and has been found" (Luke 15:31,32). There's prodigal love at its fullest. The father had loved the elder son all along. All things were his. Feel the heartbreak of the father, more excruciating than when the younger son left home. He realized that his elder son had never been at home—really.

The elder son's work was not out of gratitude. He had not accepted the father's daily flow of provision, sustenance and opportunity as evidence of love. Most of all, he did not share the father's love for his brother. Note the disturbing difference between the elder's "your son" and the father's "your brother." He had completely cut his brother off, assumed he'd never come back, and was enraged when he did. A party to welcome him home was unthinkable.

24

Before we become too hard on the elder brother, we must admit that most of us share his attitudes. How can it be that the father's acceptance and affirmation of the younger brother tell us anything about a just God? Is there no retribution for what people do with the inheritance of life? If a rascal like that can slip back into an equal status with us, why work and do what's right? Deathbed conversions make us wonder about our life-long efforts to serve God and live a productive life.

Aren't there some rewards for years of faithfulness? Yes, the joy of fellowship with our Father through the years. But when our own self-generated piety, morality and religion keep us from grace, we might as well have been squandering in the far country. We elder brothers leave the father without ever leaving the farm. The distance is measured by our efforts to be adequate on our own, constantly calculated by comparison with others.

"A darkened heart," says Augustine, "is the far country, for it is not by our feet but by our affections that we either leave Thee or return unto Thee."

How do we know that we are elder brothers? Just check our attitudes toward those who have failed, are lost, or whose behavior we abhor.

One of the most poignant ways of feeling the full impact of what Jesus is saying about us in the elder brother is to imagine what might have happened if the returning son had met his older brother on the way, before receiving the loving embrace of the father. The younger son never would have made it home. Living as a starving slave in a pigsty would be better than being starved for love and acceptance with his brother. It sets our imagination racing. How many needy people never make it back to the Father's heart because of us elder brothers in the church, the family, or society? If being at home with the Father means constantly contending with the self-righteous, judgmentalism of niggardly, indignant attitudes and words from our elder brothers, many would rather go back or stay away. Christian fellowship can so easily be turned into a house of judgment instead of grace. As one person said about a church in his city, "I had to get past the negative members to find positive meaning in my faith." Disturbing. Has anyone gone back to the far country because he or she met us first?

Considering these implications should be enough to bring us to the party! If we want fellowship with our heavenly Father, that's where we have to go—to the party, leaving our fussy standards behind.

Jesus did not finish the parable with an "all-lived-happily-ever-after" ending. Lots of dangling loose ends make us wonder: Did the elder brother ever go to the party? Did his attitude to his brother ever change? More crucial, was he ever able to admit his own need for forgiveness from the father? Jesus does not say but we suspect he didn't. Religious elder brothers often miss the Father's joy now and forever. What a tragedy!

The final curtain comes down as the father stands there with arms outstretched beseeching the elder son to come share his grace. He will not force him. That, too, is prodigal love.

We have beheld the face of God. The experience is both immensely comforting and personally disturbing. There's some of both sons in all of us. Both in me want to go home to the Father to receive forgiveness and to share His joy. The Father has already begun the celebration. He knew I would come. There's no other place to go!

3

God Knows
and Cares About You!

Luke 15:1-10: Parables of the Lost Sheep and Lost Coin

Last summer I had a preaching engagement at the Tabernacle in Ocean City, New Jersey. My hotel room overlooked the Atlantic and the busy boardwalk which parallels the seaside. Thousands of people stroll or ride bicycles along the boardwalk and frequent the famous saltwater taffy shops or the amusement parks situated along the way.

From my room I could see the endless streams of people walking aimlessly. A blend of clattering voices and the carnival sounds of the merry-go-round wafted into my room on the soft, salty, humid, summer night's breeze. A pleasant background for my time of study in preparation for my sermon the next day. My mind was focused on Luke 15 and Jesus' parables of the lost sheep and the lost coin. I did not expect that what I was about to hear over one of the speakers which adorn the light posts along the boardwalk would bring what I was reading into stark reality.

Piercing through the din was an anonymous announcement. None of the people on the boardwalk seemed to hear, respond or care. But from my vantage the words were alarming, though the announcer's voice did not express the pathos and anguish of the distress.

"A little girl about five years old, answering to the name of Wendy, has been lost. She is wearing a yellow dress and carrying a teddy bear. She has brown eyes, auburn hair. Anyone knowing the whereabouts of Wendy, please report to the Music Pier. Her parents are waiting for her here."

I tried to return to my reading. But my mind was on Wendy. Who was she? Where was she now in what must have looked to her to be a forest of legs along the boardwalk? How did she feel without the clasp of her father's strong hand? I felt heart-wrenching empathy as I pictured her clutching her faithful teddy bear, tears streaming down her face, her heart bursting with fright and loneliness.

Then I pictured her parents. That triggered my own parental concerns and flooded me with memories of times my own children had gotten lost. I wanted to start a search party all my own, or go wait with the parents. What must they be feeling? Imagine all the tragic things that could happen to Wendy: the sea, physical harm, strangers. . .

I was deeply relieved when I learned that Wendy was found. I pictured the thankful looks of love on the parents' faces and felt the joy they must have expressed. Warmth pulsated in my arms as I almost felt the tenderness of holding sobbing, little Wendy. I could hear something inside me saying, "It's alright now, Wendy.

Don't cry anymore. It's okay. We've found you. Never let go of my hand again. I love you, Wendy."

Then I looked out of my window again at the streams of humanity along the boardwalk. How many of them were lost and did not know it? Or how many felt a deep lostness inside and wished an announcement would be made about their spiritual condition? Did anyone care? I wondered how many of them knew that they needed a heavenly Father as much as Wendy needed her daddy.

Suddenly the Scripture I'd been reading was alive with existential vitality. The parables of the lost sheep and the lost coin were planted in freshly plowed feelings and thoughts within me. I was ready to experience, as well as consider, a dynamic dimension of Jesus' portrait of the Father in His parabolic autobiography of God.

An interrogating question had prompted the twin parables. Jesus had been criticized by the Pharisees for the company He kept. Guilty as charged! His love and vulnerability had attracted a needy group of friends: abhorred tax collectors, irreligious people, nonpracticing Jewish outcasts, morally suspicious failures. Sinners all, as far as the leaders of Israel were concerned. "Why spend your time with them, Jesus?" the Pharisees demanded to know. His answer was not defensive. He made no effort to explain His actions or associations. Rather He told them about God in a way that answers our deepest questions and lances our infected conceptions. Homely parables revealing a holy God. Earthly examples with heavenly vision.

Does God know? Does He care? How can He be concerned about billions of people? There is so much that forces us to feel our insignificance and littleness—our impersonal, computerized society, the lack of concern among people, the vastness of the earth with its countless races and faces and, beyond that, the astronomical intimidation of being on a planet in a galaxy, one among immeasurable galaxies. We cry out with the psalmist, "What is man, that thou art mindful of him?" (Ps. 8:4, *KJV*). And then in our hearts our own personal question, "Who am I that God would care about me?"

God's autobiographical answer to us through His Son astounds us. The parables of the lost sheep and the lost coin communicate with undeniable vividness that God is concerned about the lost, cares about individuals and is consumed with an active, seeking love for you and me.

Jesus, the master teacher, answers our questions by asking questions, first about a lost sheep and then a lost coin.

"What man among you, if he has a hundred sheep and has lost one of them, does not leave the ninety-nine in the open pasture, and go after the one which is lost, until he finds it?" (Luke 15:4). A question packed with portent. His listeners were drawn irresistibly by the drama He staged. Familiar props and players exposed a forgotten truth. Sheep and shepherds were a part of life. A hundred sheep would be a sign of prosperity. But what kind of shepherd would leave ninety-nine sheep in an open pasture to search for one gone astray? Would that be good business? Why not cut your losses and get on with caring about the flock? Why is *one* so important?

Jesus had the Pharisees—and us—where He wanted them. Surely some of them caught the impact of His illustrative query. Israel considered herself the flock of God. The imagery of God being a shepherd and His people a cherished flock, was woven into timeless testimony. David prayed, "The Lord is my Shepherd, I shall not want" (Ps. 23:1). Every worshiping Hebrew had said or sung Psalm 100 countless times: "Know that the Lord Himself is God; it is He who has made us, and not we ourselves; we are His people and the sheep of His pas-

30

ture" (v. 3). Had any of Jesus' listeners ever felt the comfort of Isaiah 40:11? "Like a shepherd He will tend His flock, in His arm He will gather the lambs, and carry them in His bosom."

But the concern was whether any of those sneering, scoffing Pharisees ever identified with Isaiah's confession: "All of us like sheep have gone astray, each of us has turned to his own way; but the Lord has caused the iniquity of us all to fall on Him" (Isa. 53:6). If they had, Jesus' parable was more than they bargained for. The leaders of Israel were considered undershepherds of their Shepherd God. Now we're getting closer to what Jesus intended. Did anyone remember Ezekiel 34? The shepherds of Israel were exposed by the Prophet for not caring for the flock: "Thus says the Lord God, 'Behold, I am against the shepherds, and I shall demand My sheep from them . . . Behold, I Myself will search for My sheep and seek them out. As a shepherd cares for his herd in the day when he is among his scattered sheep, so I will care for My sheep and will deliver them' " (vv. 10-12).

Jesus went for the jugular vein. The Pharisees' attitude to the lost tax-collectors and sinners was set in convicting comparison to the Shepherd, God Himself. The Shepherd God had come incarnate in the One who said, "I am the good shepherd; and I know My own, and My own know Me, even as the Father knows Me and I know the Father; and I lay down My life for the sheep" (John 10:14). What a contrast! The Pharisees had a saying: "There is a joy before God when those who provoke Him perish from the world." Jesus said, "I was sent only to the lost sheep of the house of Israel" (Matt. 15:24), and "the Son of Man has come to seek and to save that which was lost" (Luke 19:10). In that context we can appreciate the bottom line of the parable. God

31

Himself speaks through the shepherd who has found his lost sheep. "Rejoice with me, for I have found my sheep which was lost! I tell you that in the same way, there will be more joy in heaven over one sinner who repents, than over ninety-nine righteous persons who need no repentance" (Luke 15:6,7). That's what our God is like and that's how He relates to the lost person and the lost dimensions of our lives.

The drama of the parable has four acts, each built around key words: the word "lost" describes our condition; "go after" portrays God's searching love; "until He finds" reveals the persistence of His grace; and "joy" dramatizes the Lord's response to finding us.

What does it mean to be lost? The Pharisees had difficulty identifying with the lost sheep. They had never thought of themselves in that condition. That's the reason they had so little sympathy for others whose lost condition was more obvious. But what of you and me?

Some who read this can feel the lostness of having no intimate relationship with God. We are lost indeed, when we have never felt the love of our Father, never accepted His forgiveness or experienced His indwelling Spirit. He is in search of us who, like sheep, have nibbled our way from the pasture, searching for new turf of satisfaction and adventure.

Others of us are lost in that we no longer desire the Shepherd to guide our lives. The desire to "make it on our own" has led us to other pastures. The inbred need for either the Shepherd or the flock is negated in our wandering hearts.

Still others of us have lost our direction. We feel lost in the multiplicity of alternatives. There is no clear conviction of where our lives are headed and how each challenge or opportunity fits into a greater plan.

Some of us feel the lostness of not being loved. That

has bashed our self-esteem. We do not feel "special" to anyone, especially the significant people of our lives. The result is the lost condition of not loving ourselves.

Then there is the lost feeling of having failed and needing forgiveness and a new beginning. We feel unacceptable because of what we have said or done.

Everyone of us has felt the lost ache of broken relationships. Misunderstandings, differences, arguments, cutting words and sickening silences leave us hurting and cut off.

But by far the most tragic sense of lostness is not knowing we are lost. The undeniable evidence of that is lack of caring for those who are spiritually lost. When we become insensitive to the pain and perplexity of people who need the Saviour, and when we have little else but judgmentalism and criticism for the mess people get into—then we are most in need of a loving Shepherd to find us and bring us back to life.

In what ways do you identify with the lost sheep? Jesus wants to know! He has left the ninety-nine and is searching for you and me.

Pascal experienced the searching Shepherd when he heard His tender words, "Thou wouldst not be searching for me hadst I not already found thee." Any longing for God is because He has drawn near. The desire to know Him and recover the warm assurance of His presence is the result of His particularized, individual care for us. The sense of being found creates a desire to bring all the lost areas of relationships of life under His gracious care.

The Hound of Heaven was indefatigable in His relentless pursuit of Francis Thompson. Listen to the poet's plight.

> I fled Him, down the nights and down the days;
> I fled Him, down the arches of the years;

I fled Him, down the labyrinthine ways
Of my own mind; and in the mist of tears
I hid from Him, and under running laughter
Up vistaed hopes I sped;
And shot, precipitated,
Adown Titanic glooms of chasmed fears.
From those strong feet that followed, followed after.

The Shepherd's footfall is always there. He will not give us up. How can it be that He always knows where and how we are hiding? But skip down to the last stanza of Thompson's poem and hear the Shepherd say,

Ah, fondest, blindest, weakest
I am He whom thou seekest![1]

It is true. All our longing, restlessness and discontent is because of our search for the One who has found us. Our lostness is healed when we accept the liberating comfort that we can never wander from Him. He does know and care! At this very moment He is surrounding us with accepting love. The Shepherd's staff is a Cross!

William Barclay catches the essence of the parable's message: "There is a wondrous thought here. It is the truly tremendous truth that God is kinder than man. The orthodox would write off the tax collectors and the sinners as being beyond the pale and as deserving of nothing but destruction. Not so God. Men may give up hope on a sinner. Not so God. God loves the folk who never stray away; but in His heart there is a joy of joys when one is found and comes home; and it would be a thousand times easier to come back to God than to come home to the bleak criticism of men."[2]

That's the theme of the last act of Jesus' parabolic drama. He contrasts the Pharisees' attitude to the shepherd's joy in finding the lost sheep which is shared by his friends. There is the slight suggestion that perhaps

34

the flock was owned communally by a village or a band of shepherds. Our mind's eye dilates to catch the picture. The shepherd tenderly anoints the cut and bruised sheep. Then he hoists it upon his shoulders. The sheep relaxes on the strong muscles of the shepherd's back. Now picture the shepherd striding back to his friends, welcomed with cheers and celebration. "Rejoice with me," he calls from a distance, "for I have found my sheep which was lost!" (Luke 15:6). God Himself, carrying you and me home.

Now we can pray with David, "Save Thy people, and bless Thine inheritance; be their shepherd also, and carry them forever" (Ps. 28:9). And we can hear the Lord's promise spoken to Isaiah, "And even to your graying years I shall bear you! I have done it, and I shall carry you" (Isa. 46:4). The strong arms, which carried and then were stretched out on a cross, will hold and carry us. We have carried the burden of being lost. He's found us. Now, and forever, He carries us!

> Souls of men! Why will ye scatter
> Like a crowd of frightened sheep?
> Foolish hearts! Why will ye wander
> From a love so true and deep?
> Was there ever kindest shepherd
> Half so gentle, half so sweet
> As the Savior who would love us
> Come and gather round his feet?
> For the love of God is broader
> Than the measure of man's mind;
> And the heart of the Eternal
> Is most wonderfully kind.[3]

Jesus' second question in answer to our questions about God's knowledge and care of us follows quickly after the parable of the lost sheep. He opened our minds to the amazing truth of God's questing, searching omniscience and omniscience. Now He will press home the same basic truth, but with an alarming twist.

"What woman, if she has ten silver coins and loses one coin, does not light a lamp and sweep the house and search carefully until she finds it?" (Luke 15:8).

Why such consternation over one coin worth about 20 cents in our money? The Greek drachma was equal to the Roman denarius, the daily wage of a day laborer. The loss would be felt by most families. But more is implied here than the monetary value of the coin.

A bit of background is helpful. The women of Jesus' time wore a frontlet on their brow called a *semedi*. It was made up of 10 coins signifying a woman's betrothal or marriage relationship. A loss of one coin from the frontlet would be traumatic. More than the symmetry of the frontlet, it was significant of the fellowship the woman had with her beloved. It was not just the loss of the cosmetic beauty, but the careless loss of the completed symbol of her lover's gift that would alarm the woman. That's why she searched for the coin so feverishly. She had to find it! It meant everything to her.

The search was not easy. Homes in Palestine were small. The floors were dirt overlaid with straw. There were seldom windows to illuminate the one-room dwellings. A low door afforded little help. A lamp must be lighted to aid in the long search through the straw and dust. But the coin must be found! Careful sweeping and sifting expresses the woman's concern. Again the words "search" and "until" leap off the page. The lost coin is sought with undiminishable persistence. If a woman would do that to restore her frontlet, what will God do to restore us to fellowship? Everything! Nothing is too much, no search too long, no obstruction too great. The point of the parable: how much more than a coin, God loves and searches for you and me.

But note, the coin is lost in the house. Was it negligence? Carelessness? Familiarity breeding thoughtlessness? Perhaps. Jesus' mission to the lost in the house of Israel? Yes! But what does that mean for us today? It is possible to get lost in a church; to be on a membership roll and lose a vital relationship with God; to be so active on committees and boards that we miss the warmth of our first love; to become so involved in talking about God that we forget to talk with Him or listen to Him.

The parable of the lost sheep emphasized the individualized, caring *love* of God. The lost coin stresses the personalized *concern* of God. Both parables carry the impact that neither the flock nor the frontlet is complete without recovery of the lost sheep and coin.

Allow the healing balm of that truth to soak into the crevices of your heart. The Lord of the universe, who came as a seeking, suffering Saviour, who comes to us in the longing love of the Holy Spirit, will not be put off or dissuaded. There is no safe place to hide. He knows who and where we are. He wants to heal that negative self-depreciation that naggingly wonders why He has time or concern for us.

The twin parables end on the same triumphant note: Joy. "And when she has found it, she calls together her friends and neighbors, saying, 'Rejoice with me, for I have found the coin which I had lost!' " (Luke 15:9). Jesus wanted no misunderstanding about His intent: "In the same way, I tell you, there is joy in the presence of the angels of God over one sinner who repents" (v. 10).

It was as if He asked, "Do you want joy? There is no other way than to share God's joy over the recovery of the lost."

The other day a woman said, "I've lost the excitement of being a Christian." She confessed that she had known joy while she was astounded by how much God loved her in spite of her failures and selfishness. She also related the delight she used to have in sharing with others what had happened to her so that they might know what she had experienced. The more we talked the more a simple diagnosis became clear: she was no longer amazed and she was not caring for people.

Joy is the outward expression of the inner experience of grace. Her "dis-grace" was her lack of fellowship with the Lord and a refusal to talk about her faith with those who desperately needed to know that the Shepherd had found them. The joy returned when she once again opened her heart to the startling and ultimately satisfying good news of the cross and what God had done for her. That renewed her passion for people and their needs.

The purpose of the church in worship, study and fellowship is to rekindle the fires of love for our Lord and for people. Joy should be the identifiable mark of the people of God. Job 38:7 should be our motto and text: "The morning stars sang together, and all the sons of God shouted for joy." A church like that will join heaven in what Luther called "*Te deums* among the heavenly host." St. Bernard was right. "The tears of the penitent are the wine of angels."

As I closed the Bible that night in Ocean City, I too began to sing for joy. My heart was flooded with almost uncontainable exuberance about my Lord. Thirty years ago I was lost. He found me in a college dormitory. There have been lost times when I let go of the Shepherd, but He never let go of me. In a wonderful way I knew He had found me again in that hotel room. The joy I experienced would last only as long as the lost on that boardwalk, or on the streets of Los Angeles, or in the pews of my church, or in the homes of my parish were my purpose and passion. Before I fell asleep it seemed as if the Lord was saying, "Lloyd, if you want me, care for the lost. That's where you will find me. What you do for and with them, you will do for and with me!"

Notes

1. Francis Thompson, "The Hound of Heaven."
2. William Barclay, *The Gospel of Luke*, The Daily Study Bible (Edinburgh: The Saint Andrew Press, 1962), p. 208.
3. F.W. Faber, "Hymn."

4

The Tenant
Who Owns the House

Matthew 12:22-47: Parable of the Empty House

Empathize with Jesus. Try to feel what He must have felt when the scribes and Pharisees came to Him demanding a sign to authenticate His ministry. A sign? What more could He do? He had healed the sick, cast out evil spirits, and clearly announced that He was the Messiah. What did these pious religionists want? Would anything convince them?

Look through the Lord's eyes into the faces of these self-righteous, cautious men. Lines of constriction crease their furrowed brows. Their jaws are set in rectitude. Eyes filled with jealousy resist a steady gaze. Rigidly folded arms speak loudly the body language of resistance. Hostility shouts in every movement. They move in on Jesus like wolves on a huddled prey.

How would you have responded? With anger? Defensiveness? Hurt? Impatience? I'm sure I would have felt all that, and more.

Not Jesus. Love motivated the unvarnished directness of His response. We feel His concern for these men and the unnumbered masses under their spiritual influence. He saw beneath their robes of dignity and power to the needy persons inside. Compassion surged within the Master as He contemplated the pitiful plight of these leaders. They were in a perilous place of great danger. Their negative self-righteousness had made them, not Him, the cornered prey. They were being attacked by the forces of evil! Their emptiness was being invaded by Satan. The heart of God in Jesus reached out to them, longing to sound the alarm, to say something which could wake them from the restless sleep of neutrality and uncommitted blandness.

What Jesus said was consistent with His leadership style. He stated the truth as plainly as explanation and parable could conjugate. With piercing incisiveness, the Lord reminded them of the sign of Jonah, and then told them a story which should have made them shudder.

No sign could be given except the sign of Jonah. Our minds scurry back to the Old Testament, to the reluctant prophet who was used by God to proclaim His righteousness and power to the Ninevites. No miracles or divinations; just a clear preaching of God's sovereignty over all creation. Jonah was, himself, God's sign. His words, empowered by God's Spirit, led the Ninevites to the only acceptable response when God speaks: repentance and reformation.

It was as if Jesus was saying, "I am God's sign, just as Jonah was God's sign to the Ninevites. The word of truth I speak should be enough!" The implication was that as the Ninevites had responded to a spirit-infused

41

preaching, so should the leaders of God's people make a positive response to the Messiah in their midst. They should not need the other signs which had been performed wherever He went. "The men of Nineveh shall stand up with this generation at the judgment, and shall condemn it because they repented at the preaching of Jonah; and behold, something greater than Jonah is here" (Matt. 12:41). Greater than Jonah? Yes. The Messiah Himself. What greater sign could be given than God incarnate?

While the Pharisees contemplated that disturbing thrust, Jesus added another historical comparison. The Queen of Sheba recognized God's wisdom in Solomon, and had come to listen and learn. Jesus speaks with boldness: "And behold, something greater than Solomon is here" (v. 42). Imagine what that statement did to the Pharisees! Greater than Solomon? Who but the Messiah could have greater wisdom than Solomon? Exactly! That's all the sign that would be given. More than enough. Jesus' answer required a decision; a positive response. And that was more than the leaders could give. Their neutrality had become a guise for active resistance.

The rhetoric of explanation would not be enough to pierce these hardened hearts. Perhaps a parable could. It was out of profound love that Jesus exemplified His prophetic word with a parabolic illustration. He told a story of a man whose empty neutrality resulted in final ruination. Did the scribes and Pharisees identify themselves in the parable? That was expecting a lot. But Jesus wanted nothing less. His comparison motivated a radical story to confront the antagonists with the danger they faced. The stringency of negative religion is always the prelude to the final attack and capture by Satan and his demonic legions.

In that context, we can attempt an exposition of the parable of the empty house. At first reading it seems terribly negative. Jesus illustrates the power and persistence of evil in a grisly way. We are confronted with the danger of the indefatigable, relentless virulence of evil. Suddenly we realize that we may need to hear this parable as much as the scribes and the Pharisees.

The parable is about a man who had been delivered from an unclean, demonic spirit. The demon passed through the desert places, restlessly seeking a new place to lodge, some new victim to possess. When its search is unrewarded it says, "I will return to *my* house from which I came" (v. 44, italic added). Note the possessiveness with which the demon stubbornly calls it his house. Jesus compared an empty house to an empty life. He clearly had the Pharisees in mind when He said, "And when it comes, it finds it unoccupied, swept, and put in order" (v. 44). What a shocking description of Israel and her leaders at that time. Immaculate but empty! Repeated exorcisms through history had had little permanence.

But Jesus goes on. The demon wants to recapture the empty house in a way that his tenancy will never be questioned again. He rounds up seven other demons to live with him in the empty life. There will be little chance of future eviction with all eight of them lodging in every room! Study of demonology reveals that seven demons was the worst state of possession. This was the plight of Mary Magdalene and surely was the root of Legion's name. (See Luke 8:2; Mark 5:9.)

We are gripped by the drama. The empty house is repossessed. With fiendish glee the eight spirits move into every crevice and corner.

The point of the parable is painfully clear. A personality which has been purged of evil must be filled. Something, someone must fill the emptiness. If not, "the last

43

state of that man becomes worse than the first" (Matt. 12:45). Jesus hammers home the piercing truth for the scribes and Pharisees. And for us! "That is the way it will also be with this evil generation." And ours ... and with you and me!

We wonder how this parable fits as part of the autobiography of God. What aspect of the nature of God could be revealed in this ghastly tale? It seems to teach us more about the demonic than about the dynamic of God. And yet, as we ponder the parable in the context of the total sweep of Scripture and the message of Jesus, it dawns on us that He is leading us into a discovery of one of the most positive truths about God and His plan for our lives. The autobiography of God would not be complete without what this parable tells us about God and our intended purpose.

You and I were created to be the containers and communicators of the Spirit of God. That was God's original intention. We were meant to be the dwelling place of God. He is the tenant who owns the house. But sin evicted Him. Rebellion slammed the door in His face.

That's why Jesus came. God with us, creating a new breed of people in whom He could live. God dwelt in Jesus to call a new Israel to be His home. "And the Word became flesh, and dwelt among us, and we beheld His glory, glory as of the only begotten from the Father, full of grace and truth" (John 1:14). The ancient prophecy was realized. "Then I will dwell in your midst" (Zech. 2:11).

But we know what happened. "He came to His own, and those who were His own did not receive Him" (John 1:11). We observe the empty house is the Pharisees to whom Jesus' parable was spoken. The Messiah came to them to claim His place in their hearts. Neutrality was their nemesis.

And so Jesus turned to the common people to create a new Israel. They heard Him gladly. The disciples responded with ready receptiveness. "But as many as received Him, to them He gave the right to become children of God, even to those who believe in His name: who were born not of blood, nor of the will of the flesh, nor of the will of man, but of God" (John 1:12,13).

On the last night of His ministry before He was crucified, Jesus unveiled the liberating secret of how the empty house was to be filled. "If anyone loves Me, he will keep My word; and My Father will love him, and We will come to him, and make Our abode with him" (John 14:23). There's the positive side of what seems to be a negative parable. Then He went on: "Abide in Me, and I in you. As the branch cannot bear fruit of itself, unless it abides in the vine, so neither can you, unless you abide in Me" (John 15:4).

Pentecost became the triumphant climax of the Incarnation. As the Spirit of God had dwelt in Jesus, now through His death and resurrection the original purpose of creation had been reclaimed. The empty, receptive hearts of the apostles were filled with the Holy Spirit. God had made His home in them. Each new challenge brought fresh infilling, the remarkable lives we see spread across the pages of the book of Acts. Here was the positive example of the opposite of the negative warning of Jesus' parable of the haunted house.

Eventually the dynamic of the Spirit-filled life spread to an empty house named Saul of Tarsus. His persecution of the Christians forced him to observe their amazing power. It was Stephen's dying witness that shattered open the windows of his haunted heart. He was ready when he encountered the Lord Himself on the road to Damascus. Then through Ananias, whom he had come to imprison, the Pharisee was set free from the prison of his own powerless religiosity. After years of Spirit-filled living, the apostle Paul did more than any other Christian in history to put into writing the distilled essence of God's original purpose for His people.

To the Ephesians he wrote his deepest longing for all people. "For this reason, I bow my knees before the Father, from whom every family in heaven and on earth derives its name, that He would grant you, according to the riches of His glory, to be strengthened with power through His Spirit in the inner man; so that Christ may dwell in your hearts through faith" (Eph. 3:14-17). Paul knew that the Christians' most difficult battle was not against flesh and blood, but "against the powers, against the world-forces of this darkness, against the spiritual forces of wickedness in the heavenly places" (Eph. 6: 12).

Paul took Satan and his demonic emissaries seriously. From his own life he had learned that the only antidote to demon possession was the Spirit-filled life. The empty heart had to be filled. That accounts for the urgency of the Apostle's message about the Spirit to the Christians at Rome. "However you are not in the flesh but in the Spirit, if indeed the Spirit of God dwells in you. But if anyone does not have the Spirit of Christ, he does not belong to Him. And if Christ is in you, though the body is dead because of sin, yet the spirit is alive because of righteousness. But if the Spirit of Him who raised Jesus from the dead dwells in you, He who raised Christ Jesus from the dead will also give life to your mortal bodies through His Spirit who indwells you" (Rom. 8:9-11).

The full impact of the Spirit-filled life as the protection against the invasion of Satan is given by Paul to the Colossians. They too had had their bouts with ol' Scratch. "Christ in you, the hope of glory" (Col. 1:27), is the secret mystery of the Christian's power over evil.

I am convinced that Jesus' parable of the empty house was an anticipation of the fulfillment of His life and ministry as well as a reflection of what He observed in His people. He had come not only to defeat the powers of evil by His death on the cross, but also to evacuate the hearts of men from Satan's grip so that they could be filled with His own Spirit after His resurrection. The purpose of the Incarnation was at stake. We must consider the parable with no less urgency than He taught it to the scribes and Pharisees.

That presses us on to the second impelling aspect of the parable. It teaches us the danger of the emptiness of negative virtue. Reformation without regeneration leaves us like the empty house. Often, we are like the rulers who resisted Jesus: We have done our best to cleanse our lives of the habits, thoughts and patterns which would not be pleasing to God. We know more about what we are against than what we are for. We have a multiplicity of don'ts but little power to do. "Oughts" become our compulsion. All our energy is spent on rules and regulations to insure purity of living. We stabilize an empty house with judgmentalism. Negativism becomes the inadvertent passion of our lives. We are determined to be good people and make the world good by our example.

Too harsh? Perhaps. But how else can we explain the lack of warmth and joy among so many Christians? There are congregations, whole denominations, which have been organized around a set of rules and clearly stated disciplines if we fail. God becomes a cosmic truant officer instead of the tenant who owns the house.

But let's keep this personal. What about you and me? Has our religion released us to be life-affirming, contagious, enabling lovers of people? Do we find it difficult to be Christians in life's pressures and demands? I wonder if it could be that we have done well at the cleansing of the house, but it still stands empty, open for the restless demons—now sevenfold—to take possession. Surely this must be the explanation of the checkered history of Christianity. We can understand how people who call themselves Christians do the dreadful things they do—often in the name of Christ. Satan has occupied the house!

It's possible to live by half the gospel. The cross forgives and cleanses our sin. We can know that we belong to God and are alive forever. The other half of the truth is that we are delivered from the past to be God's dwelling in the present. We cannot live the new life in Christ without a new heart filled with Him. Following the message of Christ is impossible without the might of Christ.

The third thing this parable teaches is that there is an alarming possibility for us to be agents of Satan instead of Christ. When any relationship, responsibility or area of life is unfilled by Christ's Spirit, surrendered to Him, we can become channels of demonic influence.

Frightening? Yes! We can resist progress. Scuttle the Master's strategy for us and others. Stand in the way of dynamic movement. It can happen in our personal lives, our families, the church and society. Why is it that personal and social advancement must usually climb over the stiffened backs of Christians? Can Satan twist our thinking, distort our vision and cripple our effectiveness? He not only can, but does! Whenever we have evicted the Holy Spirit's rule and guidance, we can be sure that the emptiness will be replaced with seven demons of pride, selfishness, false ambition, competition, willfulness, distrust and arrogance. They are always outside an empty heart, waiting to repossess us. Satan stalks a Christian at every turn. He takes greater delight in invading a house which belongs to Christ but has been carelessly left unguarded and unfilled, than in bringing ruination to a house that belongs to him anyway. Our only protection is consistent communion with Christ.

Satan longs to entice us into a personal failure which contradicts our relationship with Christ. He multiplies the intensity by unleashing self-condemnation. When we are down on ourselves it's difficult to be up for life's next challenge. Christ is the author of authentic self-esteem. He helps us to forgive and love ourselves. From within our hearts, He encourages us to love ourselves as much as He does. Self-negation leaves our house open and empty. Soon it is haunted with self-doubt. We become debilitated in our efforts to discern and do the Lord's will.

The final message of the parable is the hazard of neutrality. An empty heart is completely neutral. It is not engaged in any positive good. The Pharisees tried to remain neutral about Jesus. Neutrality soon gave way to hostility. An active, positive life of living what we believe, and communicating it to others is the surest way to keep our Christianity alive. We will lose what we do not use. The only way to overcome a bad habit is by starting a creative one. The safeguard against losing our Christianity is giving it away. Any member of Alcoholics Anonymous will tell us that sobriety is inseparably related to helping others who are addicted. Christ is constantly trying to employ us in building the Kingdom of God by sharing our faith, introducing people to Him, and helping them to grow in grace. Every structure of our society is the realm of responsibility for a Christian. As long as there is injustice, prejudice, greed and dehumanization in our society, our work is not finished. Unless we are engaged in changing the world, the world will change us. Our last condition will be worse than the first, before we met Christ. Why? Because now there will be two masters in the same house. And we can only serve one master!

The parable of the empty house presses us on to grow. Christianity is more than rearranging the status quo. Becoming a Christian is more than repositioning the cherished furniture of the past in our hearts. Paul was vividly clear: "If any man is in Christ, he is a new creature; the old things passed away; behold, new things have come" (2 Cor. 5:17). Be sure the new has come into the house or it won't be long before the old will return. The indwelling Christ wants permanent occupancy. He owns the house!

5

The Hearing Heart

Matthew 13:1-23: Parable of the Soils

The television interviewer asked me to prepare several questions I would be willing to answer on a talk show. They were to be questions which would explore aspects of my life as a speaker and writer. One of the questions I submitted caused no small alarm among the people preparing the script.

"What has God been saying to you these days?"

I intended the question to give me an opportunity to share fresh insights and visions my studies and observations of life had produced. The question sparked a reaction in the host of the program as well as the scriptwriters.

"What do you mean, 'God saying to you?' Does your God talk? When do you hear Him? How do you know it's His voice? Do you claim some special pipeline to heaven?"

I did my best to clarify. No audible voice—an echo in my soul; fresh thought; insight and wisdom; convictions from ancient truth. But more than that, a communication from God comes as I read Scripture, take time for meditative prayer, listen to people, observe the Almighty's signature in nature, and live in-depth in life's challenges. God whispers in my delights, speaks in my problems, and shouts in my perplexities. He impinges on my every moment, waiting for me to listen to what He has to say. My most exciting times are when I pause in the midst of my studies and daily duties to ask, "Lord, what are you trying to say to me in this?" Suddenly what I'm reading or facing takes on new meaning. God breaks through. What He has to say is registered on my thoughts and feelings. He intends that His communication be expressed in my character and actions.

You and I are part of the sublime work of God's creation. He has created us with capacities to listen to Him. Jesus is His ultimate Word to us. In Him, God has spoken to us about what He wants to have happen to us, between us and through us in society. God's conversations with us always get back to the same subject: the Kingdom of God, His rule and reign in our hearts. All of life's experiences are occasions for fresh communication about the next steps of His strategy in discovering, discerning and doing His will. What He desires from us is what Jesus longed for as the response of the throngs of people who came to consider His message: a hearing heart.

The Master was enjoying an unprecedented popularity. People came from near and far. The crowds pressed in upon Him as He stood beside the Sea of Galilee and taught. He was forced to utilize a small fishing boat as

His pulpit. A few feet from shore, He was able to scrutinize the throng. How serious were they? Had they exercised their God-given gift of listening? Did they really know what He was saying? Did they have a hearing heart?

A life-situation parable was being dramatized nearby on the hills. The master teacher grasped the vivid illustration of His profound concern about our spiritual auditory ability. His built-in audiometer could measure that not all of His listeners were hearing Him. In the crowd before Him there were levels of receptivity. He observed a sower sowing seed on nearby hills. The ground into which those seeds fell was not all the same. The different kinds of soil gave Jesus the perfect example He needed.

The parable He told has been called both the parable of the sower and the soils. Keep both, but keep them inseparable. The titles represent two sides of a central truth: God speaks and we were created with the awesome responsibility to listen. This is one of Jesus' most autobiographical parables. He clearly identified Himself as the Sower, the seed as the Word of the Kingdom, and the soil as the hearts of the varied kinds of listeners. The penetrating question of the whole parable is disturbing: If God is speaking through the Messiah, is anybody listening? Jesus knew that there are always two parts to any communication: what's said and what's heard. And hearing was to be judged on the basis of whether what was heard was put into action. "He who has ears to hear, let him hear" (Matt. 13:9).

Join the crowd there beside the sea. That's the only way to feel the depth of love in the Master's words. Look around. The disciples listen with rapt attention. Others nod with an almost overfamiliar enthusiasm that makes us question whether they understand the cost of Jesus' message. Some seem distracted as if their minds are elsewhere, hidden behind masks of responsiveness. The Pharisees are listening but they do not hear. We feel an empathy with the many reactions in that crowd.

Jesus is compassionately concerned about the hearing capacity of our hearts. He knows all about us: what life has done to us and what we've done to ourselves to impair the delicate listening ability we have been given. As we catch His eye, He gives us a knowing look. He understands the grids we have placed over our hearts and how little can get through. Does He know about our set ideas and inflexible presuppositions? Is He aware of our prejudices, our wardrobe of excuses, our resistance to truth? Yes! In His gaze we can't seem to hide our hurts which have made us unfeeling. He knows how out of touch we are with our feelings about ourselves and others. Most of all, He is aware of beliefs and convictions which have never been put into concrete actions of obedience. Jesus understands what's happened to our hearing hearts. When He directs our attention to the sower, we know He's talking about Himself and our hearing impediment.

Four kinds of hearts are exposed in the parable's varied soils. Four very different ways of hearing the God who speaks. We need not try to fit ourselves into only one of the categories. There's a bit of all four in each of us. Our heart, in the Hebrew understanding, is the seat of intellect, emotion and will. What Jesus has to say to us must thunder through to all aspects of our hearts if we are to be made whole.

Note that all the soil is essentially the same earth. It's what's happened to it or been added to distort its purpose that delineates the kinds of soil. It's no different with our hearts!

Jesus observes the seeds which fall on the trodden path. The soil is hard. Impenetrable. The seeds dance on the surface, gusted to and fro by the winds. The birds flutter above and then descend to pluck up a ready meal. The seed and the soil need each other. But there is no productive contact. The marble-hard surface resists implantation.

The impenetrable soil represents hardhearted hearers. What happens to a person to bring him to the place where he cannot hear God? When did he close his mind, shut off his feelings and refuse to discern and do the will of God? The world's alive with the sounds of grace, but he does not hear them. How did he get that way?

Our hearts get hard because of what people do to us and we do to ourselves. The path was hard because foot, hoof and wheel had ground it into a familiar thoroughfare.

Life can do just that to our hearts. Our growing years are not easy. Each failure or rejection impacts a crust of resistance to vulnerability. We develop our defenses to cope. The pity of it all is that we lose selectivity. The good and bad are held off with equal tenacity.

The hard hearts in Jesus' audience that day beside the sea were the Pharisees. Distorted teaching about God and man had layered the hardness. Presuppositions had hardened into prejudices. Prejudice has been defined as being down on what you are not up on. The Pharisees' minds were closed to what Jesus said because they could not accept Him as Messiah. His message about the Kingdom of God could not penetrate the barriers erected by carefully defined expectations. They were not open to Him. Their emotions and wills followed the dictates of unexamined thoughts.

We could relegate the category of the hard hearts to the Pharisees if it were not for the fact that we can become one of them so easily. We can become like Jesus' friends and neighbors in His hometown of

Nazareth. "He could do no mighty work there because of their unbelief" (see Matt. 13:58).

I have observed hardhearted Christians with hearing problems in churches across our land. They have set ideas and beliefs. Customs and familiar practices developed through the years take on the authority of the Ten Commandments. Political beliefs and economic theories are baptized with holy fervor. The Americanized Jesus of our own making makes it difficult to listen to the biblical Christ. Arnold Toynbee was right: familiarity is the opiate of the imagination. We develop familiar patterns of life-style, church life and priorities which become more important than Christ Himself!

But hardness of hearing is caused by an even deeper problem. Whenever we have a conviction we do not live out, we block our sensitivity to hear further truth. We are so constituted that the final step of hearing is action on what we heard. Ruskin said that every duty we omit obscures some truth we might have known. Every thought and emotion must have a creative expression. The great danger for us as church members is the immense truth and insight we are given each week in sermons, Bible study, and fellowship. If we do not express what's impressed we will get depressed.

Periodically in my church we take a small band of our members off for a spiritual retreat. We all go through an inventory of our hearing ability. It's like a medical checkup with a doctor. We probe to discover how open we are to listen to God. The greatest single cause of impaired hearing of fresh truth is the refusal to live what we know already. At the end of one of these retreats, a prominent member said, "My Christian life has become dull and bland. I was no longer inspired or uplifted by worship or fellowship. Today, I found the reason. I hate to hear familiar truths and ideas I have refused to apply.

I had closed my mind." We talked about a few basic things this man would dare to do in subsequent weeks. I saw him recently and was delighted to learn that his hearing had been restored. His eyes sparkled as he said, "I feel like I did when I first became a Christian. It's been like falling in love again!"

The other day I went to my ear, nose and throat specialist. As a part of my checkup he cleaned out my ears. He used a powerful water pressure pump and blew out the wax and other impediments which had collected. When I looked at what had been removed I said, "Doctor, it's amazing that I could hear anything with all that in the way." His response was classic. "It collects a little bit at a time until the miracle of hearing is almost completely blocked. Like Christians who have ears but do not hear!"

The second category of hearers in Jesus' parable is the shallow heart. His explanation helps: "And the one on whom seed was sown on the rocky places, this is the man who hears the word, and immediately receives it with joy; yet he has no firm root in himself, but is only temporary, and when affliction or persecution arises because of the word, immediately he falls away" (Matt. 13:20,21).

A consideration of this kind of soil has led me to a helpful insight. Bedrock is covered over with a thin layer of soil. The seed is lodged in this soil and takes root. But the roots quickly reach the impenetrable rock. Because the roots are not allowed to grow deeply and are denied the replenishment of depth nourishment, the surface plant withers in the sun. It cannot sustain its initial growth.

What does this have to say about our hearing and our hearts? Remember that the heart is the inner core of intellect, emotion and will. If one aspect of our hearts is penetrated to the exclusion of the rest, our hearing will be faulty. We will know immediate growth, but no lasting maturity.

Think of it this way. Any one of the three aspects of our hearts may be the thin layer on top of the rock. The seed of the Word of the Kingdom flourishes there with spectacular growth, but it does not last. Jesus is determined to make us whole. He wants us to identify the part of our heart that is set in bedrock recalcitrance.

Take the emotional Christian. His encounter with Christ has been warm and exciting. He is enthusiastic and expressive. That's great, but it won't last until there is an intellectual and volitional conversion. We must love God with our minds and lives as well as our feelings. We get blown off balance when difficulties arise and we are not able to think and act under the guidance of clear thought about the gospel. So many of us have never grappled with intellectual issues. Tragedy, death, complicated ethical issues—cause us to fall apart.

But the same is true of the intellectual Christian who has never allowed Christ to deal with his feelings. Emotionally we are the products of our relationships. Parents, friends, significant others have shaped our feelings about ourselves and life. The rock beneath the thin layer of intellectual assent to the faith is made up of unresolved feelings, stunted emotions and conflicting attitudes. The impact of our relationships brings hate, jealousy, rejection, hurt. There are some of us who have been on an intellectual head-trip so long we cannot respond to life with an authentic expression of our feelings. The love of Jesus Christ can heal that. His acceptance and forgiveness can enable us to admit honestly how we are feeling and express the feelings creatively. There are some of us who find that difficult because we think we have to maintain a "Christian countenance." Underneath, we are a burning caldron of mixed feelings. When we are selective of the emotions we express, we soon become blocked and incapable of authentic relationships.

A woman shared a problem like that in her marriage. Her brilliant husband was a clear-thinking, intellectual Christian, but he was a bruised child emotionally. His self-image had been damaged by a cold, affectionless father. It wasn't until we walked back into his memories and he got in touch with that unhealed relationship that he was able to become whole.

The volitional rock is equally dangerous. We can be intellectually sound and emotionally free, but become withered Christians if we refuse to do God's will in the painful areas of obedience. It's impossible to grow without the persistent question and response: "Lord, show me what you want me to do and give me the courage and strength to do it."

Allow me to press this insight one step further. It is possible that the layer above the rock is volitional, with our minds and emotions forming the rock beneath. We are living in a day of unprecedented activism and social responsibility. That's commendable and necessary, but not at the expense of personal growth. What Napoleon said of himself can be true of any of us who seek to change society on our own strength: "Great men are meteors that consume themselves to light the earth. This is my burned out hour." Burned-out Christians are activists whose roots are not firmly planted in intellectual and emotional maturity. It is dangerous to be a reformer without constantly being reformed within. Obedience without a close relationship with the One we obey soon becomes self-generated moralism.

As I write this, the Lord is asking me a question that I must also ask of you. What's the surface layer for me and for you? What forms the rock that resists the root?

That prepares us to consider the thorny soil. Jesus observed that some seed fell into ground that was infested by weeds. That means that the soil had within it seeds of weeds as well as the newly planted good seed. Both would come up and flourish, but eventually the nutrients and resources of the soil would be sapped by the thorns. What does that have to do with hearing?

There are many voices clamoring for our attention. We can become so over-involved that we cannot hear what our Lord is saying to us. The circuits get overloaded and jam.

The other day I tried to call New York for several hours. The recorded, impersonal voice repeatedly droned, "Sorry, the circuits to New York are all in use." The same thing can happen when God tries to speak to us. There are too many people and demands calling us at the same time for Him to get through to us.

A doctor explained the untimely death of one of my members. "He tried to do too much and he succeeded!" What an epitaph!

Jesus' explanation of the crowded heart makes the hearing difficulty explicit. The Matthew and Luke accounts of the parable taken together, reveal that Jesus was concerned about the competitive loyalties of worry, riches and pleasures: "And the one on whom seed was sown among thorns, this is the man who hears the word, and the worry of the world, and the deceitfulness of riches choke the word, and it becomes unfruitful" (Matt. 13:22); "And the seed which fell among the thorns, these are the ones who have heard, and as they go on their way they are choked with worries and riches and pleasures of this life, and bring no fruit to maturity" (Luke 8:14).

The key issue is that the good seed of the Kingdom,

demanding absolute loyalty and first priority to God, is sown in a heart already committed to nourish the seeds of the weeds of our own agenda and prior commitments. The soil of our hearts accepts the Lord's seed as one among many. Worry, riches and pleasures are but headings for long lists of priorities we bring to the Christian life or keep long after we have accepted Christ as Lord of our life.

Worry over an aspect of our lives is a sure sign we are trying to accomplish our plans with our own power. When we worry over people or situations we can be sure that we have elevated the problem to first place and are not able to find adequate resources. To seek first the Kingdom of God is to listen for His guidance on what we are to do and be.

Things, whatever their monetary value, can become our "riches." What gives us security? That's the question. Material things are not bad in themselves. But if they crowd in for first importance in our lives, we won't be able to hear what God is trying to say to us. Inanimate things are very inarticulate when we need a word of hope in a crisis.

So what's wrong with pleasures? Nothing if they are an expression of our faith and not a substitute. If we are to hear God clearly, we must be able to listen to Him while we are enjoying the pleasure. That's a good test. Can we talk to God and hear His response in the pleasure? Can we hear Him say, "Enjoy! I have given you this pleasure because I am pleased with you. It is good because it is my gift." Then can we say, "Thank you Lord for this delight and for joining me in relishing it!" With that kind of listening conversation, we wouldn't need an elaborate list of don'ts. There are lots of things we would never dare do and talk to Him at the same time. These things are the thorns of sin. They must be weeded out. Sir Lancelot in quest of the Holy Grail said:

But in me lived a sin
So strange, of such a kind, that all of pure,
Noble and knightly in me twined and clung
Round that one sin, until the wholesome flower
and poisonous grew
Together, each to each
Not to be plucked asunder.[1]

There is a time when the growth of the good seed is so entwined by the thorns that it is choked to death.

When is a heart overcrowded? When is the good seed unable to grow because the resources of thought, energy, creativity and time are depleted on secondary loyalty to the thorns? If there is no time for listening to God in Bible study and prolonged meditation, we are too busy. When we are too distracted by duties and responsibilities to grow as persons, we are over-involved. When we have no time for people and are not reproducing our faith in them, we are dangerously close to missing the reason we were born. However much we do, if we're not actively involved in fulfilling God's appointment in some area of social need, we will miss the adventure of extending the Kingdom in His timing and power.

Again the sticky personal question. What are my thorns? What am I over-involved in doing that the Lord never willed for me? How about you? A radical weeding out is necessary if the soil is. to grow the good seed of the reign and rule of God. I find it helpful to ask God what weeds must go. The very question is a sign the soil is being cleared. We've admitted that the soil is not ours and needs cultivation. I have always found God ready to guide me about which weeds to pull first.

The good soil is the listening heart. When the Lord asked Solomon to name the one blessing he needed most, the young king responded, "Give Thy servant an understanding heart to judge Thy people" (1 Kings 3:9). The Hebrew means a listening or hearing heart. Jesus wanted that for everyone who thronged along the seashore. Later, in His explanation to His disciples, He revealed what that meant: "And the one on whom seed was sown on the good ground, this is the man who hears the word and understands it; who indeed bears fruit, and brings forth, some a hundredfold, some sixty, and some thirty" (Matt. 13:23). Mark stresses receptivity as the basic ingredient of the good soil. Luke quotes Jesus' illumination as, "the seed in the good ground, these are the ones who have heard the word in an honest and good heart, and hold it fast, and bear fruit with perseverance" (Luke 8:15). Considered together, the three versions stress that a hearing heart receives, responds, reproduces and is relentless.

God is speaking to each of us right now as we read this. What does He have to say? He wants us to know how much He loves us. For our sins, He wants to give us Calvary's assurance. His perspective and power are offered for our possibilities and problems. He wants to reign supreme in our hearts so we can pray, "Thy Kingdom come, Thy will be done." The Lord is ready to guide the future. He offers insight, discernment and wisdom for the alternatives which face us. Most of all, He wants to give us Himself.

A hearing heart responds with sincerity. It is an honest and good heart. Not double-minded or seeking to serve two masters. It is a prayerful heart, holding fast what God has said, pondering it until it yields the gift of understanding. Listening to God takes time and attentive effort. It means spreading out all our concerns and cares before Him and saying with Samuel, "Speak, Lord, thy servant heareth" (see 1 Sam. 3:10). And speak

He will! Each new communication is dependent on the enactment of a previous guidance. Fresh light is given if we walk in the light we have been given.

Don't miss the final qualification of hearing God. He speaks to those involved in bearing fruit in themselves and others. The fruit of listening to God is the transformation of character. The more we listen to Him, the more He will work on our personalities. He wants to make us like Jesus. The fruit of the Spirit, the productive result of communication with God, according to Paul, is "love, joy, peace, patience, kindness, goodness, faithfulness, gentleness and self-control" (Gal. 5:22,23). Take that list into dialogue with God in prayer. Ask Him to show you what's lacking and needs growth. Allow Him to give your imagination the picture of what you would be like as a fruit-filled person. Then thank Him that it shall be so!

A fruit-filled Christian is a fruitful disciple. Any person who listens to God soon hears the beat of His heart for people who do not know Him. To "bring forth fruit" is helping others to meet Him, receive Him and commit their lives to Him.

When we listen to God, He identifies the people He has made ready. He gives us the strategy, words, attitude and love for a liberating friendship with those people. The One who knows the depths of each personality can give us the key to unlock the people He appoints for us to introduce to Him. He "walks us through" our relationships, sensitizing us to the way to communicate profoundly. The people who listen to God are able to listen to people. When we speak and share we will be on target. People will be changed and will be the fruit of our listening to God.

I once had a speech professor who made me write out exactly what I expected people to understand and do as a result of my message. The same discipline should be required of a writer for any chapter of a book. This chapter will have accomplished its purpose if the reader is amazed with the awesome truth that God speaks and that prolonged quiet enables us to hear Him. But action is the final step of hearing. I would not be satisfied with what I have tried to say if, as a result of listening to God, you and I were not motivated by love to produce the fruit of what we have heard. God has spent a long time plowing, blasting the rock-bed, weeding out the thorns of the soil of our hearts. He's made us good soil. Now He has something to say. Are we listening?

Note

1. Alfred Tennyson, "The Holy Grail," *Idylls of the King*.

6
How to Live
Without Anxiety

Mark 4:26-29: Parable of the Growth of the Seed

If I could have the confidence in the midst of crises and challenges that I have after they are over, how much more abundant my life would be. I am much better at retrospective interpretation of what God has done than I am at relaxed insight about what He's doing.

After a storm has passed I can see what the Lord was doing in the tumult better than I can ride out the present storm. It's much easier for me to look back and observe the goodness of the Lord than to trust His graciousness in the fast currents of uncertainty and waiting. The area of my life where I need to grow is in patience in the process. I share this because I suspect there are many of you who identify with me in this. The process of God's evolving plan for us is as crucial as the product. But so much more difficult to endure.

I am alarmed at how little I remember of how God has worked in the past when I face difficulties in which I need the confidence that He is at work right now. How could I forget? But I do. Perhaps you suffer from impatience as much as I do. If so, Jesus' parable of the seed growing secretly is the Great Physician's personal prescription for our perturbation.

This parable follows naturally our previous study of the sower and the soil. The focus is still on the planting of the seed of the Word of God. Keep in mind that the seed is the word of the Kingdom of God: the reign, rule, and triumph of God in us, between us and in society. The impetus of the parable of persistent growth tells us how the seed grows in us, in the people for whom we are concerned, and in the unresolved problems or potentials of our lives. The parable has taught me how to be patient with myself, others, my projects and plans that all too often become an extension of my own restless impatience.

There's a progression in the disciplined process of becoming a patient person. It's based on an observation of how God works out His purposes. It grows through personal experiences of how He works in us. It is nurtured by observation of what He's doing in people we love. It has its full impact in the complexities of life when we must wait for the unfolding of God's glory. What Jesus wants to communicate to us about the spontaneous growth of the seed could change our daily lives.

The best way to experience the truth of this parable is to start with the things that make us impatient. Line them up! March them before your mind's eye. Look at each person you long to change; observe each situation that causes you the excruciating pain of unfulfilled plans. Now contemplate the nature of God and the indefatigable, relentless forward progress of His Kingdom in the world.

Only Mark records this parable. Did he see this autobiographical exposure of God's methods as a biography of how those methods had worked in his own life? I think so. He had become a Christian under the influence of the early church which met in his home in Jerusalem. The seed of the Kingdom had been planted in Mark's mind and heart during the exciting days of the expansion of the infant church. The warm and affirming fellowship of the apostles encouraged his growth as a man in Christ. He experienced the days of high adventure on the first missionary journey with Paul. Then he went through a time of disappointment and failure that did more for the growth of the Kingdom in him than the joyous times in Jerusalem. He defected from the mission with Paul. Life fell apart as he faced the painful embarrassment of his lack of courage. Barnabas helped Mark make a new start and Peter enabled the Kingdom seed in him to grow to full fruition. The germination process required death to Mark's own human adequacy.

Mark was Peter's companion; in fact, Peter called him his son (see 1 Pet. 5:13). It must have been Peter who told him about this parable. I like to think that it became Mark's favorite because it dramatized his own slow, but ultimately successful growth in Christ. Mark was a fully grown man in Christ when he sat down to write the first of the Gospels based on the life and teachings of Jesus as recounted by Peter. Mark included it years later to give courage and hope to the persecuted church. I can imagine that he smiled and felt a surge of delight as he wrote the magnificent lines of parabolic truth. It was his story. It happened to him. Now it must happen to us.

And Jesus was saying, "The Kingdom of God is like a man who cast seed upon the ground; and goes to bed at night and gets up by day, and the seed sprouts up and grows—how, he himself does not know. The earth produces crops by itself; first the blade, then the head, then

68

the mature grain in the head" (Mark 4:26-28).

That's how God does His work in the world, and in us. It's the dramatic narrative of the Incarnation. Jesus planted the seed of the Kingdom of God in the soil of history. Over hill and dale in every heart that would listen, and then, on a bare hill called Calvary, He planted Himself. The world has never been the same: a band of disciples, a Spirit-filled church at Pentecost, a missionary movement to the reaches of the world, and now the only hope for our psycho-cybernetic creation. Two thousand years, but a moment in eternity beyond calculated time. Why does it take so long? We are chained to our conception of progress; bound by our lack of vision. God is working His purposes out. The seed is planted, the blade is piercing the hard crust of our resistance. We cannot stamp it out. It's growing. The kingdoms of this world are becoming the kingdoms of our Lord!

In that context, we can enjoy the persistence of God in us. When was the seed planted in you? It happened to me as a freshman in college. I heard the good news of God's love in Christ and had my imagination turpentined by a fellowship of Christians who gave me a picture of what God meant my life to be. I accepted Christ as my Saviour. Trusting Him as Lord of my life has not come as easily. Each new surrender of the facets and relationships of my life fertilizes the seed.

Allow your mind to drift back over what has happened to you since you first gave your life to Christ. Capture the memory of that moment. Next, allow your mind the luxury of relishing the times you knew God's intervention and inspiration. We can feel the growth of the seed of the reign and rule of God. We are not the people we were. Nor are we now what we shall be.

Now we are ready to see what the parable of spontaneous growth has to say about our impatience with life and the future. Jesus' simple reminder of how the seed grows silently but persistently is a healing balm for our most virulent disease—anxiety.

Anxiety is the result of doing our own thing, on our timing and with our resources. Freedom from anxiety comes when we desire to do what God wants, when He wants it, with whom He wants it and by His power. God's work done without God's power depletes God's people.

The parable of the growth of the seed teaches us that what God guides, He provides. But between the planting and the harvesting is the waiting period when He is at work and we must wait. Peace is God's gift for the interface between the launching of what He wills and fulfillment in His way and time. That peace is the product of the confidence that while we wait, God is busy working with people, potentials and possibilities we never dreamed of or even knew existed. The Lord is spontaneous! And very original with each of us.

Jeremiah expressed the essence of this in Lamentations 3:26: "It is good that a man should both hope and quietly wait for the salvation of the Lord" *(KJV)*. He could say that because God had said to him and His people, " 'For I know the plans that I have for you,' declares the Lord, 'plans for welfare and not for calamity to give you a future and a hope' " (Jer. 29:11).

The parable of the growth of the seed is the basis of future hope rather than "future shock." Jesus wants us to experience the reliability, resources and responsiveness of God.

The process by which the seed is planted, grows and is harvested tells us that God knows what He is doing. There is order in the created world. Our lives are not determined by a nameless fate. There are physical and spiritual laws that govern the levels of plant, animal and human life. God is the ultimate architect and builder of history and our personal lives. He has resources to call into action we cannot imagine. "The earth is the Lord's, and the fulness thereof; the world, and they that dwell therein" (Ps. 24:1, *KJV*). At every moment of our anxious uncertainty, He is arranging, motivating, inspiring, preparing. The resourceful Lord has an infinite capacity to surprise us. He is responsive to our need. He wants to delight us with what He has been preparing while we have been waiting. Paul knew this after long years of experience with the faithfulness of God. "Have no anxiety about anything, but in everything by prayer and supplication with thanksgiving let your requests be known to God" (Phil. 4:6, *RSV*).

Jesus taught this parable of the omniscience, omnipresence and omnipotence of God to cut anxiety at the taproot. He was deeply concerned about the anxiety He observed in His disciples. "You must not set your heart on what you eat or drink, nor must you live in a state of anxiety. The whole heathen world is busy about getting food and drink, and your Father knows well enough that you need such things. No, set your heart on his kingdom, and your food and drink will come as a matter of course" (Luke 12:29-31, *Phillips*).

But that's not any easier for us than it was for the disciples. Food and drink is not the source of anxiety for most of us. It's the lack of trust that things will work out for us and the people we love. God has given us vision and hope. It's that very creative ability which must always be equaled by patient trust.

Rollo May suggests that our ability to hope and our susceptibility to anxiety are two sides of the same capacity. Our power of expectation engendered by the Spirit must be equaled with the assurance that what we have been led to expect will evolve at the right time and way. If we didn't have the daring to believe that things don't have to remain as they are, we'd never be anxious.

Will the seed of hope grow? Will there be a harvest? So much of life is lived in the period between planting and fruition. That's life! The alternatives of anxiety or faith are before us constantly. Anxiety is the result of putting our hopes on anything short of God and His faithfulness to complete what He's started in us and around us. Our gift to dream must be matched by dependence.

The restless bedfellow of anxiety is worry. Worry is sin. It's the outward expression of inner anxiety. Do we have confidence in God? What more must He do to prove Himself? More than creation, the Incarnation, Calvary, Resurrection, the gift of the Holy Spirit?

Anxiety needs more than a cure. It needs forgiveness. Can we accept that God will allow only what is ultimately good for us? He will grant us only those requests that are part of His plan for us. Freedom from worry and anxiety comes when we can believe that nothing will happen to us that God has not willed. He will use even the disappointments that come when others seem to thwart His best for us.

One time, in an anxious period of waiting, a friend said a harsh thing to me which finally gave me comfort: "If God wants it, no one can stop it. If He doesn't, there's no way you could pull it off anyway. So relax!"

The parable gives us some very specific steps for living with the tension of unfulfilled hopes. Once the seed of the Kingdom of God has been planted in us and begins to grow, this parable becomes the secret of how to live without anxiety. At this moment in time, we all have concerns which frustrate us. Perhaps we have launched out on a new venture we felt God guided.

Progress is painfully slow. For some of us our major anxiety is wrapped up in a person. Others are worried about a loved one who is ill. Or perhaps it's some organization we long to move forward. Whatever it is for each of us, that is our seed. It must be planted in the ground of God's resources. The parable tells us how.

First, evaluate the seed. Consider the seed carefully. Is what we want an extension of the Kingdom as best we can understand? Does it fit with His purposes? Will it bring us and others closer to Him? Is He guiding you?

Second, once we are sure of the seed, plant it courageously. Commit it unreservedly to God. Do all we can and leave the results to Him. We cannot hold on to the seed in our feverish, sweaty hands and expect the earth to do anything. Put the seed into the resourceful soil of the power of God.

Third, allow the seed to die as a part of the germination. Listen to Jesus: "Truly, truly, I say to you, unless a grain of wheat falls into the earth and dies, it remains by itself alone; but if it dies, it bears much fruit. He who loves his life loses it; and he who hates his life in this world shall keep it to life eternal" (John 12:24,25). The word "hate" leaps off the page. It is a comparative word challenging us to love Him and His plan for us more than anything or anyone else. In a way we are to hate our grasping self-determination to run our own lives, and feel abhorrence for what our control of situations and people produces. That's not difficult when we see the mess we make of things when we refuse to trust Him. It's like clutching the seed in our clenched fist and thrusting it into the ground, expecting it to grow when our hand of impervious determination keeps the soil from touching it.

The cycle of death and resurrection is in the germination process. The seed dies to itself. Then follows the long waiting while the nurture of the soil brings life, roots, a sprout, and finally a fully grown plant. All the concerns of our life must pass through the same process.

Fourth, leave the committed seed and its new root in the ground! Our temptation is to pull up the roots to see if they are growing. My family had a vegetable garden when I was a boy. The hardest thing for me was to not disturb the roots to be assured they were growing. It may be fascinating to look at the vivid light green life pressing out from the seed or bulb, but it is a sure way to kill future growth. The farmer of the parable went about his regular duties while the seed grew. He didn't go out to the field each day to dig up the seed to see if there was any progress.

There is a leisure of faith. When Jesus learned that Lazarus was ill, He went on about His duties and went to Bethany two days later to help. There is great meaning in John's account. So when Jesus heard that he was sick, "He stayed then two days longer in the place where He was" (11:6). Not to worry. God was in charge.

Next, cultivate the ground. When the first evidence of the blade appears above the surface of the soil, rejoice; but know that God intends to grow a fully mature plant. Don't harvest the blade. The fruit of faithfulness is in the grain. Watch the blade grow with adoration and praise. It's a portent of fulfillment.

Lastly, enjoy the harvest. So often we are worried so much about the next challenge that we can't enjoy what God has done with previously committed concerns. The Lord wants us to distribute the harvest by sharing what He has done for us with others. Sharing strengthens our faith and heightens hope in the people around us. If He could grow a plant out of our relinquished seeds, He can do the same for them. The final stage of harvest is the milling of the wheat so it can be baked into bread to be broken for others. Together, we can say, "To God be the glory—great things He has done!"

I have experienced the truth of this parable repeatedly in my own life. The word I dislike the most is "wait." I want everything to work out yesterday. But it's in the waiting times that I have grown as a person.

A couple of years ago my wife was seriously ill with cancer. Her own prayers about the future gave her a firm confidence that she would be well. She placed the seed of that God-given vision in the ground. Together we thanked God that what He told us would come true. The long period of surgeries, treatments and therapy seemed endless. The temptation to fear was ever-present. But God was faithful to His promise. His timing was not ours. Now she is well again, healed by the Holy Spirit.

As a spiritual leader, I have to put seeds of commitment into the ground constantly. God has given me an exciting vision for the local church in America. But repatterning the church around the mind of Christ takes time and patience. Whenever I get anxious, God reminds me of this parable. Plant the seed and leave its growth to Him!

As a parent, I have to relearn that repeatedly. God has given me three unique and special children. In each stage of their growth as persons, I have had to be reminded that they belong to the Lord. My memory verse as a parent is Philippians 1:6: "And I am sure that he who began a good work in you will bring it to completion ..." *(RSV)*. God is not finished with me or the people I love. The challenge is to trust that He always finishes what He starts. The future is in His hands!

We have beheld a salient segment of God's autobiography. Do you believe it? Then why is there still a seed in your hand? Thrust it into the ground! You can live without anxiety.

7

The Most Dangerous People in the Church

Matthew 13:24-30,36-42: Parable of the Wheat and Tares

Some time ago, I had the questionable notoriety of being listed as one of the ten most dangerous leaders of the church in America. My vision for the renewal of the church ran counter to the ideas of the author of the list. I gained some comfort in the fact that my friend Billy Graham was also listed, along with eight others whom I love and admire. The list-maker's purge of the leadership of the church was not taken seriously, and soon was publicly repudiated as one more of his vitriolic pronouncements.

The title of the list lingered in my mind for a long time. It led to a profound question. Who are the really dangerous people in the church? Or, to put it more personally: Who are the dangerous people in your congregation and mine? Our minds leap immediately to the people with whom we may not agree on a particular policy or whose priorities are different from ours. But go deeper. Every congregation has a group of dangerous people. Dangerous not to us and our ambitions, but to our Lord. Before we list them, be careful. We may be among them ourselves.

The local congregation is made up of two kinds of people. It makes all the difference for now and eternity which group we're in. The great challenge is to liberate people from one category to the other.

The church of Jesus Christ is made up of inside-outsiders and inside-insiders. The first group makes up the most dangerous people in the church. Only two people have the prerogative of determining which group you're in—Jesus Christ and you.

The inside-outsider and the inside-insider often look alike, sound similar and both believe in Jesus Christ. Their relationship to Him as Lord couldn't be more dissimilar. What's the difference?

The inside-outsider is in the church but outside a deep, intimate relationship with Christ. He believes that Jesus Christ is the Saviour of the world but has never come to know Him as the Lord of his life. There never has been a time of complete commitment of all he has and is. The power of the Christian life is experienced in daily, specific surrender of the needs, challenges, problems and opportunities of life. The inside-outsider is inside the church, but outside of an intimate, impelling, indwelling experience of Christ as Lord.

One of the most gratifying and puzzling phenomena of our time is the great number of church members who are discovering the joy and freedom of committing their lives to Christ. They are discovering the excitement of trusting Christ with their frustrations and fears.

Recently, a church member realized the power of

Christ in his life. At a party of fellow members, he shared the delight of his experience. It was very disturbing to some when he said, "I've been a Presbyterian for years. Last week I found out what it's all about to be a Christian. I've always believed that Christ was Saviour, but for the first time I know He's *my* Saviour! It's alarming to think of all the joy I've missed being an uncommitted church member. Now I know Christ as the Lord of all my relationships and responsibilities."

Perhaps it was the fact that this man had been a church officer, generous giver and leader of the church which contributed to the wonderment of his friends. But most of all, it made them wonder about themselves. Was there something missing in their lives?

This church member had become an inside-insider: inside the church and inside a personal relationship with Christ. He was no longer running his own life. Christ had taken charge as Lord. Previously Christ and the church had been two of the many loyalties and concerns of his busy life. But he was in control. He seldom prayed, except in crises. His own sagacity and strength were the source of his clever life. His plans were always within the limits of his own power and ability. The decisions he made at his office and on a church board were marked by caution, concern and dependence on human skill and adequacy. His family was filled with stress and he was disturbed when his children did not adopt his bland mixture of moralism and regulations.

Most of all, my friend was tense and tight until he became an inside-insider. As long as he remained the lord of his own life, he continued to have problems and be a problem.

He was one of the most dangerous men in his church. Why? Because his pretentious facsimile looked like the real thing. And he kept his church locked on dead center. He would not allow his church to move beyond what he had experienced. He was a stumbling block to progress.

Recently, I had a great visit with Sally and Bill Kanaga. Bill is the president of the Arthur Young Company. Sally has been an outstanding leader in her community. Both of them experienced the power of Christ long after they had been church members. Bill had been a deacon and a very generous contributor. Sally led the way in moving beyond religion to the abundant life. The changes in her life were so dramatic that they forced Bill to face the emptiness of his life in the frantic scramble for success and material security. There was a sparkle in his eye and a vitality in his voice as he told me about the time, when the carnality of his belief in Christ and his determined running of his own life became excruciatingly clear to him. Home alone one Saturday morning, this brilliant, humanly effective leader confessed the inadequacy of his own self-sufficiency and the lack of spiritual power in his life. He committed his life to Christ and asked the living Lord to come and live in him. The difference was astounding. Now he and Sally have a new marriage, a very dynamic witness to others and a responsible ministry in the business world and the New York community. Church members became filled with the power of God.

I have reflected deeply on that conversation. It was another evidence of outside-insiders becoming inside-insiders. The same thing happened to Don Seibert, chairman of the board of the J.C. Penney Company. His transformation took place as a result of sickness in his family. He realized his need for a personal relationship to Christ after years of membership in a conservative church.

There is no more crucial issue before the church today

than how to make inside-insiders out of inside-outsiders. It's never easy. Inside-outsiders think they have experienced all that there is to be discovered in the Christian life. They are dangerous because they want to do God's work in their own strength. It won't work!

Billy Graham is often criticized because so many of his converts are church members. That says a lot more about the local congregation in America than it does about the Graham crusades. Hundreds of thousands of inside-outsiders who are members of churches have discovered the liberation of a personal commitment to Christ at the crusades.

The other day I completed a series of meetings in a church in Arkansas. On the last evening I asked those who wanted to surrender complete control of their lives to Christ for the first time to stand. I was amazed at the large number of church members who stood up. One man said, "I've been waiting for 66 years to hear what you said about commitment tonight and to respond. Thanks for not taking us for granted."

There is a great movement mounting in our day. It is made up of people who are discovering that there is more to Christianity than acceptance of Christ. They are experiencing the energizing, liberating power of surrendering all they know of themselves to however much they know of Christ. The most dangerous people in the church are becoming the most dynamic. There is little distinction in believing in Jesus as the Saviour of the world. The devil believes that! The power, peace and triumph of the Christian life is available when Christ takes up residence and reigns on the throne of our hearts.

All of this leads us to one of Jesus' most disturbing parables. He had both inside-outsiders and inside-insiders among His followers. In the crowd that swirled about

Him were people who looked and acted like faithful disciples. But something was missing. They had not surrendered themselves and their loyalties and priorities to Jesus as the Lord of their lives. They became vulnerable to the control and influence of a very different lord. The problem that faced Christ was that they looked and acted like His disciples.

The parable of the wheat and the tares is Jesus' frightening analysis of the multitudes. The Lord was realistic. He knew and said that not every one who said "Lord! Lord!" would enter the Kingdom of God. In fact, there were some who were direct pawns and plants of the Evil One. What Jesus revealed in this parable helps us with the complex problem of uncommitted church members. No parable has more to say about the perplexity of inside-outsiders in the membership of the local congregation.

This parable was based on a very alarming experience in the agricultural life of Palestine, and an honest appraisal of life in any age. The greatest threat to any farmer was that an enemy might express his hostility, anger or retribution by sowing weeds in his field of wheat. At that time the most fearsome threat of a malcontent was, "Watch out. I'll plant darnel in your wheat field!"

What Jesus wanted His followers to ask was, "Am I a wheat or a weed in the field; am I an authentic follower of the Lord or the planting of the devil?"

Let's look at the parable of the wheat and the tares with that background and then at the implications Jesus drew from it as an explanation for His disciples.

A farmer planted a field of wheat. Then he went to sleep to rest from his labors. While asleep an enemy invaded his field to sow darnel, tares—a poisonous, nocuous weed which when it grows looks like wheat and cannot be distinguished until fully grown at harvesttime. When the crop was near harvesting, the servants of the householders discovered the dastardly deed. "What shall we do?" they asked the owner with consternation. His answer was based on his knowledge of wheat and tares. "Let it grow. If you weed it out now, you will destroy the wheat as well. Leave it alone until the harvest, then divide the tares from the wheat and burn the tares" (see Matt. 13:24-30).

The disciples could hardly wait to get alone with Jesus to ask for His explanation of the parable (see Matt. 13:36-42). What He told them was far more than they had anticipated.

The Lord clarified that the field was the world. The world He had come to save; the world God loved so much that He gave His only Son. The owner of the field is God Himself. The parable was a vital aspect of His autobiography. The sower of the good seeds was the Son of Man, Jesus, the Immanuel. The enemy was the devil. Now the plot intensifies. The good seeds were the true sons of the Kingdom of God; the tares were the sons of the Evil One.

Note how the metaphor has shifted from the parable of the sower we considered in a previous chapter. Before Jesus talked about planting seeds in our hearts. Now He identifies us as the seed. We are to be planted in the world. Likewise, the devil plants his seeds among the Lord's seeds. The question that focused on the disciples was, "Which kind of seed are you?" No less our question. "Which are you—am I?"

As if that wasn't enough, Jesus went on in His explanation. He said that we can identify the people who are tares by the undeniable signs: they are "stumbling blocks, and ... commit lawlessness" (Matt. 13:41). That prompts us to search the Scripture to understand the meaning of stumbling blocks and lawlessness. Only in this way will we feel the full impact of the parable.

The Greek word for stumbling block ("offend" in *KJV*) is *skandalon*. It means a stone of tripping, a snare or a fouler. Anything which causes a person to stumble. It also means anything which is offensive. Isaiah, Jeremiah and Ezekiel all use the term. In Isaiah 8:14,15, the righteousness and justice of God Himself were identified as stumbling stones for the people of Israel: "A stone to strike and a rock to stumble over, and a snare and a trap for the inhabitants of Jerusalem. And many will stumble over them, then they will fall and be broken; they will even be snared and caught." An intimation of the Incarnation is sounded in Isaiah 28:16: "Therefore thus says the Lord God, 'Behold, I am laying in Zion a stone, a tested stone, a costly cornerstone for the foundation, firmly placed.' " Jesus, the Messiah, was that stone. Jeremiah uses the same imagery to expose the willful pride of God's people: "Therefore, thus says the Lord, 'Behold, I am laying stumbling blocks before this people, and they will stumble against them' " (Jer. 6:21). The shift in Ezekiel is that the iniquity of the people had become an "occasion of stumbling" (Ezek. 7:19). In the fourteenth chapter, Ezekiel calls the idols in people's hearts stumbling blocks.

Jesus used the idea in two ways. He knew He was a stumbling block to people who were self-righteous. They "took offense" at Him. The same basic word is used. He also warned people about being stumbling blocks for others. Both of these are emphasized by Paul. When he reflected on the Incarnation and his people's rejection of the Messiah, he said, "They stumbled over the stumbling-stone" (Rom. 9:32). But Paul also cautioned about people who obstruct others with stumbling stones: "Therefore let us not judge one another any more, but rather determine this—not to put an obstacle or a stumbling-block in a brother's way" (Rom. 14:13).

The early church recognized the cross as the major stumbling stone for the Jews: "But we preach Christ crucified, to Jews a stumbling-block, and to Gentiles foolishness" (1 Cor. 1:23). The Crucifixion is a direct confrontation of our need for forgiveness and salvation. It exposes the fact that we cannot save ourselves with our own righteousness or religion.

Now to recap the meaning of these Scriptures for our understanding of the nature of a tare. When we stumble over Christ and reject Him as the only hope of life, now and forever, we become stumbling blocks ourselves. We actually suggest that our goodness is enough and that we can make it on our own. Pride is the inner germination of the seed of the tare.

Life begins when we stumble over Christ. When our arrogant pride is broken we can recognize our need and accept the gift He died to give us. The dangerous people in the church are those who celebrate Christmas, Good Friday, Easter and Pentecost without realizing and experiencing for themselves the death, resurrection and indwelling power of Christ. It's possible to hear the good news of God's love in Christ without letting Him love us personally in the depth of our need. Seems ridiculous and incredulous, but thousands of Christians attend church and call themselves Christians but never know the joy of abiding in Christ and allowing Him to abide in them. They look and act like wheat, but are tares. Our Lord says to them what He had to say to Simon Peter when he resisted the necessity of the cross: "Get behind Me, Satan! You are a stumbling-block to Me" (Matt. 16:23). We can be agents of Satan's resistance, rather than agents of reconciliation. Until we trip in our efforts to control our own lives and justify ourselves, we will cause others to stumble over our distorted example.

I meet Christians everywhere who resist the confession of their total dependence on Christ. It's possible to say we believe in Christ when we join the church and then live in our own strength and our own efforts to be adequate by our own talent and moral rectitude. There is a constant relapse into old patterns of self-sufficiency conditioned by training and the values of self-reliance admired in our society. It trips our self-image to accept that there's no way to God except by way of Calvary, that we could not think a thought or breathe a breath without God's blessing and that we cannot accomplish our reason for being without God's transformation of our personality. Tares become wheat when we realize our insufficiency and invite the Lord to take charge of our lives. The difficulties and tragedies of life are special gifts to alarm us that we may be dangerous tares being sown in the field.

The second designation of the nature of the darnel tares was lawlessness. Let's be sure we understand what lawlessness means for a Christian in the church. For many people God is an absentee landlord. We can believe that *He* is Lord of the universe yet at the same time *we* run our own lives. Lawlessness is more than refusing to be a law-abiding citizen or breaking the Ten Commandments. It is living our lives by values and goals which have never been tempered in the fires of God's will for us. We are lawless when we make decisions about what we will do and be without profound prayer. It's possible to be a respectable church member today without ever reporting in to the Lord for daily orders about what we are to say and do, spend and save.

That's dangerous. If we make our crucial decisions without prolonged conversation with the Lord in prayer, we will not only mess up our lives and others, but will miss the immense possibilities that would never occur to us without His inspiration. When an unguided, self-determined Christian is placed in a position of leadership in the church or society, he can be a menace to the expansion of the Kingdom. He can impede progress, lead off in wrong directions and cripple the potential of others.

We all know Christians whose value system is completely dominated by non-biblical presuppositions. What they believe is controlled by ideas ingrained by culture. More devastating, what they believe to be possible, denies the inspirational interventions of God and the flow of power from His Holy Spirit. Many churches are led by officers and even pastors who are dangerously self-motivated and self-limited. No wonder the local church lacks vitality, daring and excitement. We can be more convinced about the impossible than God's possibilities—carnal Christians out of power.

But Jesus' parable offers hope. The wheat and the tares are allowed to coexist until harvest. There's time for us to determine whether we are wheat or tares. The gracious patience of God, that, too, is an undeniable part of His autobiography. When we consider the parable in the light of the total message of Jesus Christ, we know that tares can become wheat before the harvest at the end of our physical life.

We can be channels of the Spirit or Satan. That shakes us in our boots. Until we yield to Christ the vital nerve center of our lives, the intrinsic self within, we have the potential of being negative, nocuous tares. That explains the checkered pages of Christian history that make us blush and the impotence of the church in our own time that makes us blanch.

The hope of the parable is that we are to cultivate the wheat rather than try to weed out the tares. We are responsible to be sure we are wheat. Our task is not to purge the tares. That's God's business. Rather than wring our hands in consternation over the satanic influence in the church through the tares, we are to grow as wheat. The judgment will come each day and on our last day. The basis of that judgment of the wheat and the tares will be on whether we have allowed the conviction of the saviourhood of Christ to become the experience of His Lordship in every facet and area of our lives. The final test of the wheat and the tares will be the extent to which we have yielded complete control of our minds, hearts, relationships, responsibilities in church and society.

The conversion of church people in our time is slowly but persistently raiding the ranks of the most dangerous people in the church. The Lord leaves us with a question only we can decide. A wheat or a tare? To ask the question of ourselves seriously and answer it with unreserved commitment to Him, is a sure sign that we are part of the wheat ready for harvest.

8

Before You Give Up!

Matthew 13:31,32: Parable of the Mustard Seed

I had a difficult time going to sleep in the hotel room in the East. My body was on California time. After I had prayed my prayers and read for hours, sleep eluded me. Finally I turned on the television set. Between the scenes of an old western movie, a 30-second spot appeared on the screen. It caught my attention. In bold letters was the message, "Before you give up, call 866-3242." I was not about to give up on anything except getting some rest, but my interest was piqued. I dialed the number and found that it was a Christian crisis-intervention ministry. The woman's voice on the other end of the line spoke before I identified myself. "Before you give up try Jesus! Can I be of any help?" I thanked her and told her that I was a Californian whose only problem was sleeplessness. She laughed, and we had a good conversation about her ministry to people who are about ready to give up. Afterward, I reflected on the many people I know who are hanging on by a thin thread, about to give up. I pictured them: people ready to give up on their marriage after years of trying; others tempted to give up hope for a friend or loved one; still others who feel that whatever they do to change things, it doesn't work.

Ever feel that way? We all feel it at times. The temptation to give up—on people, relationships, projects, hopes, and dreams. Sometimes on ourselves.

The other day I went into a sporting goods store. They had a special sale on survival kits for the wilderness camper. I looked through the supplies provided to stay alive when lost or out of touch with civilization. The booklet inside was particularly interesting to me because of my conversation with the crisis intervention ministry in the East. The booklet was entitled, *Before You Give Up!* It contained 10 things to do to survive. That started me thinking about what we give people to help them make it when lost or lonely in the wilderness of life today.

The purpose of this chapter is to claim Jesus' answer to that need. The advice to "try Jesus" may sound simplistic. How to do that is very profound. The parable of the mustard seed is the Lord's hope-filled survival kit. He wants us to know the secret before we give up.

Some of the disciples and followers of Jesus were tempted to give up. Was following the Master worth it? Would it make any difference? John the Baptist's question was beneath the surface, lurking in the hearts of most of them: "Are you the One, or shall we look for another?" Could this carpenter of Nazareth pull it off? Was He truly the Messiah? Could He affect the powerful political structure of Rome or the ecclesiastical authority of Jerusalem? Why was it taking so long? We can empathize. Evil seems so virulent. Change takes so much patience. Progress is difficult and slow.

Impatience breeds discouragement and births self-incrimination. It's then that we say, "If I only had more faith! Things would be different if I had enough faith to face life's excruciatingly slow process. My faith just isn't big enough!" As if everything depended on the size of our faith, we spiral subjectively into misguided musings about our own adequacy. The bad mood which results drains our energy and spreads to the people around us like a contagious disease.

Jesus' answer to His disciples and to us is piercing and penetrating. His antidote for our impatience rooted in our impotence is a homely parable filled with holy truth and hope. It is simple and direct. He says, before you give up, consider the parable of the mustard seed.

"He presented another parable to them, saying, 'The kingdom of heaven is like a mustard seed, which a man took and sowed in his field; and this is smaller than all other seeds; but when it is full grown, it is larger than the garden plants, and becomes a tree, so that the birds of the air come and nest in its branches'" (Matt. 13:31, 32).

This parable has three hopeful things to say to us before we give up on anything or anyone.

The first is that Jesus wants us to discover the might of the miniscule. Some background will help. The mustard plant was an herb. It was planted in gardens in Palestine at that time. There was a particular kind of mustard plant which grew rapidly from a minute seed into a bush, and then into a shrub the size of a tree. Mustard seeds were so small, the naked eye could barely see them. Yet the result was a strong-branched growth in which birds could not only perch, but build nests.

Look closely at the central character of the parable,

"a certain man." We've met Him before. This parable is part of the autobiography of God. Understood in the context of Jesus' words that the field is the world, and the Son of man the sower, we begin to grasp the meaning. The Lord Himself is the sower of the mustard seed which will grow to gigantic proportions. The seed is His gift of faith in us. When that grows in us we can be planted in the world as examples of what the power of God can do to heal discouragement.

Jesus' own life and ministry exemplified the meaning of the parable. God planted a seed in Bethlehem. He grew in wisdom and stature. Then He came forth proclaiming the Kingdom of God. His message of love set people free. The cross and resurrection followed. Indefatigable growth! Pentecost and the birth of the church unleashed His power. The mustard tree of a universal movement stands resolutely. A small beginning; a triumphant conclusion still to come. Surely the early church found great hope in the parable, as it faced insurmountable odds with a faith that had removed mountains.

When Jesus told this parable, He wanted His disciples to dare to believe that what was happening before their eyes was the beginning of the transformation of the world. God was working His purposes out. How He does that is the crucial aspect of the autobiography He was writing in His Son. The same basic miracle of God would happen in them.

That introduces the second part of the secret of survival. Jesus said elsewhere, "If you have faith the size of a mustard seed ... " When we are tempted to be discouraged, we need to remember that it's not the size of our faith, but the immensity of God's power that makes the difference. Christ lifts our inverted attention off our own insufficient faith to the immensity of God's resources for growth and change. All we are to do is plant the seed and leave the results to God.

This summer, I preached at the Church of the Lepers, in Taipei, Taiwan. The work among these rejected people was begun by a great lady named Lillian Dixon. It's called the Mustard Seed Ministry. An infinitesimally small seed of trust has unleashed the infinite power of God. Lillian believed that God had called her to begin the work. She trusted Him completely. Money began coming in from all over the world. The work expanded. Now the results tower like a great mustard tree. She was tempted often to give up. The Lord wanted to amaze the world with what He could do with a little lady who had a grain of faith. The glory is now given to Him. When I saw the healed bodies and the transformed personalities that have resulted, I was given new courage and hope.

Focus the people, problems, and responsibilities that cause you discouragement. The issue is not the size of your faith any more than the light switch is electricity. Our only task is to flip the switch.

Prayer is the sacred time for mustard seed planting. The Lord waits for us to pray, "Dear God, I am faced with problems too big for me. But I believe you are able. I trust you and want only what you have planned for me and the people I love. The worst thing that could happen would be for me to miss anything that you have arranged for my welfare."

What is true for our problems is also applicable for our growth in Christ. He begins with the smallest of mustard seed beginnings. Our faltering confession of belief in Him starts a recreative, regenerating process that never stops. We look back on that first prayer of commitment and are amazed at what the Lord has done with our character and personality.

Paul was very conscious of the miracle of what the Lord had accomplished in his life. He was not the man he had been, nor was he the man Christ would enable him to be. God gave the Apostle the patient love to affirm growth in others. He was a great encouragement for the struggling Christians in Philippi: "For I am confident of this very thing, that He who began a good work in you will perfect it until the day of Christ Jesus" (Phil. 1:6). The Ephesians were admonished to trust the future to God. Paul wanted them to know there was so much more to be discovered in Christ: "I pray that the eyes of your heart may be enlightened, so that you may know what is the hope of His calling, what are the riches of the glory of His inheritance in the saints, and what is the surpassing greatness of His power toward us who believe. These are in accordance with the working of the strength of His might which He brought about in Christ, when He raised Him from the dead, and seated Him at His right hand in the heavenly places, far above all rule and authority and power and dominion, and every name that is named, not only in this age, but also in the one to come" (Eph. 1:18-21).

God is on the move in us. He wants to make us His miracle for the world to see what He can do. And He's not finished; He's barely begun. Paul went on to remind the Ephesians what kind of people they had been when God first began His work in them. Then he confirmed the magnificent transformation that had taken place.

When we reflect on what God has done with the mustard seed of our first trusting response to the gospel, we can yield our troublesome affairs to Him. He's growing a mustard tree out of you and me. Be sure of that!

When we are a mustard tree, we can become communicators of hope to people around us who are ready to give up. The first step to a solution of any problem is to plant the mustard seed of unreserved faith. People need to be reminded of that by others who know what a difference the Lord can accomplish. We are not expected to be perfect. We are expected to be contagious infusers of viable hope. There are discouraged people everywhere in our lives. They desperately need a mustard tree to perch on. That's the final twist of the parable. Once God grows a mustard tree out of our seed of faith, the worried birds will flock to receive what we have discovered.

The parable of the mustard seed has profoundly enriched our appreciation of this dimension of God's autobiography. He has told us He is power, and that power is available to us. Before you give up, plant the mustard seed of faith and be ready to be amazed at what God will do!

9

God Can Change
Your Personality!

Matthew 13:33-35: Parable of the Leaven

"It's changed my personality!" That was the confident claim of a middle-aged entertainer who had just had a face-lift. She had gone to a world-renowned cosmetic surgeon. His artistry removed the lines that age and difficulties had plowed deeply into her cheeks. The bags under her eyes were gone. With a careful incision along her hairline, the surgeon was able to stretch out the furrows in her brow.

I had to acknowledge that the woman looked 15 years younger. The harried, pressured look her face had developed was gone.

"You look like a new woman!" I said, in affirmation of the pain and expense she had endured.

"I only hope I can stay that way!" she responded, in a concerned voice which contradicted her now smooth, china-doll face.

"What do you mean?" I asked, immediately sensing

her anxiety about the possible impermanence of her mask-like, cosmetic transformation.

"Well, the surgeon tells me that plastic surgery and face-lifting will be lasting only if there is a change in my inner patterns of thought and emotions. He says that my face is an expression of my psyche, and that I'll look the way I did again in three years unless I learn how to live. He recommended I see a psychiatrist or a spiritual advisor, to get a soul-lift that will help me keep my face-lift."

Amazing! The surgery had altered the woman's appearance enough to give her a temporary, positive self-image, but it had not really changed her personality. It would take more than a new face to make her a new person. A change in her personality would have to wait for that.

Personality change is not easy. Most of us are what the patterning of learning and experience has made us. We are conditioned creatures. Most authorities say that once a person's personality is set by early training, example and molding, it cannot be changed. The purpose of this chapter is to challenge that assumption.

Personality is the sum total of our individuality. It is the outward expression of the intrinsic person within each of us: that which constitutes, characterizes, and distinguishes us. As the entire organization of our uniqueness, personality is the composite of our essential self—innate disposition, beliefs, convictions, impulses, desires, appetites, and instincts.

The people around us know who we are through our personalities. Personality is the observable I—that which others experience, relate and respond to in the dialogue and drama of life. It is the product of all that's happened to, around, and within us. Environment, education, culture, significant people, and experience have all had a sculpturing hand in the shaping of the clay of our personality. The people we want to emulate, as well as those we reject as influential examples, have contributed to our image of ourselves. We are all in the process of developing our personalities around the picture of the person we envision ourselves to be. The person we are inside, however, will irrevocably control the personality we express outwardly to others. Any change in our personality must be a result of a transformation of the values, goals, feelings, attitudes, and self-esteem of the person who lives inside our skins.

That's where Jesus begins. He can transform our personalities!

He never used the word. It cannot be found recorded in the Scriptures. And yet, everything Jesus said, did, and does radically alters and reshapes personality. The Lord is deeply concerned about our personalities. He has called us to be His people in order to remold us in His own image, and then send us into life as liberated personalities. What He does for us is in preparation for what He wants to do through us in the world.

The parable of the leaven is the parable of the transformation of personality and, subsequently, the transforming power of a Christ-centered personality. It dramatizes how the Kingdom of God changes us and then how we, as changed people, affect the world. Jesus tells us how the gospel gets into us and, then, how we are to get the gospel into the world.

"The kingdom of heaven is like leaven, which a woman took, and hid in three pecks of meal, until it was all leavened" (Matt. 13:33).

Leaven was a little piece of dough which had been kept over from a previous baking. (Breadmakers today call it "starter.") While it was stored, it fermented. After a time, it was ready to be kneaded into a new batch of dough. It pervaded the entire dough with its transforming influence. The dough would change its nature and size through the silent, rising impact of the leaven.

This was Jesus' homely illustration of hope. It described how He was working in history, how He works in us, and how we are to work in the world.

Clearly, the Master saw His own Incarnation as leaven. The power of God was being kneaded into the dough of humanity. His life would alter the shape of history. Imperceptibly at first, then undeniably. Jesus was the fullness of God infusing new life. Just as the leaven subdues or conquers the dough with its power, so too the gospel was at work beginning a new creation. Christ brought an entirely new element into life: the gospel of the Kingdom of God, the reign and rule of God in all of life. Christ's life and message was the insertion of the leaven; His death infused its power; His resurrection released its pervading dynamic; His presence in the Holy Spirit is now permeating the whole of life. The bread is rising!

The kingdom people are the leaven of the Kingdom of God in society. The individual is always the key. The whole dough of humanity is made up of its separate parts. The leaven transforms every particle of the dough. That means you and me! The Lord leavens us and then uses us to leaven society. He transforms our personalities and then displays to the world what He can do with a person who seeks first His Kingdom. Let's consider exactly how this happens.

The leaven of Christ enters our life when we accept the love and forgiveness He offers us. We know that we are accepted just as we are. But He will not leave us there. Once the leaven of His presence enters our life, it begins to reorganize the total dough of the person we are. Everything is touched by the insistent infusion. Christ's persistent love pervades and penetrates our total person. That He has taken charge of us is comforting; how He transforms us is often very uncomfortable.

He begins with what has made us what we are. Our previous experiences are exposed to His scrutiny. "What has made you what you are?" He asks. "Let's examine each relationship of your formative years." One by one, He leads us through the corridors of memory. He affirms the positive experiences, and helps us to forgive and forget anything that has warped us. Then He helps us to see ourselves as we are. He reveals to us how we come across to people.

First, He enables us to enjoy the strengths of our personalities. Then He penetrates into the attitudes, experiences, and habit-patterns that cripple our growth and debilitate our relationships with others. All of the eccentric traits which reveal that we are off center, away from Him, are exposed one by one. The Potter of personality reveals how we would look, sound, and act if those traits were surrendered to Him.

The leaven works inadvertently. The more we focus our total attention on the leavening Lord Himself, the more we become like Him. That's the exciting adventure of Christian growth. The indwelling Lord is up to nothing less than making us like Himself! Our task is not to try to develop Christian virtues, but to yield ourselves to Christ. The virtues of Christlikeness grow naturally.

I constantly hear people saying, "If I could get out of the way; if I could only get rid of self, I would be more of the Christian I was meant to be." That's absurd! It's like the dough refusing to be dough. Just as every particle of the dough is transformed by the leaven, so our lives are transformed by the indwelling Lord. He is in us and we in Him. No one would dissect rising dough to discern what is the dough and what is the leaven. The two are so inseparably intermingled that the union is imperceptible. The issue is the ever-expanding scope of Christ's penetration in our personality. Jesus' promise is also a command: "Abide in Me, and I in you" (John 15:4). That's the secret of a transformed personality.

A personality inventory helps to focus how thoroughly the leaven has penetrated. Here are some questions I ask myself:

How would I describe my personality?

If I could change any aspect of my personality, what would I change?

How would the people closest to me describe my personality? What do I think they would suggest needs changing?

Would I like anyone else to have a personality like mine? Why? Why not?

List five assets of my personality. Now list five liabilities.

If Christ were to write a critique of my personality, what would He write?

All of that is in preparation for creatively introspective prayer. We have opened ourselves to listen to our Lord. Now take a prolonged period of uninterrupted silence. Picture your personality. Now ask for the picture of what the leaven wants to liberate you to be.

The last aspect of the inventory is to write down what you have learned. Keep a logbook with your Bible. Make a list of areas of your personality where the leaven needs to work. Record daily what you experience of the Lord's changes in your personality. You will be amazed; the people around you will be delighted and thankful!

I know this inventory works. When I became a Christian and the leaven entered my life, I was a jumble of objectionable personality traits. My insecurity manifested itself in distractive patterns. As a drama student, I was always on stage. I talked like I was reciting Shakespeare. Misuse of the gifts of intellect, voice, and presence got in my way, tripping me in my movement toward people. The warmth of Christ in my heart was often contradicted by an aloofness. Perfectionism, inbred in childhood, made me judgmental and critical. Ambition made me competitive, more for my own achievement than for communicating Christ.

Then, early in my new life in Christ, I discovered the liberating power of the parable of the leaven. It has disturbed me ever since. Now, many years later, the Lord is still at work shaping my personality. He's not finished. Nor will He ever be. I am sure that on the day I die, I'll be aware of the next steps to be taken, new areas to be touched by the leaven.

The adventure of working with people is maximized for me because I can share the pilgrimage of personality transformation with them. The most exciting times of my life are when I can be part of the Lord's implantation of the leaven in people. It's a delight to watch people change and grow after they have entered the Kingdom and allowed the reign and rule of Christ to be the leaven in their personalities.

The other day, I read a grim commentary on human nature: "If a man is a philanderer, he will always be a philanderer to the end. It is only in novels that a miracle occurs in the last chapter that makes the drunkard reform and become sober, the grouch sunny and sweet-tempered, the miser generous and open-handed, the shrew so mild that butter wouldn't melt in her mouth. In real life these things never happen. People continue to be what habit and usage have made them."

I don't believe that! Everything in my own experience and observation of people in whom the leaven of the Lord is at work convinces me that personality can be changed.

Look at the disciples. What a study of unleavened dough they were when Jesus began to work with them! In the band of disciples Jesus had a strange mixture of insecure, pushy, introverted, insensitive, arrogant, competitive personalities. He called them so "that they might be with Him." That's when the leaven slipped into the crevices of their psyches. Like the woman of the parable, the Lord hid the dynamic of His Lordship in their hearts. The process began. The kneading was penetrating during the days of the Master's ministry, as they listened to His words and watched His actions. But it wasn't until after Pentecost that the Leaven Himself took charge of the disciples and made them apostles. More than an example from without, the Lord became a reorienting energizer from within. The new creation Jesus promised in the coming of the Kingdom was now populated by new creatures. But the Leaven was not finished with them even then. The pages of Acts describe the continuing transformation.

There's no more vivid and dramatic illustration of Christ's power to change personality than in Saul of Tarsus. A psychological profile on the rigid, determined, compulsive personality of the Pharisee assigned to persecute the Christians would suggest that flexibility and metamorphosis would be impossible. Then he encountered one of the people he was determined to destroy. Stephen's witness to the living Christ, and the radiance of the Lord upon his face while he was being stoned to death, made an irresistible impression on Saul. What the leaven had done in the martyr's life began its work in his executioner.

Then, on the road to Damascus, Saul met the Leaven Himself. Blinded by the encounter, he staggered into Damascus. A few days later, Ananias, whom Saul had intended to imprison, was the kneading agent who enabled the Leaven to begin His transforming work on the Apostle-elect. The Lord said to Ananias, "Go [to Saul], for he is a chosen instrument of Mine, to bear My name before the Gentiles and kings and the sons of Israel" (Acts 9:15). The most exciting account of personality transformation resulted.

Paul's own account of his growth as a man in Christ tabulates the transformation. References to it are in many of his recorded messages and in almost all of his epistles to the early church. The third chapter of Philippians traces how the leaven worked in the dough of his personality. He tells us what he was as a Hebrew of Hebrews, a zealous persecutor of the church, and a self-righteous religionist. Then he describes what Christ had done for him. Righteousness with God through the grace of the cross reoriented his nature. Knowing Christ personally was the key. Christ was the goal; the prize of his life. Maturity for Paul was a life completely surrendered to, filled with, under the control of, and immersed by the indwelling Saviour, "who will transform the body of our humble state into conformity with the body of His glory, by the exertion of the power that He has even to subject all things to Himself" (Phil. 3:21).

What the Lord did to transform Paul became the compelling content of his message. Wherever he went, the Apostle introduced people to the Saviour and encouraged them to grow to full maturity as new creatures in Christ. His message was, "If any man is in Christ, he is a new creature; the old things passed away; behold, new things have come" (2 Cor. 5:17). How this happens is explained in passages like Romans 12:2: "Do not be conformed to this world, but be transformed by the renewing of your mind, that you may prove what the will of God is, that which is good and acceptable and perfect." Paul goes on to show how the renewed mind is manifest in a personality that is gracious, forgiving, warm, and considerate. He believed that we can have the mind of Christ as the guide and control of our personality.

In Paul's prayer for the Ephesians, we catch a glimpse of what the Apostle longed for all people: "I bow my knees before the Father, from whom every family in heaven and on earth derives its name, that He would grant you, according to the riches of His glory, to be strengthened with power through His Spirit in the inner man; so that Christ may dwell in your hearts through faith; and that you, being rooted and grounded in love, may be able to comprehend with all the saints what is the breadth and length and height and depth, and to know the love of Christ which surpasses knowledge, that you may be filled up to all the fulness of God" (Eph. 3:14-19). There's a vivid description of the leaven which God puts within us.

On the basis of that, Paul could challenge the Ephesians to grow in mature Christian personality: "I, therefore, the prisoner of the Lord, entreat you to walk [live] in a manner worthy of the calling with which you have been called, with all humility and gentleness, with patience, showing forbearance to one another in love" (Eph. 4:1). The Apostle wanted the new Christians to realize their full potential, to "attain to the unity of the faith, and of the knowledge of the Son of God, to a mature man, to the measure of the stature which belongs to the fulness of Christ. As a result, we are no longer to be children, tossed here and there by waves, ... but speaking the truth in love, we are to grow up in all aspects into Him, who is the head, even Christ" (Eph. 4:13-15).

I think Paul was referring to what we call Christian personality. "In reference to your former manner of life,

... lay aside the old self, ... that you be renewed in the spirit of your mind, and put on the new self, which in the likeness of God has been created in righteousness and holiness of the truth" (4:22-24). The letter to the Ephesians concludes with admonitions that flow naturally from this: "Be imitators of God ... walk in love, as Christ also loved you ... walk as children of light" (5:1,2,8). The leaven of the Spirit of Christ fashions us in the image of Christ.

The same instruction is given the Colossians. When the word of Christ dwelt in them richly, they would have an outer personality of compassion, kindness, humility, gentleness, forbearance, forgiveness, and encouragement.

What Christ has been in us as the leaven, we are to be in the world. Once we have been leavened, we are to be the leavening agent of the Kingdom of God in the world. We are kneaded into the dough of society by our Lord. Our influence in the lives of others is like Christ's influence in us: pervasive, penetrating, and permeating.

Observe how Christ-centered personality becomes His leaven in the world. As the leaven pervades each aspect of our inner person, the result is manifested for others to see. We should be the source of repeated questions: How did you get the way you are? How can I find what you have found?

That makes our evaluation of the extent Christ is evident in our personalities a crucial issue. A negative, cold, unloving personality is a contradiction of terms. Not everyone is endowed with physical attractiveness. But each of us is capable of becoming an attractive personality. Christ's love and warmth can do that for all of us. Paul's question to the Corinthians demands an answer: "Who sees anything different in you?" How would you answer?

Our personality is our window to the world. People will be able to see what can happen to them by observation of what is happening to us. Leaven is observable only as it's working, not after the bread is baked. Our task is not to become "perfect," but to expose the leaven as it's working in us. As we share what the Lord is doing as well as what He's done, we will make contact with other struggling persons. Vulnerability and openness create contagious communication about the adventure of the Spirit's transforming work.

The test of a leavened personality is the number of people with whom we have been able to share our faith. Any Christian who is allowing the leaven to work in him will be besieged by people who also want to discover the dynamic.

The parable of the leaven is both confrontation and cheer. It confronts us with what Christ wants to do in our lives, and cheers us with the good news that no one of us needs to remain as he is! Where is the leaven at work in you right now? With whom have you been called to be the agent of leavening? Christ will not be finished until He has transformed every part of us, every person around us, and all of society.

10
The Treasure Is You!

Matthew 13:44-46: Parables of the Treasure and the Pearl

The theme song of the college conference was Ralph Carmichael's winsome confession of complete commitment, "He's Everything to Me." Each evening the collegians would close the day by singing the words that expressed the unreserved trust of a personal faith.

In the stars His handiwork I see,
On the wind He speaks with majesty.
Though He ruleth over land and sea,
What is that to me?
Till by faith I met Him face to face,
And I felt the wonder of His grace,
Then I knew that He was more than
Just a God who didn't care
That lived away out there.

And now He walks beside me day by day,
Ever watching o'er me lest I stray,
Helping me to find that narrow way,
He's everything to me.
He's everything to me.[1]

As I watched the joyous faces and heard the gusto of the singing, the words affirmed my own longing to have God be everything to me. The days of the conference had been filled counseling students. They were wrestling with the problems of conflicting loyalties: studies, career plans, dating, marriage, success, and self-images. Their burning questions were: "How can I put God first in my life? I really want to mean it. How do you make a full surrender of your life to know and do the will of God? Why is it so difficult to be a true Christian?"

The words of the song gave me God's answer for my final message. You can't say, "He's everything to me!" until you can say and believe, "I'm everything to God!"

That's the exciting truth Jesus communicated to His disciples in the twin parables of the hidden treasure and the pearl of great price. He had called His inner band into intimate conversation. It was to these men who had responded to His message and were His followers that He gave the secret of how to make the Kingdom of God everything to them. He had given several parables of the Kingdom to the masses, as we have seen in our exposition of the parables of the sower and the leaven. Now to those who believed in Him, He explained the surpassing value of the Kingdom and the way to enter into the full joy of the reign and rule of God in their lives.

The twin parables deal with the will. The issue is knowing and doing the will of God. The disciples had to want that more than anything else. Jesus gave them the motivation in these parables. They are autobiographical and biographical. We will miss the full impact

108

unless we see both what they tell us about the King of the Kingdom and the subjects of the Kingdom. The motivation of the second is dependent on the first. Let's look for both as we dig out the deeper meaning of the parables.

"The kingdom of heaven is like a treasure hidden in the field; which a man found and hid; and from joy over it he goes and sells all that he has, and buys the field" (Matt. 13:44).

We can feel the emotions of the plowman working the field. He had plowed it many times before. Feel the hot sun beating down, the sweat rolling off his brow, the weary hands gripping the slivered plow handles. Sameness, demanding labor, monotony. Then suddenly the plow hits an obstruction. Another rock to be dug out and carried to the side of the field! He got down on his knees and began to dig with his hands. Clump and clod were removed. The hard earth resisted movement. Then the man's hand broke through and he touched the obstruction. Not granite, but the top edge of a chest! The man's heart began to beat faster. Could it be—? He knew that treasures were often hidden in the ground. There were no banks. People resorted to the earth to hide their valuables. When war or calamity drove them off their land they would bury their treasures, hoping to return to claim them. The plowman dug furiously, remembering the rabbinical "finders keepers" law of the time. Excitement surged through him as he ripped the chest open and beheld the jewels and curios sparkling in the sunlight. But then a terrible fright jabbed his mind. Had anyone seen him? He carefully covered the chest, replacing the earth, so no one would suspect. Then a plan formed in his mind. At all cost, he must have that field so the treasure would be his. Joy gripped him as he liquidated all other assets to buy the field. Nothing was of value in comparison to possessing that treasure!

Jesus has captured our interest. Who is not fascinated by hidden treasure? We all can identify with the plow-man.

Now that He has riveted our attention, He goes on to tell another parable. The message seems the same and yet it is distinctive. We are drawn into the drama of a man's search for valued pearls.

"Again, the kingdom of heaven is like a merchant seeking fine pearls, and upon finding one pearl of great value, he went and sold all that he had, and bought it" (Matt. 13:45,46).

The one-sentence account gives wings to our imagination. We feel the intensity of the search for the best of fine pearls. The quest, the longing, the persistence. The man knew pearls. He had spent his life studying them, bartering one for another, upgrading his collection as he traveled from village to village. He had heard of *the* pearl of unsurpassed perfection and beauty. We wonder if it was one that had been the cherished possession of Cleopatra, valued at over $400,000. The merchantman thought of little else. His every conversation focused on it, hoping to glean some new information on where he could find it. He dreamed about it. His conscious mind was never on anything else.

And then one day he found it! When he saw it, he knew his relentless search was worth the tireless energy. The cost? Name the price! The man had to possess the pearl! He could not contain the joy he felt. Everything he had—possessions, other pearls, life itself—was more than worth the cost. We can empathize with the ecstasy he felt when he finally possessed the pearl of great price. "It's mine! It cost me everything, but it's mine!"

We are left to ponder the powerful truth Jesus is telling us. Our first response is, "What means that much to us? What would we value as highly as a treasure or a pearl? Does God and His Kingdom mean that much to us?" Then we look at the parables again. There's a deeper meaning. Suddenly it dawns upon us. As we contemplate it, we feel the wonder of the sublime serendipity. The parables of the treasure and the pearl tell us about the purpose of Jesus' passion and the passionate purpose that He unleashes in our lives.

Jesus is saying, "You are the treasure! You are the pearl of great price! I have found you!"

Check the context in which Jesus spoke the parables and the truth breaks forth. His explanation of the parable of the tares of the field gives us the needed key: "The one who sows the good seed is the Son of Man, and the field is the world" (Matt. 13:37,38). He is the leading character in most all of the parables He had been teaching.

Here, He is the plowman, the merchantman. God with us saying, "You are everything to me! No cost is too high!"

Our mind's eye dilates on Calvary. That's how much it cost. The suffering, shame, and agony of the cross was the price He paid for you and me. Hebrews 12:2 thunders in our souls: "Fixing our eyes on Jesus the author and perfecter of faith, who for the joy set before Him endured the cross, despising the shame, and has sat down at the right hand of the throne of God." That's how much He loves us. He came for us, lived for us, died for us, was raised up for us. The familiar parables flash with new meaning.

Now we can plunge deeper into the metaphors of the Master. The treasure reminds us of the many times God had told Israel that she was a "special treasure among all the peoples, for all the earth is Mine" (see Exod. 19:5). The pearl metaphor is drenched with meaning. It complements the treasure in the field in that it reveals how much God treasured His people, and what must happen to us to realize His love.

Pearls are the result of invasion and injury. They are products of a living organism. A grain of sand gets within the oyster and injures it. The oyster then covers over the injury with macle and mother-of-pearl, layer on layer, until the pearl is fashioned. The wounding is the source of the wonder.

The word pearl is used only once in the Old Testament. Job said, "The price of wisdom is above pearls" (see Job 28:18). But it was not one of the significant words or symbols of Israel. Why then did Jesus speak of great price? His metaphors were carefully selected. I believe that He had the metamorphosis of the pearl in mind. The Kingdom of God would not be fulfilled without the terrible wounding of Calvary. He knew what was ahead. Isaiah had made that clear. The Messiah would be "wounded for our transgressions." And yet, from Golgotha's wounds the world would be won.

Only the power of love can make us realize how much we mean to God. Our self-deprecation debilitates us. Life's blows form negative self-images and lack of self-esteem. How can we accept the love God offers? We are not worth the Incarnation; we have done nothing to deserve a love like that. The Lord knows the injury and the wounds of our experiences. And He uses them to make a pearl. The magnificent metaphor is twofold: what Christ means to us and what we mean to Him.

The point is this: You and I are central in the strategy of the Kingdom. The rule of God must begin within us, then reside between us, and eventually pervade all areas of life. God has elected us to be the channels of His plan and purpose in the world. The Kingdom must enter into us before we can enter into the Kingdom. That's exactly what Jesus wanted the disciples to realize. Once they knew they were treasured by God, they would give everything to possess the treasure of the Kingdom. When they realized that they were pearls without peer to God, they would sell all they had to obtain the pearl of great price—knowing and serving Him. The passion of our Lord liberates us to fulfill the purpose for which we were born.

So often the gospel is preached or taught in the grim ambience of what we must give up before we can realize God's grace. That is backwards. What God has done for us is the only adequate motivation for what we are to do and be in response. We can "seek first the Kingdom of God" only after we know that He has sought us, and having found us, loves us with acceptance and forgiveness which knows no boundary. Paul experienced that. He could say, "For to me, to live is Christ" (Phil. 1:21), because Christ had lived for him. The Apostle's passionate purpose flowed from that: "More than that, I count all things to be loss in view of the surpassing value of knowing Christ Jesus my Lord, for whom I have suffered the loss of all things, and count them but rubbish in order that I may gain Christ . . . that I may know Him, and the power of His resurrection" (Phil. 3:8,10). That's the essence of the meaning of the parable of the treasure and the pearl. Love responding to love. The cost of discipleship must always be considered in the light of what it cost our Lord to make us disciples.

This is what Paul wanted the Ephesians to realize: "I pray that the eyes of your heart may be enlightened, so that you may know what is the hope of His calling, what are the riches of the glory of His inheritance in the saints" (Eph. 1:18). The saints, the members of the church at Ephesus, needed the encouragement of affirming again that they were Christ's inheritance. If they could accept who they were as chosen people, they would be able to choose to do the Lord's will: "Therefore be imitators of God, as beloved children; and walk in love, just as Christ also loved you, and gave Himself up for us, an offering and a sacrifice to God" (Eph. 5:1,2). We know what we are to do when we receive what He's done for us. What is true for us as individuals is true for the church as a fellowship and a life-changing agency of love in the world: "Christ also loved the church and gave Himself up for her; that He might sanctify her, having cleansed her by the washing of water with the word, that He might present to Himself the church in all her glory, having no spot or wrinkle or any such thing; but that she should be holy and blameless" (Eph. 5:25-27).

The purpose of Jesus' passion was the creation of a new people, the church. Precious treasure to bless the world. Peter knew what that meant; it had happened to him. His words to the church flow out of the depths of his realization of his value to the Lord: "But you are a chosen race, a royal priesthood, a holy nation, a people for God's own possession, that you may proclaim the excellencies of Him who has called you out of darkness into His marvelous light" (1 Pet. 2:9).

The boldness of the early church was rooted in this amazing grace of God. The unbelievable courage we witness in the book of Acts was engendered by the Cross. Christ crucified, risen, present, was the motivation of the vitality and viability of the new breed of loved and forgiven people who modeled and mediated the Kingdom of God. The church became the dramatic demonstration of God's eternal purpose for His people.

Now, hundreds of years later, the parables of a treasure and a pearl call us to an unreserved response. What stands in our way of selling all, giving all, committing all? Is there anything that can match the value of being God's cherished person?

Augustine answered that question: "What I feared to be parted from was now a joy to surrender. For Thou didst cast them forth from me, Thou true and high sweetness. Thou didst cast them forth, and in their place didst enter in Thyself, sweeter than all pleasures."

Jesus said, "The kingdom of God is within you" (Luke 17:21, *KJV*). When He reigns supreme in our hearts we can pray, "Thy Kingdom come, Thy will be done on earth as it is in heaven." That means that His will becomes the passionate purpose of our lives. All our worthy ambitions must become secondary to our ultimate purpose. The lesser pearls of our pleasures, plans, priorities, and popularity must be surrendered to claim the pearl of the absolute rule of God in all of life's relationships and responsibilities.

The great need of our time is for Christians to live out the implications of the Kingdom of God. That requires study, prayer, imagination, and commitment. The more we come to know Christ and spend prolonged periods in prayer with Him, the more aware we will be of His guidance and direction. We will be able to imagine what our life could be if it was filled with Him and motivated by His love. If we ask Him He will reveal what we are to do and say to *be* His love to others. He will expose the contradictions in our personal and interpersonal lives. The needs in our society that break His heart will break us open to specific caring. Get close to Christ and injustice will disturb us out of bland inactivity.

So many of us who claim Christ as Saviour have never dared to trust Him as Lord. Why is this? He gave us the answer: "He who is forgiven little, loves little" (Luke 7:47). Love enables love. We must know what we mean to God before we can discover what He wants us to mean to the world. When we realize we are the treasure for whom Christ died, we will treasure doing His will at all costs!

Then we can sing:

> Love so amazing, so divine,
> Demands my soul, my life, my all.

Accepting that we are everything to God frees us to say, "He's everything to me," and finally, "He's Lord of everything!"

> He found the pearl of greatest price,
> My heart doth sing for joy;
> And sing I must for I am His,
> And He is mine for aye.[2]

Notes

1. Ralph Carmichael, "He's Everything to Me," copyright 1964, Lexicon Music, Inc. ASCAP. All rights reserved. International copyright secured. Used by permission.
2. *The Parables and Metaphors of Our Lord*, G. Campbell Morgan, D.D., Fleming H. Revell Company, New York, p. 77.

11
The Virtue of Viability

Luke 5:17-39: Parables of New Patch and New Wine

There's a great difference between the God of our experience and our experience of God. It's possible to become so dependent on our previous knowledge and understanding of God in our lives that we become closed to new discoveries and growth. We can reflect with gratitude on the ways God has worked in our lives in the past and miss the interventions of His love right now.

There are Christians who can recount with elaborate detail how they first discovered God's grace in some experience of need or challenge. Often the treasured memory becomes more important than God Himself. His question is, "What have you allowed me to give you and do for you lately?"

A sure sign of a vital Christian is viability. He or she is open to grow and capable of freedom and flexibility. Faith is dynamic, not static. Fellowship with God is an adventure which is never completed. He wants us to be open and receptive to new truths about Him and fresh encounters with Him in our daily life. He is never finished with us and, therefore, we are never finished growing. Whatever has happened to us, it is only a prelude to what God is about to do. He is engaged in a momentous transformation in each of us. We have hardly begun to become the person He is ready and able to liberate us to be. There's never a time when we can settle into satisfaction or complacency. The Lord is on the move in you and me.

And yet, there is something in all of us which longs for the tragic tranquility of memories rather than forward movement. We resist the penetration of the Spirit of God into untouched areas of our personalities and habit patterns. We want to say, "Lord, I've learned enough for a while. Just allow me to enjoy life as it is without any crises or difficulties which force me to change and grow!"

Many of us have built a whole theology on our personal experiences of God. Soon our experiences build us. They become limitations to further development and expansion of our understanding. We become rigid and immobilized. We insist God must always do what He's done and be for us what He's been.

Life is filled with predictably unpredictable events. We can never freeze-frame God and be sure that we know all there is to know about Him. The moment we think we have captured all the "unsearchable riches" of His nature, He breaks out of our carefully fashioned mold. True, He is "the same yesterday, today and tomorrow," but all that He is takes eternity to realize. There's a special joy given to "What's next, Lord?" teachable saints. The unfolding drama of life is for the unveiling of aspects of His nature that we will never

118

learn if we become comfortably settled on dead center.

I know this to be true for my life. When I am finished with my careful categories of how God deals with me and am sure that the best God has to give has been given, He forces me to face my spiritual immaturity by giving me an opportunity or problem which is so far beyond my strength that I am amazed that I could ever have been satisfied with my previous relationship with Him.

The God of my experience is constantly in competition with my fresh experience of God. But He will not allow me to break the first commandment and have other gods before Him—not even the idol of my dependence on the past. I have discovered that my tenacious hold on reflections of great experiences of the past is really fear of the future. The false security of the familiar must constantly be replaced by trusting God with the complexities and uncertainties staring me in the face today.

The parable of the new wine in old skins and the new patch on old cloth expose the inadequacy of trust in our experience of God. They tell us that whatever we have known of God can be like an old, dried, cracking wineskin, or a worn, shrunken piece of material. The new wine of fresh experiences will burst the old skin, and the unshrunk patch of new insight will tear the old material.

The parables are a forceful part of the autobiography of God. They both proclaim a central truth: God is more than whatever we know of Him; He is Lord of the now; and He is about to break forth with new revelation that will demand new openness from His people.

The parables were prompted by the Pharisees' consternation over what Jesus did and said that challenged their experience of God. Their God was a God of history. He had revealed His nature in crucial events and pronouncements that had become the basis of the Hebrew religion. Passover, Exodus, Sinai and the Ten Commandments, the glory of the kingdom, the Temple and the prophets of old were sacred. The tragedy was that the leaders of Israel were locked in on the firm belief that the God who spoke was not speaking in their age. They did not expect new acts of intervention from the Almighty. The Law and all the annotated rules which applied the commandments to life were all they needed. The rituals of the sacrifice looked back to what God had done rather than anticipating what He would do. Customs and rites which commemorated the spectacular events of their history became an obsession. Finally, the festidious practice of their rituals became a replacement for intimate, present communion with God Himself.

A petulant pride had developed over being God's special, blessed, called and chosen people. Forgetting that they had been blest to be a blessing, they became exclusive. Their uniqueness was maintained by an esoteric, shrouded separation.

No wonder Jesus got into trouble with the officialdom. In Luke 5:17-39 we see the battle lines drawn. Pharisees and teachers of the law had come from Jerusalem to investigate the ministry of Jesus. What they observed Him do and heard Him say brought their angry judgment. When we follow Jesus through each event of this passage we can understand their reaction and His response in the twin parables about the unpredictable, dynamic nowness of God which demands newness from His people.

When some men brought a paralyzed friend on a bed for Jesus' love and care, they found that they could not get into the house where the Master was teaching because of the crowd. So they tore open the roof and lowered their friend down in front of Jesus. The Lord discerned the paralyzed man's need for forgiveness and healing. Affirming the faith of his friends, Jesus said, "Friend, your sins are forgiven you" (Luke 5:20).

That stretched the old wineskin of the Pharisees' and scribes' experience of God. "Who is this man who speaks blasphemies? Who can forgive sins, but God alone?" (v. 21). They were not willing to accept that the God who had forgiven His people so magnificently in the past could forgive through a rabbi from Nazareth. What they would not consider was what Jesus then plainly proclaimed. God present in the Son of Man, the Messiah, could and would forgive sins. Look at His bold claim and clear self-identification: "In order that you may know that the Son of Man has authority on earth to forgive sins"—He said to the paralytic, "I say to you, rise, and take up your stretcher and go home" (v. 24). The man's healing followed His forgiveness. Jesus always knows what we need first and most.

Everyone was seized with astonishment and fear. Even the scribes and Pharisees joined in saying, "We have seen remarkable things today" (v. 26).

The next event was no less challenging to the official leaders' dry and parched wineskins. Jesus called a tax collector named Levi to follow Him. Tax collectors were among the most abhorred people in Palestine. They were in collusion with Rome in the collection of very steep taxes. But the intense anger for tax collectors came from the fact that in addition to the regulated tax, they could levy any additional amount they wished and keep it for themselves. A Jew would speak of tax collectors, harlots and Samaritans with equal disdain. The quislings were excluded from worship and the rights of their religion and national heritage.

And Jesus alarmed the officials from Jerusalem by

121

calling Levi to be one of His disciples. That was worse than claiming to be the Son of man and forgiving sins. How could that fit into their experience of God? Everything they had been taught from childhood about how to treat a tax collector was contradicted.

But the disputation between Jesus and the investigation committee from Jerusalem reached a crescendo when Jesus accepted Levi's invitation to attend a reception at his house in order to introduce the Lord to some of his old tax-gathering friends. Levi wanted them to know the Lord who had changed his life. An evidence of our newfound joy is that we want everyone to share what has happened to us.

That did it. The rage of the scribes and the Pharisees burst out in open accusations. They grumbled at Jesus' disciples saying, "Why do you eat and drink with the tax-gatherers and sinners?" (v. 30).

The Lord's response was a further messianic claim. His reference to the bridegroom was very telling. The messianic age was to be like the joy of a wedding banquet feast. Jesus again identified Himself as the Messiah.

Life with Him was to be like that of the bridegroom's attendants while they were with the bridegroom. Joy was the dominant note of the celebration.

Some historical background helps. In Jesus' day there was a full week of celebration following a wedding. Everyone who attended was relieved of all religious observances that would lessen the delightful merriment. The messianic age would be like that. Jesus the Bridegroom had ushered in a time of unprecedented blessing from God. In that context, the Lord answered the scribes' and Pharisees' criticism: "You cannot make the attendants of the bridegroom fast while the bridegroom is with them, can you? But the days will come; and when the bridegroom is taken away from them, then they will fast in those days" (Luke 5:34,35).

The Lord had contradicted the leaders' experience of God in three drastic ways: the contemporary presence of the forgiveness of God in the Son of man, the inclusiveness of love calling a tax-gatherer and the feast with those judged as sinners. This had been more than the leaders could take. Jesus tried to help them understand their frustration with Him by giving these twin parables. He was more concerned about the needs of people than the ancient rules and regulations. God was doing a new thing in the Messiah and the presuppositions of the leaders prevented them from experiencing it.

The parables of the wineskins and the old garment were the Lord's way of introducing the interrogating officials to themselves. What He was saying was: This is what you are like— your experience of God is like an old wineskin or an old garment. You cannot contain or accommodate the new revelation of God before you.

Three things grip our attention in these parables from the autobiography of God. They tell us that God is an innovator, that His Incarnation in the Messiah is the new wine and the new patch, and that we have been called to contain the tumultuous dynamic of His Spirit today. He is the Lord of new beginnings: "Behold, I am doing a new thing" (see Isa. 43:19), is His watchword through history. And His promise is sure: "And I shall give them one heart, and shall put a new spirit within them" (Ezek. 11:19). The new covenant would be established through the Messiah. He is the persistent, relentless newness of God. An old wineskin or a patch on a garment would not do.

God is the original innovator. The word for new, *kainos*, that Jesus used in the parable, means to make new or to make as if new, fresh. Each new day of life is to give us opportunities to feel the freshness of His love. He can take our affairs and make them an occasion for the innovative thing He wants to do in us. Our God has all power, resources and people at His disposal to break through our defenses with possibilities we never dreamed possible. All He needs from us is an openness expressed by spreading all of our problems, relationships and responsibilities before Him. At this very moment He is preparing the innovation that will bring a solution or answer that no amount of cleverness or planning on our part could have devised.

But no gift the Lord can give is better than the gift of Himself. Jesus is the new wine. More than answers to our problems, we need the power of His presence. Our minds and hearts have been made for Him. We will return to the same truth often in our study of the parables. We have been called to abide in Him and He in us. That's the secret meaning of the parable of the new wineskins.

We are to present the Lord with a fresh wineskin of viability each day and in each new situation. We cannot depend on previous experience. If we do we will be like the wineskins that burst.

Jesus took a familiar image of our old wineskin to explain what happens when the new wine of His presence and guidance fills us. In that time the skin of a goat was coated with pitch and sealed to make a bag. The neck was the opening; it was closed tightly after the new wine, freshly pressed from the grapes, was poured in. Then the fermentation process began. The new skin was soft and flexible, capable of taking the expanding, tumultuous fermentation process. It stretched as the wine fermented.

The reason an old bag could not contain the new wine was that it had already been stretched to capacity. It had become dry, cracked, and inflexible. The fermentation process was sure to burst the skin, so that the bag would be destroyed and the wine lost.

We wonder if Jesus had the words of Job on His mind. "Behold, my belly [heart] is like unvented wine, like new wineskins it is about to burst" (Job 32:19). Or was He thinking of the time when the representatives of Gibeon came to Joshua and pretended their depravity by their broken wineskins: "And these wineskins which we filled were new, and behold, they are torn; and these our clothes and our sandals are worn out because of the very long journey" (Josh. 9:13). We cannot be sure.

But what is certain is that the leaders of Israel were the wineskins Jesus had in mind. And us! Who can escape the incisive implication? Not I.

The Lordship of Jesus Christ cannot be poured into the old skin of our settled personality structure, presuppositions about life, prejudices about people, plans for the future and predetermined ideas of what He will do or how we will respond. The dry, cracked bags of the past will burst; we will lose our cherished religion and Him as well.

Once the Lord takes up residence in us a dynamic process begins by which everything is made new. He reorders the tissues of our brains so that we can think His thoughts. Memories are healed and liberated. Values and purposes are reoriented. Our image of ourselves is transformed. He is satisfied with nothing less than molding us into His own image. The miracle of the new creation begins—and never stops. The old person in us is made into a new person. That's the inside story of conversion and sanctification. We become new creatures in Christ.

The outside story is focused by the parable of the patch on an old garment. The point the Lord is making is that we need a new garment, not a patched old one. We cannot patch up our old self with a fragment of the gospel. The imagery of clothes and clothing in the Scriptures make the idea all the more impelling. The Lord came, lived and died to clothe us with the righteousness of God. Paul reflected on what our response should be: "Put on the new self, which in the likeness of God has been created in righteousness and holiness of the truth" (Eph. 4:24). "Put on a heart of compassion, kindness, humility, gentleness and patience" (Col. 3:12). The wardrobe of a new person in Christ is not tattered, patched and restyled. It is new—made of the character of Christ Himself.

The twin parables of the wineskins and the patch are desperately needed in the church today. There are some of us who have never experienced the new wine of the indwelling Christ at all. Our bags are empty. But most of us are about to burst because we have offered Christ a dry, cracked, used wineskin. We are disturbed by the demands of following Christ in our inner hearts, with people or in the problems of society. Shifting the metaphor, the fabric of our religion is tearing because we have patched our self-sufficiency with the patch of just enough of the gospel to make us uncomfortable.

All this leads me to a personal decision I hope you will share. I have learned a great deal through study of Scripture and years of fellowship with the Lord. But I suspect that my most exciting years are ahead. How about you? If so, I want to surrender any false pride or dependence on the past and make a fresh beginning. My past experience of God can never substitute for the experience of God today. "Lord, here is a fresh wineskin; fill me. Here is my naked need; clothe me with your character." Now I can't wait for what the Lord will do!

12

Knowing What You Want and Wanting What You Know

Luke 7:31-35: Parable of the Children at Play

If you were to die today, would you have accomplished the purpose for which you were born?

What would you say is the purpose of your life? How would you define your ultimate purpose and your unique personal purpose?

How do you think God would answer those questions about each of us? He has a primary purpose for all of us which we share in common. But He also has a secondary purpose for each individual to accomplish which is a part of that primary purpose.

I have found it a rigorous but, eventually, releasing discipline to refocus my purpose—repeatedly. When I am able to recapture the reason I was given life, I experience a new freedom to live with joy and abandon. In that context, I can honestly say that if I were to expire today, I have discovered the reason I was born. Then I can rediscover the personalized purpose of my life. This liberates me to prioritize the opportunities and challenges of daily living.

When either our ultimate or unique purpose becomes clouded or confused, we find that we lose an essential quality of life: earnestness. We are no longer direct, zealous, fervent. Earnestness is distinguished by deep feeling and conviction, resoluteness and dedication.

When we drift from a deep, intimate companionship with God, we become negative, critical, judgmental and recalcitrant. We resist the repeated overtures of God's love. Neutrality and detached aloofness eventually result. We become respectably unresponsive. It happens to all of us at times. The telltale signs are equivocation, vacillation and pretense.

That's what happened to the Pharisees. They rejected John the Baptist and resisted Jesus' ministry. Don't forget that they were the religious leaders of the time. What happened to them, can happen to us. We can get just enough religion to make us rigid, but lose our purpose which releases power.

It was in response to this critical, spiritual sickness that Jesus told the parable of the children at play in the marketplace.

"To what then shall I compare the men of this generation, and what are they like? They are like children who sit in the market place and call to one another; and they say, 'We played the flute for you, and you did not dance; we sang a dirge, and you did not weep' " (Luke 7:31,32).

Jesus was a careful observer of life. He drew His parabolic illustration from the common things of life. Every one of His listeners had observed children restlessly trying to find a game to play on a long, hot afternoon. Some wanted to play "weddings" and others wanted to play "funerals." The division of desires separated the group in the marketplace. They taunted each other with pique and petulance. One group cried, "We wanted to play wedding and you wouldn't play our game!" The other responded with the chant, "But we wanted to play funeral and you wouldn't do what we wanted." They couldn't get together to enjoy a make-believe drama. Each wanted his own way. The children didn't know what they wanted. They ended up enjoying neither game.

There's a great difference between childlikeness and childishness. Jesus often used a child to exemplify the honest, enthusiastic, unequivocal response to life He wanted from people. "Except you become as a little child ... " But in this case Jesus depicts the most unattractive characteristic of immaturity: the trifling, fickle, uncooperativeness of a bored, spoiled child. The children in the marketplace were really saying, "If you don't do what I want, I won't do what you want. But I don't even know what I want. If you were to do what I think I want, I'm not sure even that would please me!"

What comes before and after the parable makes Jesus' message undeniably clear. Luke's commentary introduces the parable; Jesus' explanation makes it inescapable.

One of the most disturbing statements in Scripture is the key to this parable: "But the Pharisees and the lawyers rejected God's purpose for themselves, not having been baptized by John" (Luke 7:30). The parable of the children at play was Jesus' dramatic characterization of the leaders of Israel who rejected the purpose of God. Jesus knew what they had done to John the Baptist and would do to Him. They didn't like John because he was too ascetic; they didn't like Jesus because of His affirmation of life. John was written off as one who had a demon; Jesus was not taken seriously because He ate and drank wine with tax collectors and sinners. They played one off against the other. John was too serious; Jesus not serious enough. What did they want?

Jesus' point is that the Pharisees did not know what they wanted. But beneath the uncertainty was a very determined resistance to God. They did not want Him! A religion of rules and regulations had become their diminutive god. Both John and Jesus called for repentance and acceptance of the absolute reign and rule of God. "The Kingdom of God is at hand!" It's the tragic condition of religious people who do not know God that they do not really know what they want or want what they know to be true.

What a scathing exposure! It was as if Jesus said, "Listen, you say you want God, but your actions and words expose that you don't. You talk about God's judgment, but you did not willingly accept one who proclaimed it and called all of you to repentance. You say you long for the Messiah to come, but when He is here you search for reasons to reject Him. You are childish! If you had the wisdom of God, you would recognize His truth in the messenger sent to prepare the way for the Messiah and in the Messiah Himself. You have developed the miserable sickness of religious pretense and no longer desire what you prattle and pray about aimlessly!"

The Lord has given us a very significant chapter in His autobiography of God. God is earnest. The Messiah knew that. He was the incarnate expression of the earnestness of God to save His people. Jesus knew why He had come. When the multitudes found Him in a lonely place praying, He expressed this earnestness: "I must preach the kingdom of God to the other cities also, for I was sent for this purpose" (Luke 4:43). Later in the last week of His ministry in Jerusalem, He articulated it again: "Now My soul has become troubled; and what shall I say, 'Father, save Me from this hour?' But for this purpose I came to this hour. Father, glorify Thy name" (John 12:27,28). God's response rings with indefatigable earnestness. "I have both glorified it, and will glorify it again" (John 12:28). That glorification culminated in the cross and the resurrection. Now we are the recipients of eternal life through Christ—if we are earnest! The Lord demands that above all else.

Now the parable takes on a very personal focus. We can no longer enjoy observation without participation. We are part of the drama which is staged in this parable. Jesus came. What have we done with the truth of His message and the gift of His forgiving death?

Jesus comes. How shall we receive Him?

Jesus is coming. What is the hope we have to share? No one can read this parable seriously without asking: What would I have done with Jesus of Nazareth? Our answer depends on what we are doing right now. We will have missed the point of the parable unless we are forced to identify with the children in the marketplace and the childish Pharisees they exemplified.

The parable challenges us to clarify and claim our purpose and live it with absolute earnestness. Our ultimate purpose is Jesus Christ: to know Him, allow Him to love us, love Him in response and love others as He has loved us. Each of us is called to live out that purpose in the unique circumstances and opportunities of our individual lives. That will mean several crucial things:

Our personal relationship with the Saviour will recreate us in His image. He is to be our purpose and passion. We are to long to know Him and make Him known to others.

Our concern will be to discover and do His will in all of life. He will deploy us in situations and with people where we can be effective for Him. We will know what we want: Christ. We will want what we know: His indwelling power.

The earnestness Jesus wanted from the Pharisees was expressed years later by a converted Pharisee named Paul. Prior to the Damascus road, he neither knew what he wanted nor wanted what he knew. His whole life was committed to destroying what he was against. A personal encounter with the loving Lord transformed his purpose. After years of growth in personal relationship with the Saviour, Paul exemplified energetic earnestness.

The Apostle's letter to the Philippians is filled with directness of purpose, deep feeling, conviction and unreserved commitment. What a contrast to the Pharisees who motivated Jesus' parable about equivocation. Leaf through the epistle and listen to an earnest man:

"For to me, to live is Christ" (Phil. 1:21).

"But whatever things were gain to me, those things I have counted loss for the sake of Christ. More than that, I count all things to be loss in view of the surpassing value of knowing Christ Jesus my Lord, for whom I have suffered the loss of all things, and count them but rubbish in order that I may gain Christ, and may be found in Him, not having a righteousness of my own derived from the Law, but that which is through faith in Christ, the righteousness which comes from God on the basis of faith, that I may know Him, and the power of His resurrection and the fellowship of His sufferings, being conformed to His death; in order that I may attain to the resurrection from the dead" (Phil. 3:7-11).

On the basis of this purpose Paul could forget what lay behind and reach forward to the prize of the upward call of God in Christ Jesus (see vv. 13,14).

In the Colossian letter Paul articulated why Christ

was life for him: "He is the image of the invisible God, the first-born of all creation. For in Him all things were created, both in the heavens and on earth, visible and invisible, whether thrones or dominions or rulers or authorities—all things have been created through Him and for Him .... For it was the Father's good pleasure for all the fulness to dwell in Him, and through Him to reconcile all things to Himself, having made peace through the blood of the cross" (Col. 1:15,16,19,20). The purpose of God in Christ had become the purpose of life for Paul. Christ was everything to him because Christ had done everything for him. That's earnestness: Christ is all or not at all!

Until we can say that we will be like the children in the marketplace. It's possible to call ourselves Christians and resist Christ. Like the Pharisees we can religiously say we anticipate the coming of the Messiah and reject His approach. We can be church members and refuse the implications of His direction of our personal and social life.

I talked to a church officer in a midwest church recently who had drifted from earnestness to equivocation. He said, "I am sure about what I don't want, but I don't know what I want. I'm against about everything that's proposed, but I am at a loss when challenged to make a positive suggestion for what we should be doing. I fuss over insignificant details of church administration and have become critical of almost everyone and everything." What a pitiful condition.

Be sure of this: if we don't know where we are going, we will be negative and critical of where others want to go. The issue is our relationship to Christ and our surrender to His guidance and direction. Church boards can be like a marketplace with opposing factions childishly complaining, "You weren't for my motion, so I

133

won't be for yours." All because the Lord was disregarded and denied complete control. Exciting things happen to individuals and congregations when we are earnest about the Lord of the church.

A woman came to me about her marriage. She was sure her husband was her problem. She said, "If my husband would only change, we could make a go of this marriage." I listened to her dissatisfied complaints for what seemed like hours. Finally I asked her to list 10 things she wanted her husband to do and be. In a subsequent visit with her husband I tried to communicate her needs to him. We talked at length about what it would take to satisfy her demands. He made a commitment to try. I kept close contact to see how things were going. The man made every effort to change, but whatever he did, it was not enough. Weeks later, the wife came to see me again. She blurted out, "Now what am I going to do? My husband has met all my demands, but I'm still unhappy. What's wrong with me?"

The answer to that question was in her relationship with Christ. Though the woman was an active church member, she had never given Christ complete control of her life and relationships. All her religious activity was a smoke screen for her lack of commitment to Christ. Her husband's efforts to change only exposed her own need to change. Underneath her words was the deep desire to get out of the marriage. She was too religious to think of divorce. When her husband became a Christian and began growing spiritually, her own lack of earnestness was exposed. I'm happy to say that's not the end of the story. At a Day of Discovery Retreat sponsored by our congregation, she met the Saviour about Whom she had talked and organized activities for so long. Now she knows what she wants and wants Whom she knows.

I was deeply gratified by the statement of one of my members who visited me the other day. "Lloyd, something happened to me in church last week. I felt the presence of the Lord as I sat in the pew. When you said, 'The living Lord is here!' I said to myself, 'That's really true.' I had come to worship not really expecting to either meet Him or sense His special touch on my life. But as the service proceeded, I was made aware of all the areas of my life that had never been brought under the guidance and control of the Lord. That's why I'm here today. I want to take the Lord seriously."

That's it! To take the Lord seriously. What would that mean? Does the Lord have charge of all that there is of us? Our hearts, relationships, jobs, money, hopes and plans? He wants nothing less!

Recently my congregation decided to give a special offering to world missions. Each of us was challenged to ask the Lord to guide us in the amount—above our regular giving pledge—we would make. We had to dare to believe that the Lord would guide an amount that He would provide. Some very exciting things happened. Many people made pledges beyond what they anticipated their income would allow. An excitement swept throughout our congregation as people's earnestness was rewarded by monies from unexpected sources. The Lord guided the pledge and provided the means. One woman wrote me, "I'm on a fixed income. I was astonished when I felt led to pledge an additional amount for missions because I had no idea where the money would come from. A week later, I got a check in the mail for the exact amount I had pledged. Isn't God good! All He needed was an open channel to pass the money through." The woman had been earnest and the earnest Lord of all creation unleashed the money because she could be trusted to do what she had promised.

The same is true of the unlimited power of the Holy Spirit. He waits for us to dare to attempt things beyond our strength and talents. When we do He provides wisdom, faith, discernment and resources we never dreamed were available. If we take Him seriously, our life will be punctuated by miracles.

A couple I know have a gift of healing. I have kept a documented list of the spectacular physical, emotional and spiritual healings God has done through these two. We lunch frequently to swap stories of God's interventions. Each time I am refreshed and renewed by the evidences of the relationship between their earnestness to trust the promises of God and the results in blessings to people. These adventurers really believe that God is faithful to His promises. They have drawn on the untapped resources of God because they fervently believe that the purpose of their lives is to care for people. They know what they need and need what they want. How unlike the children in the marketplace!

Any exposition of Jesus' parable eventually leads us to the resurrected Lord's incisive word to the church at Laodicea: "I know your deeds, that you are neither cold nor hot; I would that you were cold or hot. So because you are lukewarm, and neither hot nor cold, I will spit you out of My mouth" (Rev. 3:15,16). The word for lukewarm is *chliaros* meaning nauseating and tepid, probably in reference to the mineral springs directly opposite Laodicea at Hierapolis. The Lord wanted the Laodiceans to be hot, *zestos*, in their passion for Him and His purpose in their lives.

Any earnest response to Christ must be based on His bold offer to us: "Truly, truly, I say to you, he who believes in Me, the works that I do shall he do also; and greater works than these shall he do; because I go to the Father. And whatever you ask in My name, that will I do, that the Father may be glorified in the Son. If you ask Me anything in My name, I will do it" (John 14:12-14).

That presses us to clarify what we want. If it's in keeping with His will for us and we are in earnest, He will bless us beyond measure. This is the only creative cure for the children at play in the parable, the Pharisees they characterized, or us today. The Lord says, "What do you really want?" If it is best for us and the people around us, it shall be ours for His glory and our enjoyment. His personal word to each of us is, "Until you want what I want for you, you will be troubled in your views and your desires; easily displeased with yourself and others and out of harmony with me and yourself; full of reservation and distrust. If you give your heart totally to me, you will find peace and true contentment." If we accept His offer, soon we will know what we want and want what we know. Our purpose will be to glorify Him and enjoy Him forever.

The earnest Lord of all says, "For I know the plans that I have for you ... plans for welfare and not for calamity to give you a future and a hope. Then you will call upon Me and come and pray to Me, and I will listen to you. And you will seek Me and find Me, when you search for Me with all your heart" (Jer. 29:11-13). There's a purpose which demands an earnestness now and for all eternity. Instead of playing games, we have a game plan for a truly exciting life.

13

While at the Banquet, Come to the Banquet!

Luke 14:1-24: Parable of the Great Feast

The parable of the great feast. Dangerously familiar. Repetition of hearing and reading makes it difficult to understand its deeper meaning. But this is a parable which is comprehended only when it is experienced. Its deeper meaning has license to elude us until we go to the only place from which we can see, feel and hear the pathos of this magnificent aspect of the autobiography of God: the heart of Jesus. Prayer alone will make that possible. The parable must be prayed. "Lord, what were you thinking and feeling when you spoke this parable about love's invitation and our equivocating excuses?" He invites us into His heart. Our hearts beat with His— and then are broken by what we see with His eyes and hear with His ears.

The invitation to attend a banquet at the home of a

leading Pharisee was very significant to the Master. He knew He was God's Messiah and that the messianic age had been symbolized by a joyous banquet in Israel's literature and liturgy. Only the day before the Master had talked about it: "And they will come from east and west, and from north and south, and will recline at the table in the kingdom of God" (Luke 13:29). For Jesus the long-awaited age had come. No banquet, especially among the leaders of His people, could be attended without the deeper meaning reverberating in His heart. The Lord's perspective becomes ours as we enter the banquet hall. Did the Pharisees know who was their "honored" guest? Did they catch the turning point of history being staged before their eyes?

From the moment we enter the banquet hall with the Master, we realize they did not. We've been in the same kind of situation before with the Lord. The Pharisees did not either accept or appreciate the One for whom the banquet was being given. It could have been a messianic banquet if they had. The Pharisees were at the banquet but had not come to the banquet—really.

We look through the eyes of the Master at the caution and reserve of the host and the other invited guests. They watch Him closely. His every word and movement are being scrutinized. The air is hostile and competitive. This is not a celebration, but a clever way to evaluate the Lord. Accolades and acclaim from the people had reached a high pitch. It was the duty of the Pharisees to decide for themselves. Messianic claims had been whispered and now were being made boldly wherever He went. We can feel with the Lord the rejection He felt in the mood of ambiguity about Him in the leaders' minds. This could be the messianic banquet if only they knew that their guest was indeed the Messiah.

But the Pharisees had other things on their minds.

Who would be given the seats of honor at the banquet? Everyone seems to be maneuvering for the seats closest to the host. Some brush by us and the Master in a frantic effort to be recognized and honored. Others seem to have forgotten the reason they had come. Propriety and protocol dominate the mood. We overhear conversation among the Pharisees which alarms us. "When I came, I expected to be the guest of honor! I gave the host a seat of prestige when he was at my home. How can he dare do less for me when I come to his banquet?!"

It was the Messiah's party and no one knew, not even the host. They had asked the Lord to come to investigate the messianic claims about Him but that seemed secondary to the personal, not-so-hidden agendas written on their faces.

When the scramble for the best seats was finally over and everyone had reclined at tables, a shocking thing happened. It was so amazing it took the Pharisees' minds off themselves for a moment. All eyes turned to Jesus as a man suffering from dropsy made his way across the banquet hall and stood in front of Him. Everyone seemed impatient with the interruption of the intruder—except the Messiah. What finer sign from God could be given than a personification of human need in this man. The messianic banquet would include all of God's people—the sick, the lame, the poor. God knew what He was doing.

The Master knew what was going through the pious leaders' minds. Would He break the law and heal on the Sabbath? He penetrated their inner thoughts of disdain and asked them their own question: "Is it lawful to heal on the Sabbath, or not?" (Luke 14:3). Look at their faces! They are aghast that He knew what they were thinking about so critically. No one should have been surprised by the appearance of Providence's delegate.

140

Every Pharisee there should have remembered that when the Messiah came all days would be like the celebration and rest of the Sabbath. God was the director of the drama in the Pharisee's banquet hall. The tragedy was that they did not grasp it. If they had, they could have come to the party while they were at the party!

From inside Jesus' heart we can feel His compassion for the sick man. What a privilege we have to experience the love of the Lord for one person in need. That's how He feels about us when we hurt or are debilitated! Notice that all of Jesus' concentration is suddenly focused on the man. Power surges through His divine hands as they hold the man firmly, tenderly. We look at the release and joy on the sufferer's face as Jesus assures him that he is healed.

That should have been enough to justify the messianic claims that had prompted the Pharisee's banquet. We survey the body language of the others around the table —the same aloof judgmentalism! We want to shake them and awake them to the realization that this is indeed the Messiah and they could come to the messianic banquet while at the banquet in their fellow Pharisee's house. But that was exactly what they were missing.

At least the healing won Jesus a hearing for some very incisive teaching. People were more important than the regulations of the Sabbath. While He had their attention, He went on to expose the competitive squabble about who had been given the most distinguished places at the banquet. The proper thing for the wrong reason. They were more concerned about their dignity than they were about the dynamic guest whose spectacular ministry had prompted the banquet.

No wonder Jesus pressed the point about the lack of humility He observed and the distorted values in reciprocal invitations to banquets. The Messiah was with them and the banquet was so much more than one more social obligation. But they were not aware of the awesome drama of the incarnation that was happening in their midst.

It was while the Master was speaking that He was interrupted by a man who blurted out a nonsequitur which pierced His heart. Do you feel it? Slogans in anticipation of a momentous occasion of the messianic age had become trite by thoughtless repetition. The Jews had a saying which had become hackneyed with pious pronouncement. The messianic longings were refortified by a "the best is yet to be" shibboleth. It had been repeated so long and often, it lost its meaning. But not for the Messiah Himself. What must have alarmed Jesus was that the man chanted the saying without realizing that the hope was being enacted right there before his eyes. With pomp and ceremony, the Pharisee said, "Blessed is everyone who shall eat bread in the kingdom of God!" (v. 15). It was as if he said, "Won't it be wonderful to eat bread with the Messiah when He comes!" What he did not recognize was that the Messiah had come. The Pharisee was at a messianic banquet and didn't know it!

Now we can understand the urgent implications of the parable of the great feast. It was prompted by the occasion but, much more, it focuses God's loving invitation to the messianic banquet and explains why His people did not come. Once again Jesus uses a parable to introduce the Pharisees to themselves and expose their refusal to take His ministry seriously.

"A certain man was giving a big dinner, and he invited many; and at the dinner hour he sent his slave to say to those who had been invited, 'Come; for everything is ready now' " (vv. 16,17).

The "certain man" is God. This, too, is a part of His

autobiography. The parable reminds us of the preparation of the ages for the advent of the Messiah and the limitless joy the Lord wants to share with us. Indeed, everything was ready. God had come Himself to live among His people. It was time to celebrate!

We feel the anguish of Jesus' experience of rejection by the leaders of His people as He continues the parable. "But they all alike began to make excuses. The first one said to him, 'I have bought a piece of land and I need to go out and look at it; please consider me excused.' And another one said, 'I have bought five yoke of oxen, and I am going to try them out; please consider me excused.' And another one said, 'I have married a wife, and for that reason I cannot come' " (vv. 18-20).

A great deal has been made of the different excuses in expositions of this parable. The main point, however, is that any excuse would be offered at all! The invitations had been sent out long before the event and the parable implies that they had been accepted. When the banquet time arrived, and the invited guests were reminded of their commitment, they sent superficial excuses to the host. Each excuse is incongruous and absurd. There was a supercilious equivocation in each.

Who would buy a field without going to see it first? Land was very valuable in Jesus' day. The purchase of property was a serious matter. Only the most affluent could delegate the negotiation for acquisition of land. And even if the man had bought property, going to see the land was not the reason for breaking a previous promise to attend a feast. There was a deeper reason the man refused to go. He was distracted by his material possessions.

The second man's excuse was no more believable. Five yoke of oxen, ten oxen, indicated great wealth. It would be very unusual for anyone affluent enough to buy ten oxen to try them out himself—he would have his servants do that. The flimsy excuse was an affront. No one would buy oxen without first being sure of them. If the man's oxen were his hobby and he wanted to see how they would work the field, he could find another time to do that. The truth was that he didn't want to go to the banquet. The excuse hid the real reason. He had told a white lie.

The last man's evasion was ludicrous: "I've married a wife; I can't come" (see v. 20). Deuteronomy 24:5 gave him scriptural justification for his excuse. For a whole year after being married, a man was relieved of duties and responsibilities usually required of him. He did not have to go to meetings or war. The ancient translations of the passage really mean that a man was to be free for a year to cheer up his wife. We wonder why that was necessary!

Again the excuse was a smoke screen. The man could have gone to the feast. He used a legality to justify his absence. Beneath that was the true reason: he didn't want to go.

The thing Jesus wanted to communicate was that the people's longing for the Messiah was not authentic. Pride and religious self-sufficiency made it impossible for them to recognize Him when He came and to follow Him with obedience and commitment. The excuses made by the three men only heightened the complex resistance that had invaded the hearts of God's people. The thing they said they wanted most of all was not the desire of their hearts.

The Master has drawn us into the parable. We find ourselves in those three reluctant guests. Do we really want the Kingdom of God if it means the absolute rule of the Lord in our lives? We talk a great deal about our need for Christ in our lives. How much do we want

144

Him? Why are we so quick to make excuses when He invades our lives and wants to take charge of our minds and hearts? Is there the possibility that we want our relationship with Him on our own terms? What's the real reason for you? For me?

The end of the parable is a very significant aspect of God's autobiography. His Son tells us plainly that God will bypass people who equivocate and will fill His banquet with people who recognize their need and desire to be with Him: "And the slave came back and reported this to his master. Then the head of the household became angry and said to his slave, 'Go out at once into the streets and lanes of the city and bring in here the poor and crippled and blind and lame.' And the slave said, 'Master, what you commanded has been done, and still there is room.' And the master said to the slave, 'Go out into the highways along the hedges, and compel them to come in, that my house may be filled. For I tell you, none of those men who were invited shall taste of my dinner'" (Luke 14:21-24).

Did the Pharisees know what Jesus was implying? They were the invited guests who refused to come to the banquet while they were at the banquet. And so are we. Our excuses echo in our souls. We have been confronted by the graciousness and severity of God. He invites us again and again. But there is a time when our persistent refusals will fire His indignation. That leads us to an honest facing of why we trifle with the Almighty God. The invitation is given again, written in the blood of Calvary. Sheer grace.

The other day I had an experience that focused the meaning of the parable for me. My family was having a very special celebration. A piercing question from one of my sons suddenly shocked me into realizing that I had drifted off into private thought.

145

"Hey Dad! Where are you?" he asked.

It should have been obvious where I was. I was seated at the head of my dining room table and taking part in the celebration. But my son realized that even though I was present physically, my attention was elsewhere. A pressing problem I had on my mind when I came home captured my attention. I was not at the party in presence, thought or emotional investment.

The question, "Hey, where are you?" could well be asked of us all repeatedly. We can miss the great things God is doing and revealing all around us. It's possible to be in church and not be there. We can hear the magnificent truths of the gospel and not experience them. We can also be absent while participating in Christian fellowship. God's gifts of people are offered and we are not awake to the unique, cherished expression of His love that He has wrapped up in human personality just for us. The natural world around us can sing its doxology of praise to the Creator, but we do not hear. God has written His signature in the amazing surprises of His grace, but we cannot see it.

The messianic age is now. We are the Messiah's people. The banquet table is teeming with the blessings of love, forgiveness, indwelling power and unlimited hope. While at the banquet, come to the banquet!

14
The God
of the Successful

Luke 12:13-21: Parable of the Rich Fool

The title of this chapter may have alarmed you. The God of the successful? What do you mean by that? Is God only concerned about successful people? What about failures? Isn't the Bible filled with accounts of what God did with failures in spite of their inadequacies? Yes, but what would you call what they accomplished when they allowed God to love and use them? Would you call that success?

Success has become a dirty word in some Christian circles. We look down our noses at successful people. Often when describing what a person was before conversion we allude to his worldly success as if the new life in Christ will now make him a worldly loser.

Is the Lord against success? Doesn't He want us to use our gifts, multiply our resources and maximize our opportunities? Why are we critical of successful people?

What is this love-hate implication we give when we condemn prosperity all through the year and go to the prosperous at stewardship time to collect the results of their industry? We honor successful entertainers and leaders, and at the same time give the impression that if they really loved Jesus they would sell all and go into the professional ministry. Is there anything wrong with being successful?

We must define our terms. Success is the favorable or prosperous course or accomplishment of anything attempted. The word implies the result or outcome of a plan, purpose or effort. A successful person is one who obtains what he desires or intends. He accomplishes what he sets out to do.

Those definitions are benign enough. There is nothing wrong in fulfilling a purpose or in accomplishing a goal. The crucial issue is the nature of the desired end. True success is measured by that.

The title of this chapter is a play on words. We will play it in several keys. The question is, "Who is the God of the successful?" The "G" may be upper or lowercase. It is possible to create a god of our own making and build our ideas of success around our idol. Some of us have made success itself our god. We can deify our ideas of prosperity and miss the relationship with the true God. The Lord God who is Creator, Sustainer and Redeemer of the world does want us to be successful—but according to His goals, plan and design. The authentically successful have Him and His will as the measurement of their success.

Look at it this way. God had a purpose in the creation of the universe. He has been moving toward the accomplishment of that purpose throughout history. On this planet He created plant, animal and human levels of life. He created man to love Him and receive His love. He gave us the wondrous gift of free will so that we could choose to love Him and cooperate with Him. His intention for us was sublime companionship. But when we rebelled, He was not outdone. He came to us Himself to expose His nature and reveal His ultimate purpose for His people. The Lord dwelt among us full of grace and truth. He lived, died and was raised up so that our sin of separation and rebellion could be forgiven.

The same creative Spirit who made us, who came to save us, and who defeated the power of sin and death, continues with us. His post-Pentecost home is our forgiven and receptive hearts. From within us, He calls us to work with Him in making our lives, our relationships and our world what He intended them to be. Jesus said that we were to be perfect (*telos*) as God is perfect. The word *telos* in Greek means end, goal or purpose; to accomplish that end or purpose. Success, then, is cooperating with God in establishing the Kingdom of God in our hearts, all of our affairs, our personal relationships, and our society. Whatever else we accomplish during the years of our life, however much we accumulate or acquire, unless we discover a personal relationship with Christ, seek to do His will in all of life and test everything according to His purpose, we will not be successful. Right at this moment God wants to make us successful—on His terms, by His power, and on His timing. He is the God of the successful.

Now, on that basis, would you say that the rich man in the parable in Luke 12:13-21 was a successful man? Read the parable again; note the context. Someone in the crowd of Jesus' followers had demanded, "Teacher, tell my brother to divide the family inheritance with me" (v. 13). Jesus was not about to get into a family squabble over the reading of the will. He saw a deeper problem in the person's face and words. "Man, who appointed Me a judge or arbiter over you?" He retorted (v. 14). He was that in person as the Messiah, but the man had not acknowledged His Lordship. Jesus' answer may have been different if he had. What Jesus heard and saw in the man was greed, not a true plea for justice. The Lord's words bite: "Beware, and be on guard against every form of greed; for not even when one has an abundance does his life consist of his possessions" (v. 15). While the man was still staggering from that verbal blow, Jesus taught what tradition called the parable of the rich fool. It was in direct response to the man's confusion about what constitutes success.

A rich man's productive farm yielded fine crops. His barns became full to overflowing. What to do? Finally he exclaimed, "I'll tear down my barns and build new ones! Then I will have room for further expansion. I'll be able to sit back and relax with enough stored away for years to come. I can take it easy—eat, drink and be merry!" (see Luke 12:18,19).

Success? In a way. He had accomplished what he set out to do—and more. But he had missed the purpose of his life. His voice of assurance came from within himself, an echo of his own frenzied accumulation. The voice of God interrupted his self-accolade.

"Fool! Tonight you will die. Now who will get all you have acquired?" (see v. 20).

Jesus adds His commentary to the startling story: "So is the man who lays up treasure for himself, and is not rich toward God" (v. 21).

The pronouns used in the parable expose the wrong kind of success. "I" is used six times; "my" is used five times, with a self-gratifying "you" referring to himself, thrown in for good measure. The man's whole life was inverted in on himself.

The man "reasoned with himself." He talked to the

wrong person. His dialogue with himself was circular refortification of his self-image and presuppositions. No one else was consulted for perspective; least of all God. His goal to achieve ease, and to eat, drink and be merry was the measurement of his success. His decisions about what to do with his multiplied prosperity all had to fit that purpose. The possessive pronoun possessed him: "My crops, my grain, my barns, my soul." The last was the fatal assumption. He talked to his own soul to get the answer he wanted on how to support his addiction to the habit-forming narcotic of materialism.

The word for soul used here is *psuchē*. It refers to the mental capacity. The rich fool was not in touch with his soul at all. What he was saying really was, "Just think, my mental plans will be achieved. What I thought to be important will be accomplished—I will be at ease while I eat, drink and am merry."

Driving mental images like that are seldom that easily satisfied. I suspect that he would never have been able to relax and enjoy the fruit of his labors. If he ever did, he probably would be haunted with the greater purpose of using his wealth for those who needed it more than he did. Possessions eventually possess us, if they are our mental goal. Materialism is a hungry suckling—never satisfied. More! More! The fatal trick of the mind.

We are responsible for our *psuchē*. What we think about ourselves, life and our purpose form our destiny. There's an old saying, "You can't take it with you." Not true! We will take what our thoughts have determined us to become. We all live forever. The question is how, where and with whom. We will take the person inside us along. Devoid of our physical body and the material possessions that have insulated us from reality, the inner person will live in communion with God or without Him.

151

Death lurks at everyone's door. Sooner or later, like the knock of death in Sibelius' "Valse Triste," the music suddenly ends abruptly, the frantic whirling of the dancers stops, and we must answer the door.

The God of the successful wants to know what kind of success our guiding thought has produced. The words of God to the man in the parable are like thunder: "You fool! This very night your soul is required of you; and now who will own what you have prepared?" (v. 20). Follow the implication of the word for soul and we have a startling realization of what is required when death knocks imperiously. We will be accountable for our mental hierarchy of values. A tabulation of what our thinking did with the gift of life will be demanded.

The "wealth-addict" must now look at crops, grain, and bigger barns for what they are—poor facsimiles of the reason he was born. He has nothing to take with him except the miserable person he has shaped in his own distorted image. Frightening!

Now observe the contrast in the word Jesus used in introducing the parable. "Beware, and be on your guard against every form of greed; for not even when one has an abundance does his life consist of his possessions" (v. 15). The Greek word for life is *zōē*. The meaning is essential life, as contrasted to death. Jesus came to give us more than abundance of things. He lived, died and rose again to offer us the gift of abundant life—now and forever. When He speaks of life it is the composite of the mind, soul and spirit; the intellectual, emotional and volitional person within our bodies. The words, "a man's life," mean the immortal person within us which the death of the body cannot destroy. He came in order that the immortal, deathless life in us may have eternal life. That implies relationship with God now and forever.

Eternal life is richness toward God. True success!

Jesus' closing words of the parable make it undeniably clear. "So is the man who lays up treasure *for himself*, and is not rich toward God" (v. 21). Anything that keeps us from being rich with God now will debilitate our eternal life with Him forever after our physical death.

Therefore we are urgently pressed to consider what richness toward God is about. The sharp focus of Jesus' message is that our spiritual wealth is inherited, not earned. A free gift is offered. Richness with God begins in a relationship with Him. Love and forgiveness are given without measure. Christ died and rose again to reconcile us with God. When we respond and accept His grace we are born again. Life begins anew. Companionship with God Himself is given to us.

Our richness toward God grows as we surrender the direction, goals, and purposes of our life to "seek first the Kingdom of God." The passion of our life becomes seeking and doing the will of God.

Inadvertently, we begin to grow in Christlikeness. Paul spoke of the riches of the glory of the mystery of Christ in us, the hope of glory (see Col. 1:27). From within, our mental disposition about life is reformed around the Lord's goals and strategy.

Daily, and hour by hour, God guides us as we share in His work. We begin to realize that all our opportunities are given for a purpose. Every person and situation is an occasion for us to cooperate with what God wants to accomplish.

The Lord's agenda for us always includes people and society. A part of our richness is to be able to share hope with individuals by introducing them to the new life in Christ. That requires listening, love, identification and involvement. The more we give away our spiritual wealth, the more it grows and means to us. Concern for people can never be separated from caring about the practical needs of their lives. God has entrusted resources to us to meet the physical, emotional and spiritual needs of people. There's nothing wrong with wealth—if it is shared with others!

Richness toward God develops as we allow Him to use us in the areas of responsibility He's entrusted to us. Each of us has influence. We are where we are, have the power we have, and are able to accomplish what we have because of the providence of God. It's when we say, "Lord, there is nothing I have achieved without your grace!" that we are able to ask Him to use us to claim the arena of our responsibilities. Our homes, churches, schools, jobs, neighborhoods and communities belong to Him. He has placed us in them to live out the implications of radical obedience. He wants us to succeed there. The Lord is on the move in society and wants us to join Him.

In that understanding of richness, we can confront the troublesome problem of riches. Anytime the acquiring, saving, parlaying or inordinate preoccupation with wealth keeps us from richness toward God, it is not only wrong, but dangerous. It has the possibility of causing us to miss the purpose of life. That's what happened to the man with the wrong kind of success in the the parable. When death knocked, he was not ready. Actually he had died, barn by barn, as he grew further and further away from his ultimate purpose. His god was success; he never got acquainted with the God of the successful.

The rich fool has no one to thank but himself. When the time came for him to die, his possessions were dumb. They could not speak to assure him that it had been worth it. That's the final tragedy of the parable. The rich fool thought he would finally reach a day when he could eat, drink and be merry. Jesus promises us this abundance right now—whether we ever get another barn or not. I suspect that's what He had in mind by the parable: the abundant life is available; death cannot end it; physical demise is but a transition to greater abundance.

My friends Geoff and Betty Kitson led what they called a "workshop for worriers" at a conference. God has given these two adventurers a secret to unlock worry. Their lives were committed to "barn building" until they both discovered true wealth in Jesus Christ. Now what they have is poured out for people. Betty is deeply involved in helping children with remedial reading. Geoff has come out of a secure retirement to communicate Christ to individuals as the leader of the Faith at Work movement. Over dinner the other evening, my wife and I were deeply moved by the vitality and viability of these two contagious people. God is using them mightily. They are succeeding on God's terms. All the drive, ambition and creativity they have is invested in the Kingdom business.

Now we are back to our title of this chapter. God is the God of the successful. When we give Him our lives, relinquish control of our possessions, seek His will in all things, we will succeed. As someone said aptly, "God don't make no failures—He helps them!" and I say He helps them succeed on His terms and for His glory.

15
Christians with a Tang

Luke 14:25-35: Parable of the Uncompleted Tower

A young lad whose excitement for sports outdistanced his devotion to studies, brought home his report card. He put off showing it to his parents as long as he could. Finally, the moment of truth could be avoided no longer. His parents read the grades with concern, but not surprise. Then they read his teacher's comments in the report: "Johnny does well at school, but he could do much better if the sheer joy of living didn't impede his progress!"

I can picture Johnny in that classroom, wriggling and waiting for recess or the time for play at the end of the afternoon. At that stage of his life being a pitcher was more important than algebra or the facts of history.

We smile, and remember how it felt. Then we reflect on the teacher's analysis. Not true! The joy of living never impeded anyone's progress. It inspires it.

Someone asked me what I wanted for my life and the

people I love. The words of Johnny's teacher came to mind. I long for all of us to experience the sheer joy of living.

So does Jesus. And He tells us how. Luke 14:25-35 is a compilation of several of His parables that describe the nature, conditions and resources for abundant living. This is a passage that needs to be interpreted from the bottom up.

Do you ever want to skip over to the end of a novel to see how it comes out before reading the unfolding mystery? I do. That's what we must do with this series of parables in this passage. They all lead up to the climax in verses 34 and 35: "Therefore, salt is good; but if even salt has become tasteless, with what will it be seasoned? It is useless either for the soil or for the manure pile; it is thrown out. He who has ears to hear, let him hear."

Jesus came to enable Christians with a tang—destinctive, sharp, pungent. Salty Christians with an incisive quality that seasons the life of others and society. Saline saints bring zest and gusto to life. Like salt, they bring out the best of the flavor of living.

That's the kind of an enabling process focused in the parables that precede the parabolic saying about tangy disciples. The whole passage is a marvelous unity. Luke has combined parables in a progression and chronology of thought. Great multitudes followed after the Master. He wanted them to realize what they were doing. They were encountering a demanding God. He had committed all in the Incarnation; He wanted nothing less from those who responded. Jesus states the cost of discipleship with alarming clarity. His followers must put Him, and the living God He incarnated, first in their lives— before family and friends, plans or ambitions. In this context, He introduces the demand of the cross. Count the cost!

157

The parable of the uncompleted tower verifies the truth. As if that were not enough, He follows quickly with another parable—the king's rash warfare. All of this is to dramatize a traumatic truth—don't begin discipleship without understanding the high cost of faithfulness. The Lord must be put first before possessions, as well as family and friends. But then, as if for rewarding relief, Jesus tells us about salt with a tang. It's all worth it if the cost of discipleship results in the sheer joy of living as God intended. The demands are small indeed if they produce a person with zest, savor, flavor! The banal blandness will be gone. A breakthrough to the discipleship will radiate in a vitality, freedom and joy that can be found no other way. We will have the pungent, penetrating aroma of Christ. Life will be exciting. Christ's demands will have delivered us from the mediocrity of secondary loyalties.

In the Sermon on the Mount Jesus said, "You are the salt of the earth. But if salt loses its savor, wherewith shall it be salted?" (see Matt. 5:13). That's the question. Not only how to become a salty Christian, but what do we do when we lose our tang? Jesus came to call, equip and deploy a new breed of humanity who would do what salt does: bring preservation, purification and libation to the world.

I want to consider what it means to be Christians with a tang, utilizing the impact of all of these parables. Nine crucial aspects are inherent in this passage. Each one helps us to inventory our supply of salt.

First, tang in the Christian life comes from the indwelling Christ Himself. He is God's salt in life: "If anyone comes to Me ... " (v. 26). Salt works by association. It must be placed in food to bring out its taste. Christ challenged us to abide in Him and to allow Him to abide in us. A personal relationship results from com-

158

ing to Him. We come to Him because He has first come to us. The words, "If anyone comes to Me," means "to follow after," to become a loyal disciple. When we do, all of our natural capacities are maximized just as food is flavored by salt. Christianity is a personal relationship with a living, vitalizing Christ.

Second, the salt must penetrate: "... and does not hate his own father and mother and wife and children and brothers and sisters, yes, and even his own life, he cannot be My disciple." The word "hate" is comparative, meaning by comparison to our love for Christ. Any Scot knows that salt must be added to oatmeal before cooking, not afterward. If it is salted after cooking, all you taste is the salt. In a similar way, Christ can never be added as an afterthought of an already full and committed life. Family loyalties often can stand in the way of ultimate loyalty to Christ. We can try to use the Master and His power to fulfill our desires and plans for the people we love and still give Him the one place He will not accept: second place.

The words, "even his own life," are crucial for an understanding of what Jesus meant. Our "life" means our vision, image, plans, personality and priorities. If we want to become effective salt of the earth, the Lord's salt must completely pervade the depth of our being. The reason so many Christians miss the joy Christ offered is that there has never been a decisive surrender of their ego.

The amazing thing about this verse is that it gives us the key to becoming people who can love our own lives and other people with liberating, in-depth love. Once we love Christ more than ourselves or other people, we are empowered to invest ourselves in creative caring. There's a lively, salty gusto about our love. It's not self-conscious, studied or bartered. An attractive, winsome lover of people is one who has been liberated from self-consciousness. He can affirm others, build them up, help them to live fully—because his love is not squandered on the insecurity of self-concern.

Third, the cross is the power of our salty tang. We can only imagine how disturbed Jesus' followers were when He said, "Whoever does not carry his own cross and come after Me cannot be My disciple" (v. 27). The cross was an instrument of execution. We are sure Jesus' listeners were alarmed about carrying their own cross. They had not understood His intimations about His own cross; now He told them they too must bear a cross. We can identify with their consternation.

What Jesus meant was that they must follow Him with complete loyalty. His cross would give them power for the cross of obedience they would assume. Remember the cross meant love and faithfulness for Jesus. He went to Calvary out of love for a sinful world, in absolute trust that God would use His death as a sacrifice for the sins of all people.

The cross of Christ is the basis of our passionate concern for people. As forgiven people we have the salt of forgiveness to heal the wounds of people, purify their distorted lives, and set them free from the bondage of guilt and jaded memories. As the salt of the earth we can communicate hope of a new life, a new beginning and a new relationship with God.

When carrying our own cross means death to ourselves and our self-will, we are born again. We are resurrected with Christ for a new life of loving others as He has loved us. The impelling vigor of that is the source of our compassion for and acceptance of others. Our cross implies a willingness to suffer for people that they may know Christ's love for them. That's what Paul meant when he stated the longing of his life: "That I may know Him, and the power of His resurrection and the fellowship of His sufferings, being conformed to His death; in order that I may attain to the resurrection from among the dead" (Phil. 3:10,11).

Fourth, a tangy Christian is one who is unreservedly dependent on Christ's resources to meet Christ's challenges. The parable of the builder has a hidden meaning. At first glance we accept the surface meaning that it challenges us to be sure we have what it takes to be a disciple. "For which one of you, when he wants to build a tower, does not first sit down and calculate the cost, to see if he has enough to complete it?" (Luke 14:28). The deeper meaning of the parable is that we, on our own, will *never* have enough of what it takes.

Some time ago I led a funeral procession through a graveyard to an open grave. As I walked between the gravestones with the pallbearers following closely behind, I was startled by an epitaph on one marker. "Here lies a man who had what it takes!" was chiseled in bold letters. I reflected on that long afterward. Did the man order that brash accolade in his will? Or was it the analysis of friends and family? What would it mean to have what it takes?

Jesus wants to make clear that what He guides He supplies. Discipleship is not mustering up our own resources to have what it takes, but receiving from our Lord what is required in each new situation and relationship. If a builder sits down to calculate the cost, he will know he cannot finish without help. There were telling instances of incompleted towers in vineyards in Jesus' day. That's why He utilized the known experience for this parable. "Otherwise, when he has laid a foundation, and is not able to finish, all who observe it begin to ridicule him" (v. 29).

The secret of the Christian life is in its impossibility.

It was never meant to be lived on our own wisdom or power. A Christian with tang is one who dares to believe that, because the Lord is present, there is no limit to the miraculous interventions of His power that can invade the impotence of our daily lives. We salt life with a vibrant expectation. When everyone else is negative and cautious, a salty Christian asks only two questions: "What does the Lord want?" and "How can we receive the unlimited resources of His power?" A person with that kind of expectancy will flavor the dull gruel of depleted human potential. Every person, family, and church needs people who have not lost the savor of a bold belief in the possibilities the Lord is ready to unleash.

Fifth, a salty saint is a source of courage in life's battles. The parable of the king's warfare seems to have the same meaning and intention as the parable of the builder. But look again. The king in battle deals with conflict. Jesus came to do battle with the forces of Satan. He called His disciples to be soldiers in that battle. That's the key to understanding the parable of the king preparing for battle: "Or what king, when he sets out to meet another king in battle, will not first sit down and take counsel whether he is strong enough with ten thousand men to encounter the one coming against him with twenty thousand? Or else, while the other is still far away, he sends a delegation and asks terms of peace" (vv. 31,32).

The Lord wants us to realize that we will lose the battle with evil without Him. A Christian with tang realizes that the gates of hell cannot prevail against him if he knows the indwelling power of the Lord. Jesus gives the two alternatives to dependence on His strength. We become immobilized and never get into the battle, or we make peace with an entangling compromise. The point is that Jesus has called us to warfare with evil in people and the structures of society. Life will always seem like a battle with ten thousand men against twenty thousand. But that is so that, like Gideon, we can depend on the Lord and not on the size of our own troops. Our amazement will be over what the Lord can do to win the battle for us. We always have a majority when the Lord is on our side. The joyous tang of a Christian is the result of the confidence that we cannot lose. We have the limitless power of the Holy Spirit for life's conflicts. That's the source of the freedom that pulsates through us.

Sixth, the people who are the salt of the earth are no longer possessed by their possessions. "So therefore, no one of you can be My disciple who does not give up all his own possessions" (v. 33). We wonder what that means for us. Are we to sell all we have? Or, is there a more profound meaning? I think the Lord meant that we are to give up our right to have and hold life's possessions. We are liberated disciples when we want only what will bring us closer to our Lord and aid us in our obedience to Him. A possession is wrong only as it gets in the way of immediate and complete allegiance. When money, or the things it can buy, makes us give a second thought to doing what we feel the Lord guides, we have an inordinate, debilitating subservience to things. The unencumbered saint is one who seeks first the Kingdom knowing that whatever he needs will be provided. That makes for a laughing, loving, unbound, attractive Christian with tang.

Seventh, the salt of the earth is replenishable disciples. We can dare to give ourselves away carelessly because of a basic spiritual law: we only have what we give away. There is a spendthrift quality to Christian tang. We are not holding stations for spiritual insight, understanding and power. We were meant to be channels of the river of life to others. Jesus told us that within us would flow rivers of living water—artesian, constantly bubbling up with new inspiration. The more we give God, the more we can receive from Him.

The Lord's question begs His own answer given in His total life and message: "Therefore, salt is good; but if even salt has become tasteless, with what will it be seasoned?" (v. 34). The answer is exemplified in the long hours the Master spent in prayer. He was replenished by the Father for the pressures and demands of the Incarnation. The secret was in the admonition He gave the disciples, "Come away by yourselves" (Mark 6:31). The Greek really means, "Come away for yourselves." The Master knew that the disciples would wear out unless they loved themselves enough to be refortified by prolonged times of quiet with the only undepletable source of spiritual energy.

Christians with tang constantly are being refilled with discernment and wisdom beyond their own ability. I am convinced that this is the source of the eighth quality of tang. We are enthusiastic, energetic and exciting people when the Lord replenishes the saltiness. Our energies are insufficient for life's demands when we begin caring about people. I find that strain engulfs me when I try to be adequate on my own resources.

The other evening I arrived at church to lead a Sunday evening service completely exhausted. Before the service, I had a deep time of fellowship and prayer with my elders. They discerned the source of the energy drain in worry over an impossible load of detail and uncompleted tasks in preparation for the new program year. I had begun to take the whole responsibility on myself. Grimness and self-doubt invaded my mind. When they prayed, laying hands on me, I felt a new freedom to let go of my control and receive the Holy Spirit for the burdens. After prayer we all went into the sanctuary to lead a communion and healing service. The Lord answered the elders' prayers. I felt new energy, enthusiasm and excitement begin to flow again.

The world desperately needs energetic Christians with a lively verve for life. But we cannot give what we do not have. Only the Lord can refurbish enthusiasm.

Coupled with enthusiasm is humor. This ninth quality of tang comes from taking the Lord seriously so we don't have to take ourselves and life so seriously. Christians are not noted for their humor. Robert Louis Stevenson returned from church and was delighted to say, "I've been to church and I am not depressed." All too often church and church people are depressing because they have lost the tang of laughing at themselves. Our Lord wants to liberate overly grim, uptight Christians. His forgiveness should make us much more tender on ourselves and others. It frees us to share and laugh with others over our mistakes and blunders. Then the people around us are free to accept their own humorous humanity. A sure sign that we have become salty saints is in the quality and quantity of our humor.

Rufus Mosley was once asked, "Did Jesus laugh?" His response was, "I don't know, but He sure fixed me up so that I could!" So say I.

The sheer joy of living! We have been called to be Christians with a tang. There's a new image of life for our imagination. What would it be like for you today to be the Lord's flavor, seasoning and zest? Picture how you would act, what you would say if the nine ingredients of salt were evident in you.

165

16
Beyond Duty to Delight

Luke 17:1-10: Parable of the Unworthy Servants

I was called to the hospital late in the night. A highly respected member of my congregation was in serious condition. He was suffering from a terminal disease and was not expected to live. His outstanding career in the business world had distinguished him, and his contributions in the church and community had made him a very highly respected person. He had been a tireless worker in Christian causes, a tither of his sizable income, and an admired example of Christian character.

When I arrived on his floor of the hospital I found his room was next to an infamous criminal. There were policemen outside the door. Inquiry revealed that the prisoner had been shot in an exchange of gunfire at the time of his arrest for robbery. A patrolman had been killed in the line of duty by him. The prisoner had a bullet lodged in his chest. The prognosis was that he would live to stand trial. When I learned his name, I identified him as a person whose irresponsible life had been marked by a long line of petty thievery, rape and imprisonments.

My friend and the prisoner couldn't have been more different. One was a contributor to society; the other a leech. My parishioner had made his mark for upbuilding the community; the criminal had become a blight on everything good and creative. Why was one, who had paid his dues to society's improvement, dying, and one, who had wasted his life, going to live?

I sat in the waiting room with my member's wife. She was asking the same question. I waited with her through the excruciating vigil of anxiety. All that could be said to her had been communicated. I tried to give comfort and courage. The pain of uncertainty about her husband's prognosis and the nerve-jangling anxiety stretched into the dawn hours of a new day. Exhaustion and frustration finally released her to say what she was thinking and I was feeling. I noted her wringing her hands. Her eyes dilated to pinpoint precision. She swung around in her chair and met me eyeball to eyeball. Her voice was staccato and piercing.

"Listen, Pastor. You'd better talk to God. There are two people on this floor in serious condition. One is going to live and the other die. It's not fair! That criminal has no right to live and my husband has. You should tell God that my husband has a break coming. He's spent his life working for God. He has given himself doing good for years. He deserves a break. God owes him a big, fat miracle; and I expect you to tell Him so. If that criminal lives and my husband dies, it will prove there's no justice or reward in this life!"

My response was to tell her about God's love and to comfort her in her grief. I reminded her that her husband had not done good to build up a reserve of preferential treatment. The Lord was not finished with either of the critical patients on that floor. He would deal with both in His own way. Death would not be an ending for her beloved. Comparisons were irrelevant. Each of us passes through the narrow door of God's judgment individually. But God would not pull off an impossibility for one because he was good and condemn another because he was bad. He wanted both to live forever.

The long drive home from the hospital, as the sun began to rise, gave me time to reflect on what the woman had said. She spoke out of duress, but beneath her expression of the seeming injustice of it all, was a firmly held presupposition. She believed life was a balance scale. Her husband had done his part loading his side of the scale. Now it was God's turn. Or was it? Her words tumbled about in my mind. They sparked other memories of familiar statements about the system of rewards by which so many people live. I heard the often-repeated sentiments: "What did I do to deserve this? After all I've done for God and people, why did this happen to me?" The same confused convictions pervade our relationships: "I give and give, and nobody seems to appreciate my efforts." "I give my wife all she wants and she never considers what I need!" "Nobody seems to recognize my efforts—my kids, my fellow workers, my friends at church." "What's the use? Who cares that I do what's right and give myself and my resources to make this a better world?" Sound familiar? Ever feel that way? Who hasn't?

We expect rewards. It's built into our system of give and take. Life has its duties, relationships their obligations, and work its responsibilities. But what should we expect in return? Most of us love to be loved, give to receive, work to be praised and paid handsomely.

It's a part of our ethic. Whole schools of psychology

have been built around the idea that personality is shaped by strokes and patterned by pats on the back. B.F. Skinner has shown us the power of reinforcement, or lack of it, for behavior modification. Eric Berne has exposed the games people play and revealed the power of strengthening strokes. We all know about the enabling initiative of affirmation to encourage people in a pattern of behavior which is in keeping with what we want from them. Our childhood training has engrained the I'll-love-you-if syndrome in our psychēs.

We project that to God. Our belief is that we can store up a spiritual savings account to draw on when life levels its blows. We think our goodness conditions His grace in our crises. The distressed wife in the waiting room articulated our prejudice more than we may want to admit!

The "parable of unworthy servants" stands in bold contradiction. Jesus believed in and practiced the power of affirmation. He gave people a liberating image of who they were because of God's love. But He did not teach a system of bartered goodness and rewards.

Luke 17:5-10 is shocking. It attacks our motivations and cuts into our value system. Our ways of relating to God and each other are contradicted. Look carefully. He meant what He said!

The context brightens the impact. The disciples had finally come to grips with the cost of following Jesus. No wonder they exclaimed, "Increase our faith!" (v. 5). The Lord told them a parable about the quality, not the quantity, of the faith they asked for: "If you had faith like a mustard seed, you would say to this mulberry tree, 'Be uprooted and be planted in the sea'; and it would obey you" (v. 6). Limitless power was available to them. But how should it be used and for what purpose? An intimate relationship with God alone could direct the dynamic. Absolute obedience to Him would be required. Most of all, their use of their faith in the performance of deeds of mercy would not earn a status with God. He could not love them more than He did already. They needed to be sure of that. The parable of the "unworthy servants" told them a great deal about God and more about their self-justifying efforts than they may have wanted to face. They could never be proud or self-satisfied, whatever they did for God in the expression of their newly-found powers. There would be no place for an "I've got a right to desire a blessing for my use of faith" idea of entitled preference.

The parable of the mustard-seed potential for their ministry opened them up for the penetrating, larger truth of Jesus' next parable which is our focus in this chapter. They were excited by what was offered them. Now they had to learn how to offer themselves to God to use the power humbly and creatively. It gave them no rights, but a lot of responsibility! We are as disturbed by the story as the disciples must have been.

"But which of you, having a slave [servant] plowing or tending sheep, will say to him when he has come in from the field, 'Come immediately and sit down to eat'?" (v. 7).

Absurd! No servant expected that. Work from dawn to dark did not earn an appreciation banquet. It was a servants' obligation to work for the master. His work was not finished after the day's labor. The master's meal was to be prepared. Only after the master had eaten and drunk could the servant expect to be replenished by nourishment. The disciples knew that! Why this parabolic illustration? Jesus baited the query. He was about to hook His followers with a startling truth.

"But will he [the master] not say to him [the servant], 'Prepare something for me to eat, and properly clothe yourself and serve me until I have eaten and drunk; and afterward you will eat and drink'? He does not thank the slave because he did the things which were commanded, does he?" (vv. 8,9).

The disciples' and our response is, "Of course not! But Jesus—what's the point of all this?"

He's not reluctant to tell us: "So you too, when you do all the things which are commanded you, say, 'We are unworthy slaves; we have done *only* that which we ought to have done'" (v. 10, italics added).

Well! That's a twist. After we have done our duty, have we no right to expect a reward? The *King James Version* is even more direct. "We are unprofitable servants: we have done that which was our duty to do." We are indignant. Is there no compensation for doing our duty?

A prayerful exposition reveals two answers. One follows the other like day the dawn. The first is this: God owns us; He does not owe us anything. He's not accustomed to sending thank you notes for our efforts. Thankfulness is a human response, not a divine expression. He's not thankful for us or our faithfulness. We cannot manipulate His blessings by our beneficence.

That's hard for us to accept. The whole fiber of our life is woven by the back-and-forth movement of the shuttle of our works and expected rewards from God. We think that He will love us if we are good, bless us if we are effective, care for us if we are efficient. We barter for His acceptance. We promise to stop some habit if He will give us what we want. We will do a loving and forgiving thing to be sure we can count on His approval. Our prayers are a negotiation for the best deal we can get. Giving money is to be assured of financial success. Acts of mercy are to insure that we will be given His mercy. But God owes us nothing—whatever we do for Him.

After all we've done we still must say, "We are unworthy servants. We did only what was our duty."

The piercing point in this: The thing we do for rewards, we should do because it's our *duty*. That's not a popular word in our time. We hear a lot about freedom and grace these days. What we do does not earn salvation, we are told. True. But the result is that many of us do very little. We presume. Christians gather in churches every Sunday to collect "unemployment compensation." The sanctuary is a "duty free" shop for bargains.

Some time ago I took a special course on fund raising. We were taught how to raise support for the church by appreciation. The course prepared us to be able to write 75 different kinds of thank you notes. The expert in funding indicated that people give when what they give is appreciated and recognized. I was not disturbed by that. Affirming people is basic to my ministry. But I couldn't help but wonder why the people of God needed to be coddled and cajoled to do what was elemental to their discipleship.

Most churches would explode with new ministry and mission if church members followed the biblical injunction to tithe. Recently, one of my larger contributors cut down his contributions. He did not think he was properly thanked for his giving. The question I posed to him was why he gave: gratitude to God, or need for human recognition? There is no limit to what congregations could do if people gave as a normal part of their responsibility for the human space they occupy. Gratitude and praise should soar beyond that.

So much that is needed in our society is a part of basic Christianity. We should not need special motivation for honesty, integrity, righteousness and justice. That ought to be as normal as breathing, eating and sleeping. Expressing love and forgiveness should not be a big thing. It's basic Christianity. Feeding the hungry and caring for the poor doesn't warrant a brass band recognition. Allowing the plumb line of Christ's message to fall on our decisions and policies in business is normal Christian living. Why are we so excited when some Christ-oriented, biblically-guided Christian does a costly act of obedience? Big deal! After we've done what's required, we still must say: We are unworthy servants; we did only what was our duty.

Many of us must honestly admit that we're still back in the Middle Ages. We have our own kind of indulgences and treasury of merit. A new Luther is needed, or perhaps a rereading of the old one, to help us realize that we can never accumulate I.O.U.s from God as a part of our spiritual portfolios. He has no outstanding bills held by us. We are forever in His debt, however much we give or do.

Frederick Faber was on target in his hymn:

Thou owest me no duties, Lord!
Thy being hath no ties.

An inventory of our duty to God is sometimes helpful —always disturbing. If we made a list of the normal, daily, routine elements of Christian living, what would they be? Prayer, obedience, faithfulness, tithing, acts of love, caring for people, involvement in the church, extending the Kingdom of God to every realm of society— that's only a beginning. All because we belong to God. We should not expect a citation for these! When we've accomplished all this we are still at the starting line ready to begin the race of adventuresome Christianity. That's found in the second thing this parable communicates.

Beyond duty is delight. And delight transforms how we do our duties. Faith is its own reward. There is a joy we experience when we serve the Master before ourselves. To put God first in our lives enables a breakthrough from a duty-bound life.

The psalmist found that, "I delight to do Thy will, O my God; Thy law is within my heart" (Ps. 40:8). Paul caught the exuberance of this: "For I delight in the law of God, in my inmost self" (Rom. 7:22, *RSV*). He went on to say that his delight was constantly at war with the lesser motivation of obligation. We all know what that's like. We need a fresh release each day to live our lives motivated by love alone, not by calculated self-justification. Delighting in God Himself and what He's done for us transforms how we do our duties. It does not exonerate us from responsibility; it enthuses us to live and act as a response to amazing grace.

This is what Paul tried to communicate to the Corinthians. "For the love of Christ controls us, having concluded this, that one died for all, therefore all died; and He [Christ] died for all, that they who live should no longer live for themselves, but for Him who died and rose again in their behalf" (2 Cor. 5:14,15). The further sweep of the passage rejoices in the new creation through Christ and the new life we have in Him. Most of all—a new motivation. When Paul said that the love of Christ controls us he used a Greek word that focuses the driving power of delight: *he agapé tou Christou synēche hēmas. Syneche* here means not only held fast or held to, but to be pressed, forced, compelled, driven. The love of Christ is the instigation and inspiration of the Christian life. We want to please God because He has shown His pleasure in us. The fulfillment of our duty is an expression of gratitude. And we'll never be finished with that. We need no reward to motivate us. The cross, an empty tomb, an indwelling Lord is enough!

Augustine caught this: "Give me thine own self, without whom, though thou shouldest give me all that ever thou hast made, yet could not my desires be satisfied." This same profound thought is expressed by Thomas à Kempis, "It is too small and unsatisfactory, whatever thou bestowest on me, apart from Thyself." There is no greater joy than fellowship with God, now and forever. That's what Jesus was teaching in the parable. Being a servant of the master was reward enough. Not only will we want to work all day, serve Him first, but we will also look for new ways of expressing the gratitude of simply belonging to Him. The parable is a crucial part of the autobiography of God.

If we are willing to be indefatigable servants, we can go on to become friends of the Master. The delight of friendship engenders the faithfulness for our duties as servants. At the close of His ministry Christ ushered His disciples into a level of friendship that would liberate their lives as servants of God. "No longer do I call you slaves; for the slave does not know what his master is doing; but I have called you friends, for all things that I have heard from My Father I have made known to you" (John 15:15).

That friendship gives us power to serve. It is not just for enjoyment but for our employment in discipleship. Christ does not give us strength for our schemes. Our ambitions and plans are secondary; the Master's will is primary. We must stay close to Him to know how to invest ourselves in His causes with people and society. When we realize that we are undeserving persons whom Christ has saved from a meaningless, wasted, frustrated life to a life of purpose, joy and hope, we will want to be instruments through whom He will do the same for other persons.

Then we can pray like the old Scot: "Lord, this is John, reporting in for duty." And there will be fresh assignments every day. We'll never be finished. The sense of unworthiness will come not from disobedience, but from the realization that we have only touched the surface of what needs to be done. But what is done will be accomplished with delight!

A doctor I know asks himself a question as he walks from the hospital after his rounds. "Have I done all I can?" Good question!

Robert Schumann said that he always tried to play as if a master pianist were in the audience. There's only one person in our audience we have to please. His name is Jesus!

Now that the King has gone this way.

Great are the things of every day.

The question asked about Job was the wrong question: "Does Job fear God for nought?" (Job 1:9, *KJV*). Are there no rewards, compensations, residuals? The real question is "Does Job fear God for God?" Friendship with the Lord makes the Lord Himself our only reason to do our duties with delight.

A man closed a letter to his friend, "Casually Yours." That would be an appropriate end for many prayers we pray. Casual indeed! Luther's question challenges our easy discipleship: "What will Almighty God say about it in the end?" William James frequently remarked that the more ideals a man has, the more contemptible is he if the matter ends there; if there is no courage shown, no privation undergone, no risks incurred to get the ideal realized. Somewhere Dostoevski said, "Love in practice is a harsh and terrible thing compared with love in dreams. It is for love in practice that the world waits."

The parable of the unworthy servant stands as a constant reminder that there are duties, obligations and responsibilities to being a Christian. However much we do, we are never finished. But our unfinished tasks are to be faced in the gratitude for the finished gift of Calvary.

The One who accomplished that for us offered a further promise for those who serve the Master before themselves. Our interpretation of the parable concludes with reference to when the servants will be served. When He returns, those who have served out of love, and not for reward, will be part of His banquet of joy. "Blessed are those slaves whom the master shall find on the alert when he comes; truly I say to you, that he will gird himself to serve, and have them recline at table, and will come up and wait on them" (Luke 12:37). That's the glorious picture of the Second Coming, and also of the blessing of heaven. The One who was a servant on our behalf on the cross, who washed the disciples' feet to show them how to serve Him by humbly caring for each other, will welcome us as honored guests. I suspect He'll catch our eye as He serves us individually and ask, "Did you do all you could?"

My friend who was suffering in the hospital died the next day. God did not pull off the miracle the wife felt her husband deserved. The Lord did not owe him a special blessing. His life had been full of them. What his wife never understood was that the good things he had done were out of gratitude, not for special preference. He believed in Christ and had served faithfully out of love. Somehow he had not been able to communicate that to her through the years. Her presuppositions about rewards revealed her own need to love God for Himself and not for what He might do for her. As for her husband, God was glad to receive him into the fulfillment and consummation of the eternal life which had begun years before his death. Assurance of that made him the relentless servant of God he had been.

17

God Wants to Give
You a Gift

Luke 11:1-13; 18:1-8: Parables of Importunity

Have you ever wondered why we find so little time to pray? And when we do take time, why is it often an unsatisfactory experience? Have you ever been frustrated by what seemed to be unanswered prayer? Are there times when you wonder why prayer appears to be a dynamic dialogue for some, while for you it's often a monotonous monologue, as if no one were listening? Does prayer change the course of events, or is it simply to change us to be able to live in what seems to be irrevocable and unchangeable?

We wonder about prayer. What is it, really? How can we pray effectively? Why do we resist its power?

We join the disciples in expressing our need: "Lord, teach us to pray!" The Lord's answer in Luke 11 was to give them a model prayer which I like to call the Disciples' Prayer. Then He told a humorous parable. It must be considered along with its twin in Luke 18. Both parables expose the humor of Jesus. He knew that the disciples' deepest question was not how to pray but, knowing as much as they did about the power of prayer, why didn't they pray?[1]

The answer to that was so challenging that the Lord used humor to make His point. Laughter is always the best preparation for confrontations with truth.

Will Rogers once said that everything is funny as long as it's happening to somebody else. Jesus goes way beyond that. He used humor to free us to laugh at ourselves. He gets us laughing at a humorous situation in a parable and then, when we are loosened up with laughter, He identifies us in the ridiculous incongruity.

This is exactly what Jesus did in the twin parables of the friend at midnight and the persistent widow. Don't miss the humor of these very human stories!

Picture a typical one-room Palestinian house. It's divided into two parts. The main floor is used for the family's life during the day, and as a stable during the night. At one end is a loft where the family eats and sleeps. At sunset the cattle are brought in and the door is tightly bolted with a crossbar. Soon afterward, the whole family goes to sleep in the loft, the cattle settle down, and all is dark and quiet.

Then at midnight, when everyone is sleeping soundly, a persistent knock beats on the heavy wooden door. Who can that be at this hour of the night? Imagine getting out of bed, threading your steps through the sleeping family, climbing down the ladder, making your way through the cattle and then finally opening the door. An old friend has come to the village and has no place to stay. What to do, but invite him in and make a place for him. Customs can be compulsions. The friend has to be fed! Not only because he is hungry and tired. It is an unpardonable lack of friendship and hospitality to fail to offer a meal. Eating was a sacramental expression of the bond of loyalty. To refuse was to make an enemy.

The midnight visitor must be important to the sleepy host, who is aghast to find he has no bread to express his solicitude. What can he do?

His neighbor will help! Or will he? His family also has bedded down for the night. What will he say if awakened? Will he help? There is nothing to do but try!

The scene shifts to the neighbor. His house is the same. The only difference is that he has small children. Anyone knows how long it takes for them to go to sleep! Surely they will be awakened by a midnight knock.

Regardless, the man has to get bread for his visitor. All his urgency is channeled through his fist as he begins pounding wildly on the neighbor's door. Long silence. "Knock again, they're still asleep!" he says anxiously to himself. It seems like an hour before there is a response. The neighbor's voice is angry and perturbed: "Who's there? What do you want at this hour of the night?"

"Friend, lend me three loaves; for a friend of mine has come to me from a journey, and I have nothing to set before him" (Luke 11:5,6). Long silence again. What will he say?

Likely response. "Do not bother me; the door has already been shut and my children and I are in bed; I cannot get up and give you anything" (v. 7).

The neighbor turns over in bed, determined to go back to sleep. But the children are now wide awake. "Who was that? What did he want? Is it morning? Can we get up?" The cattle, too, are restless. The whole household is disrupted. Again, the persistent knocking.

"What a neighbor! He will wake the whole village for three loaves of bread." Finally, there is no other alternative than to get up and give him the bread he needs.

We laugh. And then Jesus asks us, "Well, what would you have done?" We are still chuckling when we respond, "Why, of course, we'd have to get up and help our neighbor."

Then, suddenly, Jesus is into serious conversation with us. He's drawn us into a comparison we didn't expect. If a man finally would respond because of the importunity of his neighbor, would not God, who "neither slumbers nor sleeps" (see Ps. 121:3) answer our prayers? "And I say to you, ask, and it shall be given to you; seek, and you shall find; knock, and it will be opened to you" (v. 9). The utter availability of a gracious, loving Father! Jesus has once again used His "more than that" method of teaching. How much more will God respond to us if we go to Him—at any hour of the day or night. "For everyone who asks receives; and he who seeks finds; and to him who knocks it shall be opened" (v. 10).

The warm humor of the parable has prepared us for further human illustrations which touch our hearts. "What if a son asks for a fish. Would any father give him a snake instead?" The fang of a snake and the little hand of a child flash before our minds. Our feelings rise. "Or if he asked for an egg, would he give him a scorpion?" Everything tender and humane in us recoils. "Of course not, Jesus!" Our emotions are raw from those illustrations. That's just what He wanted. Fertile soil for the planting of truth. "If you then, being evil, know how to give good gifts to your children, *how much more* shall your Heavenly Father give the Holy Spirit to those who ask Him?" (v. 13 italics added). Jesus knows us, doesn't He? We can grapple with the obscure. The obvious al-

181

ways takes us longer. Often a lifetime. For some people, discernment of the obvious never comes!

We'll have to come back to that. Meanwhile, Jesus has us laughing at another story. A dignified judge is having a difficult time keeping his propriety (see Luke 18:1-8). A certain widow is absolutely ubiquitous in her persistent tracking of his steps everywhere. He can't get away from her. She's at his door in the morning, confronts him in the marketplace, interrupts his conversations with esteemed associates, disrupts his court, and is waiting for him when he comes home at night. The appeal is always the same: "Give me legal protection from my opponent!" (v. 3). A woman, much less a widow, had few rights at this time. If the rabbis prayed daily, "I thank Thee God that you did not make me a woman!" we can imagine the attitude toward widows.

All the more reason that the judge's friends begin to tease him about his inability to get rid of this widow. He is known as a hard, impervious judge, who constantly refortifies his self-image by protesting that he does not fear God or respect any man. But he meets his match in this widow.

The incongruity is laughable. She is no retiring, self-effacing burden on society's benevolence. She is a tough lady who knows her rights and is not about to let up on the judge until she realizes them.

The disciples must have had a good belly laugh over the contradiction between his statement of his authority and his growing fear of the widow's threats: "Even though I do not fear God nor respect man, yet because this widow bothers me, I will give her legal protection, lest by continually coming she wear me out" (v. 4,5).

The humor is found in a more accurate translation of "wear me out." Actually, this phrase is rooted in a bit of slang which means, "hit me under the eye." Translators have tried to suggest that Jesus would never have used slang, and that it meant shadows under the eyes, or fatigue; thus "wear me out." Not so! I think He quoted the judge as fearing that the woman would give him a black eye. "Lest she come and beat me" is a literal interpretation of the Greek.

Some lady! The judge had met a Tugboat Annie or a Ma Kettle. He wasn't so all-powerful as he pretended.

The parable ends with a question and statement that the humor has prepared us to hear: "Now shall not God bring about justice for His elect, who cry to Him day and night, and will He delay long over them? I tell you that He will bring justice for them speedily. However, when the Son of Man comes, will He find faith on the earth?" (vv. 7,8).

Once again Jesus has used the "how much more" of convicting comparison. If a persistent, scrappy widow, who is a dangerous nuisance to a hostile, unrighteous judge, can get him to rule favorably in her case, will not the ultimate Judge of the universe act on behalf of His people with justice and mercy? The obvious again. How can we miss it so often? If humor is rooted in the incongruity of the human scene, this is the ultimate incongruity. Jesus has used humor to catch us off guard to say some very crucial things about God and prayer as the mother tongue of our relationships with Him.

Following our interpretation of the parables as the autobiography of God, we are pressed to ask: What is the central theme in these twin parables about the essential nature of God? What has He told us about Himself and how we can communicate with Him?

Jesus has lifted up a flashing diamond of illuminating truth. Its brilliance brightens the dark places of our minds. God is one who listens and responds with a gift beyond our wildest expectation. Our deepest questions about prayer can be answered. I want to deal with three of these questions we all ask at times. They come from the depths of the human struggle.

The first question is, Why is it so difficult for most of us to find time to pray? It is strange, isn't it? The reason is our profound misunderstanding of the nature of God. Jesus has cut to the core of the two major reasons that we do not find time to pray. We find time to do what we want to do. What goes undone is rooted in a deeper issue. Many of us do not find time for prayer because we think of God as a reluctant neighbor, or as a judge of our failures and inadequacies. Our conception of prayer is often that it's to overcome God's reluctance, or as a guilt-ridden accountability time for an inventory of our sins. Neither motivates us toward communication.

On the human level, we will do anything we can to spend time with a person who loves, accepts, and affirms us. A loved one who heightens our self-esteem and gives us fresh courage for life's battles is cherished, and conversation flows naturally.

In the parable of the friend at midnight, Jesus wants us to know the ready availability of God. He knows our needs before we ask Him. In fact, He creates in us a desire to ask for what He is more ready to give than we are to ask. God keeps an open door—day and night. He does not need to be awakened.

But just as we often project onto other people our reluctance to have a deep relationship, and then accuse them of being distant or unfriendly, we do the same with God. Jesus corrects this transference. To be sure we understand, He characterized God as an unreservedly willing and receptive listener. He created us for Himself and gave us the gift of prayer so that we might talk with Him and He to us. Prayer is dialogue with a Friend who longs to love us and to have us love Him.

And yet, training and conditioning have made Him little more than a judge for our uneasy conscience. He is judge of all of us, to be sure, but unlike the unrighteous judge of the parable, His love outdistances His judgment. We all need the objectivity of a reliable standard. But we all fail in spite of our best efforts. It's when we know we have sinned that we need both a just judge and forgiving Father. Just as a child often resists companionship with his father when he needs his love and forgiveness most, so we also resist prayer when we have failed. But God is a righteous judge. Jesus wants us to be sure of that. The world would be more of a shambles than it is without the Ten Commandments, and the greatest commandment of the Master—to love God and our neighbors as ourselves. And when we don't, God forgives, and helps us make a new beginning.

The twin parables on prayer have been greatly misunderstood as teaching importunity as a virtue of prayer. I believe that Jesus not only wants us to know how much greater God is than either the reluctant neighbor or the unrighteous judge, but also to realize that prayer is more than an exercise in persistence. He wants us to see the frenzied rapping at the door and the imploring of the unrighteous judge as expressions of inadequate prayer. If God is our Father and forgiving judge, He needs to be told of our need only once. Repeated prayer is not to remind Him, but to thank Him.

When we see God as "much more" than the neighbor or the judge, we can envision our prayers as so much more than banging down a door that is already open, or of convincing a judge who has already ruled in our favor.

Tell God once, and then thank Him a million times over that He has heard us, already forgiven us, and is active to answer our requests in a way that will bring ultimate good and creative growth in our lives.

That leads to the second pressing question we all ask about prayer: Why does it *seem* that some prayers are unanswered? The impact of these parables and Jesus' explanation of them is that all prayers are answered. Some prayers, however, are delayed until they are developed. God does not answer some prayers immediately because what we are asking for needs to be perfected for our good. I am very thankful that God has not answered some of my prayers on my schedule. I was not ready. Nor were the people around me. But in the painful period of waiting, what I asked for originally was changed radically. His silence was His blessing. I grew, but also my perception of what was best was honed and sharpened. Under the fires of centering love, the dross was being burned off. When I finally was ready to want what the Lord wanted, the answer came speedily.

But I must honestly admit that usually I can see this truth only in retrospect. The difficult problem is to know it in the waiting period. It's then I need to know that nothing happens without God's will or timing. He knows what's best, and when.

I experienced this reality the other morning. My personal devotional time gave me specific, practical help in a waiting period I've been through on a concern that is dear to my heart. I had awakened with a pervading sense of impatience. Why was God waiting so long to answer? My reading that month had been in Romans. Romans 5:1-5 was next up for study and meditation. It spoke to my condition: "Therefore having been justified by faith, we have peace with God through our Lord Jesus Christ, through whom also we have obtained our introduction by faith into this grace in which we stand; and we exult in hope of the glory of God. And not only this, but we also exult in our tribulations; knowing that tribulation brings about perseverance; and perseverance, proven

186

character; and proven character, hope; and hope does not disappoint; because the love of God has been poured out within our hearts through the Holy Spirit who was given to us." The thing that gripped me was that my hope was in God, not in a solution to my problem. Suddenly I realized that the thing I needed most was for the love of God to be poured into my heart. That never disappoints us. I was released and able to let go of my time schedule; to accept the fact that, regardless of whether I was given what I asked for repeatedly, it was secondary to my hope, rooted in the love of God. I had a very different kind of day because of what God said to me through this magnificent passage of Scripture.

Jesus gave us the formula for petitionary prayer. Ask, seek, knock! We are to make our concerns known. The seeking period is the perfecting time. The knocking is surrendering the direction that the seeking time has revealed. The Greek implies that we are to keep on asking, seeking, knocking. That's not to get God's attention, but to appropriate His attentiveness. To ask is to make our request known; to seek is to receive the Lord's perspective on our petition; to knock is to ask for what the Lord has guided us to pray. He wants us to move from "I want," to "Lord, what do you want?" to "I will!" As we carry on a continuous conversation about a petition, our verbs become more viable. What we think we want may not be best for us. Then we are given freedom to want what the Lord shows us He wants for us. Finally we are free to say, "Dear God, I will to do your will."

Now we are ready to consider the third and deepest question: "If God knows what we need, and anticipates our prayers before we ask Him, what's the purpose of prayer?" Jesus makes the answer abundantly clear in these parables. God wants to give us a gift. More than answers to prayer, He wants to give us *Himself.* "How much more shall your Heavenly Father give the Holy Spirit to those who ask Him?" (Luke 11:13). The one blessing God will not give until we ask, is His own indwelling Spirit. He will surround us, protect us, guide us, watch over us, arrange life's serendipities for our good; but He withholds His Spirit until we cry out for nothing less than an intimate, immediate infusion of His life in us. The ultimate purpose of prayer is to make that request. After that, prayer is communion with God, lingering in His presence, enjoying His companionship, and delighting in His gifts of wisdom, knowledge, love, and praise. Anyone who is filled with the Holy Spirit does not need to be convinced to take time for prayer. All of life is prayer without ceasing.

Jacob exemplifies this transition. His prayers went from requests, to longing to know God's name, and finally to "I have seen God face to face" (Gen. 32:30). The same was true of Moses. In his early ministry he besieged God with demands for His power. A much more abundant life began for him when he simply prayed, "Lord, show me your glory!" (see Exod. 33:18). He no longer wanted God for what He could do for him or the people, but now he wanted God for God Himself. Paul went through years of what seemed to be unanswered prayer about his personal needs, until he was liberated to say, "All I want to know is Christ!" (Phil. 3:10, *Phillips* also see 1 Cor. 2:2).

Mother Teresa of Calcutta put it clearly. "Prayer enlarges the heart until it is capable of containing God's gift of Himself."

When we know that, we will be able to laugh with God at ourselves and the carnival of life. The ultimate purpose of our life will have been accomplished and we will be able to see the humor of the comedy of anything less. Whenever we lapse back into the furor of feverish importunity, we can pray with the laughter of heaven.

18
The Prayer
God Won't Answer

Luke 18:9-14: Parable of the Pharisee and the Publican

I have a friend who claims he has discovered the hidden power of meditation. He takes time each day to be quiet; to gather strength for the challenges and opportunities of each day. During his meditation, he refortifies his belief in himself and in his gifts to win in life's battles. He talks to himself with an ego-boosting affirmation: "You're okay. You can make it. Nothing is too great for you to conquer if you believe in yourself!"

My friend asserts that his meditation is a form of prayer. He attests that it gives him great confidence and courage.

We smile. That's not prayer! The man is not praying; he's talking to himself, not God. Exactly. Our reaction is to be critical. But then it dawns on us that this man's meditation may exemplify the praying of many of us. Much that we call prayer is little more than a dialogue with ourselves.

In the previous chapter, I made the bold statement that God answers all prayers. The title of this chapter seems to be a contradiction. Not so! There are some so-called "prayers" God won't answer. God neither hears nor responds to them. The reason is that they are not addressed to Him. It's possible to think we are praying when all we are doing is refortifying our presuppositions and ruminating within the cycle of our perception of reality. We can even address the Almighty with familiar titles of the deity, repeating shibboleths of tattered phrases. The result is still the same: a pious conversation with ourselves! Our humility is vitiated by pride.

Jesus exposes the prayer that God won't answer in the parable of the Pharisee and the publican. He told the parable for people like my meditating friend—and for all of us at times. The Master tells us something about God and the quality of humility which is a prelude to prayer power. His purpose was to alarm and help "certain ones who trusted in themselves that they were righteous, and viewed others with contempt" (Luke 18:9). Who of us can evade the broad sweep of that convicting net of truth? The concluding phrase of the parable draws the net inescapably: "For every one who exalts himself shall be humbled, but he who humbles himself shall be exalted" (v. 14). Jesus has a great deal to say to us about why our prayers are often so ineffective. The problem is not just our prayers, but the dominant focus of our total life.

"Two men went up into the temple to pray, one a Pharisee, and the other a tax-gatherer" (v. 10). At first analysis both men have much in common. Both were Jews, or they would not have been admitted in the temple. Both had a desire to pray. And both addressed God. The similarity ends there. The prayers they prayed could not have been more different.

We are tempted by conditioning to categorize all

Pharisees as hypocrites and all publicans as misunderstood, misjudged collaborators with Rome. Jesus was not that simplistic, but His reversal of expected roles catches our attention. Surely His listeners were alarmed. The prayer prayed by each of the men should have been expected of the other.

The Pharisee's prayer is illustrative of the prayer God won't answer. Jesus tells us why: "The Pharisee stood and was praying to himself" (see v. 11). The words may mean that he prayed quietly, or inaudibly, in the privacy of his own heart. But I think Jesus meant more than that. Certainly the prayer he prayed never reached God. It was confined to his closed inner chamber of self-sufficiency. He addressed God, but his hurdy-gurdy rhythms of self-assurance went unheard by God. They contradicted the basic qualification of a "humble and contrite heart."

We listen to the Pharisee's prayer and are disturbed to find its contents too familiar for comfort: "God, I thank Thee that I am not like other people, swindlers, unjust, adulterers, or even like this tax-gatherer. I fast twice a week; I pay tithes of all that I get" (vv. 11,12).

The prayer reached no further than the temple roof. It was not prayer at all. The respected religious leader has given us a model not of prayer, but of pride. There were four reasons why God would not answer this prayer.

The prayer was comparative. The Pharisee took the wrong measurements. He compared himself with the tax collector looking down on another human being rather than up to God. The comparison was not only odious, but opportunistic. He grasped an opportunity to lift himself up by putting another down.

Our status with God is not based on being better than others. We are to be all that God has gifted us to be. Yet, we must honestly admit that we share the Pharisee's distorted, defensive insecurity. We, too, smack our lips in consternation at other people's failure and inadequacies. When we observe what they do with the gift of life, we are arrogantly judgmental. God should be pleased with us for the way we handle our affairs. Even our most eloquent expressions of thanksgiving are often saturated with elevated pride. God has given us the only acceptable basis of comparison: Jesus Christ. Suddenly our side-glances at the less fortunate or those caught in the web of compulsive sin, are not acceptable. Who can possibly measure up? No one. But that realization makes way for the possibility of prayer.

Note also that the Pharisee's prayer was based in externals. His pride was built on the unstable foundation of what he had done, not what he was. Both what he did and abstained from doing were on the surface. He had accomplished it all himself. There was no dependence on God for his impeccable life. The Pharisee had done it all without God. If only he had prayed, "God, I am so thankful that you have given me the strength and fortitude to withstand these temptations." He should have known that God was not impressed with self-righteous, self-sustained perfectionism.

But we must go deeper. Jesus wants us to understand how pride twists and distorts our capacity of self-scrutiny. Our minds were meant to be truth-gathering computers. The Pharisee's prayer disturbs us with the realization of how our minds can play tricks on us. We can ignore reality and forget things that are not on the agenda of our conscious or subconscious perception. It's possible to delude ourselves into thinking that we are right with God because of our own accomplishments and goodness. We can see what we want to see whether it's true or not. Our minds rationalize to protect our egos. Most of all, we can resist the need to change and grow by making our brand of righteousness our status with God. The mind will fight to make us secure—even at the cost of fighting God!

That's why some of our supposed prayers never reach God. The purpose of prayer is to see things as they are: ourselves as we really are, and God as He has revealed Himself to be. God wants us to come to grips with the true person inside us—our hopes and dreams, failures and sins, missed opportunities and potential. When we are honest with what we want and compare it with what He wills for us, we can pray a prayer He will hear and answer.

The fourth reason the Pharisee's prayer never reached God was that it lacked humility. Authentic humility is an outward expression of gratitude, honesty, and courage to grow. It asks and answers three crucial questions: What do I have that I was not given? Who am I, really? What are the next steps of the adventure of growth for me? The Pharisee could not dare to ask any of these penetrating questions. He believed that he had achieved all that he had accomplished on his own strength. There was no radical self-awareness. No incisive introspection. He did not dare! But most debilitating of all, he was satisfied with himself. It is a tragic state of self-deception when there is no yawning gap between our perception of where we are and where God would have us be as persons. Arndt was right: "Das wesen der demuth ist muth." The words rhyme in German, but the lively truth survives translation. "The essence of humility is courage." Indeed! Humility is the courage to dare. Whatever we have learned, we have barely scratched the surface of true knowledge. Our personalities are still clay, to be molded into the image of Christ. Our relationships are inadequate expressions of the love God has unreservedly given to us. Our goals are still within the limits of our meager talents. We have barely begun to live. Humility is an unheeded teacher.

The parable is part of the autobiography of God, like all the rest. God is humble and expects nothing less from His people. He who needs no one, humbled Himself in creating us so that He might love and be loved. Never satisfied with man's rebellions, He humbled Himself and became one of us. Immanuel exposed His humility. "Come to Me, all who are weary and heavy laden, and I will give you rest. Take My yoke upon you, and learn from Me, for I am gentle and humble in heart; and you shall find rest for your souls" (Matt. 11:28,29). The invitation was to share the humble heart of God. In substance, Jesus was saying: All who recognize their need, and can't make it on their own can experience the comfort of God and be given strength to be what He has meant them to be.

Paul dramatically describes the humility of the Incarnation as the model for a humble disposition: "Have this attitude in yourselves which was also in Christ Jesus, who, although He existed in the form of God, did not regard equality with God a thing to be grasped, but emptied Himself, taking the form of a bond-servant, and being made in the likeness of men. And being found in appearance as a man, He humbled Himself by becoming obedient to the point of death, even death on a cross. Therefore also God highly exalted Him, and bestowed on Him the name which is above every name, that at the name of Jesus every knee should bow, of those who are in heaven, and on earth, and under the earth, and that every tongue should confess that Jesus Christ is Lord, to the glory of God the Father" (Phil. 2:5-11).

In the same way, God can highly exalt only those who humble themselves. This is no flattering homage to God without gratitude, honesty, and daring. It is the humility of dependence, obedience, and willingness to do God's will.

The pride of the Pharisee was based on his lack of need for God. He didn't need God to help him accomplish his limited view of righteousness. Nor did God need his fictitious prayers.

The publican's prayer is a startling contrast. He desperately needed God. "But the tax-gatherer, standing some distance away, was even unwilling to lift up his eyes to heaven, but was beating his breast, saying, 'God, be merciful to me, the sinner!' " (Luke 18:13). Note the article "the." We trip over it. The tax-gatherer saw himself as the greatest of sinners. Probably with honest cause. As we noted earlier, tax-gatherers were infamous for collecting the required tax plus more for themselves. They were permitted by Rome to keep anything they could squeeze out of people. The Jews despised their political prostration under the heel of Rome. Tax-collectors of Jewish heritage became a symbol not only of what Rome's authority inflicted, but of what depth of depravity some Jews were willing to fall to for profit. What they did with the profits was often expressed in a life-style of affluence and profligate excesses. Jesus did not exonerate this with His accolade for the publican's prayer. What He did do was expose the taproot of true prayer: the need for God.

We wonder what brought the publican to the point where he saw himself as *the* sinner. What broke through the acquisitive barrier and forced him to see the real person he had become? Jesus recognized his prayer as an expression of humility. Who would ever have thought of this compromising publican as humble? What was it that brought him low so that he could rise to the sublime heights of this prayer? We don't know. But we can imagine, just based on our own experience.

Life does have a way of leveling the growth of proud self-satisfaction. It's tragedies and crises can suddenly diminish the resources of self-sufficiency. It is a special gift of God when we are forced to admit that we can't make it on our own.

But does that mean that we have to confess that we are sinners, especially *the* sinner? Don't we ever outgrow that state of contrition? Even if we admit that we are sinners, aren't we saved by grace? Isn't that what Christianity is all about? Must we hit bottom again and again to be able to pray humbly? And aren't there things we can do to clean up our act so that we have something to show God as the fruit of our humility?

We misunderstand sin. As we have noted in other chapters, it's not only separation from God, but also from our purpose and potential. We never outgrow our need for God's love, forgiveness, guidance and indwelling power. As I write this I am aware of areas of my life and relationships where I need God desperately. My opportunities, not just my failures, drive me back to Him constantly. Assurance of grace initiates aspiration to continue to grow. God is not finished with us. Therefore we are never finished.

Right at this moment, as you are reading this, are you conscious of things said or unsaid, done or left undone, that jab at your conscience? Who can live any day without a disturbing sense of missed opportunities as well as of overt sins that have hurt ourselves and others?

Paul called himself the "chief of sinners" (see 1 Tim. 1:15) at a time when he was the leading advocate of the grace of God. He was constantly pressing on in the upward call of Christ Jesus. The closer he got to the Lord, the greater was his need for Him.

The most devastating word Jesus ever spoke about

anyone was, "They have their reward." There was no place to grow. They were dead before their time. The reward of human acclaim and recognition is a reward that precludes the need for the only satisfying reward: relationship with God, eternal life now and forever.

The conclusion of the parable reveals how God responded to the preying of the Pharisee and the prayer of the publican. He did not hear or respond to the pride of the Pharisee. The humility of the publican was recognized and given the ultimate gift: justification. The Pharisee, says Jesus, went to his home unjustified, while the publican was justified. One had the feeling of being right with God which the other did not. Pride always leaves us unfulfilled and unsatisfied. Humility opens the floodgates of the heart of God; it's the basic ingredient of any prayer that God *will* answer.

How can we discover this crucial quality of humility? No one ever achieves humility by seeking it as an end in itself. It's a by-product of something much deeper. Jesus clarified that in the Beatitudes. In His description of blessedness, the truly joyous life, He delineated the ingredients of authentic humility. It's rooted in the fertile soil of spiritual poverty which recognizes our need for God's power; it grows by a profound grief over what we have done with the gifts of God; it is nurtured by a meekness that longs for the guidance of God; it is strengthened by mercy (gracious love for others); and it flowers in a dominant desire of the heart to know God and do His will at all costs. If we desire humility, our first concern is for these qualities. The Beatitudes really are a portrait of Jesus Christ Himself. That's the secret of humility. The deeper our life grows in Him, the more humble we will be. Then we can pray with confidence.

19
Shrewd Saints

Luke 16:1-17: Parable of the Unjust Steward

I had a good visit with one of America's most successful businessmen on a cross-country flight recently. He
has risen from a very humble background to immense
wealth. I asked him the secret of his success. His response was very interesting.

"Shrewdness!" was his one-word reply.

I was shocked by his frankness.

He went on to say that he spent every waking hour
thinking, scheming, planning, developing and putting
deals together. In it all he had tried to be completely
honest in all his affairs!

I couldn't help but admire his single-mindedness. He
knew what he wanted and left nothing to chance. He
worked hard to achieve his goals. All the power of his
intellect, the strength of his seemingly limitless energies,
the determination of his iron will and the resources of
his calculated discernment of people were employed to
accomplish his goals.

When it seemed natural and unforced, I shifted our conversation into what the man believed about God. There was a long silence. He admitted that he had not taken any time to think about that. He was astonished by my response: "If you ever put the same time, energy and will into being a disciple of Jesus Christ, you would be a contemporary Apostle Paul."

The man's response was thoughtful and reflective: "Nobody has ever challenged me with that!"

The conversation with my traveling companion made a deep impression on me. It forced me to wonder if I could say that Jesus Christ meant as much to me as this man's career does to him. That led me into a long analysis of people I know in business, entertainment, government and sports who invest uncalculable personal thought and resources to get ahead. No cost is too high; no sacrifice too demanding. Scheming, study, rehearsal, practice and determination are committed as a small price for perfection and success. I often wonder what would happen if Christians took following Jesus Christ as seriously as these people take getting ahead.

We have grasped the jugular vein of the parable of the unrighteous steward. Jesus wanted to teach one central truth in this very startling account. There is no parable with as many enticing dead-end possibilities as this one. We can go astray down any one of them and miss the main point. Remember that parables were taught by Jesus to focus one point. This parable is not an allegory in which each aspect and character is representative of facets of the homily. Let's look for the one thing Jesus was trying to communicate to His disciples, to the Pharisees who listened, and to us!

A rich Jew had a steward to whom he entrusted his investments and the collection of interest. Usury was forbidden for Hebrews. The steward became the factor to oversee the multiplication of the master's wealth so he would never have to be implicated in the nasty business of lending and collecting high interest. As often happens, the steward began to act as if the master's money was his own and squandered it for his own aggrandizement and pleasure. The day of reckoning finally came. The master called for an accounting of his investments before dismissing the steward from his service.

The steward was now faced with a crisis. He was too old to work and too proud to beg. What could he do? A shrewd strategy formulated in his mind. There's a Greek word used that takes six English words to define. If we were to use just one word it would probably best be translated as "aha!" or "eureka!" The unjust steward got hold of the live wire of a clever idea. It was as if he said, "Aha! I've got it!"

While the master's debtors still thought the steward was employed, he summoned and delighted them with a magnanimous offer: "How much do you owe my master?" To the one who said, "A hundred measures of oil' (about eight hundred gallons), the steward told him "Take your bill, and sit down quickly and write fifty." Then he said to a debtor who owed over a thousand bushels of wheat, "Take your bill, and write eight hundred" (see Luke 16:6,7).

The steward had a plan. He knew that soon he would be destitute and friendless. He had to make some friends at any cost in order to have a few favors to collect when he was out of work. His idea was that he could demand that the debtors take him into their homes and care for him after he was sacked.

When the steward's master learned of the clever deed, he was impressed with his resourcefulness. We are not told whether he was reinstated in his position or not. He was praised! Quite a reward for a manipulation which would further diminish the master's potential profits.

What did Jesus want to communicate to His disciples and the Pharisees? How does this parable fit in the autobiography of God? Jesus' own explanation helps.

Jesus commended shrewdness: "The sons of this age are more shrewd in relation to their own kind than the sons of light" (v. 8). The word "shrewd" means keen, artful, astute and innovative. It has taken on negative blight in our time. The Lord used the word in a very positive way. He admired forthrightness, energetic planning and complete devotion to a purpose. There is nothing wrong with creative strategizing. It's alarming that people who make no pretense of knowing and loving God are more dedicated to the multiplication of their resources than the people of God are about the cause of spreading the gospel and about the Kingdom.

I talked to a great actor. He has gained fame and acclaim for his stage and screen roles. There is a shrewdness about the man's development of his career and the use of the money he's rewarded with for his dynamic interpretation of the roles he plays. I asked him how he accounted for his success. "Hard work!" was his first reply. He went on to explain that he gets up at five in the morning to jog to keep in physical shape. Nothing is left undone or unstudied to be sure he has a vivid portrayal of the parts he's assigned. I felt his intensity, pertinacity and limitless commitment. I wondered about how many Christians give as much thought to the drama of life and their roles as saints of God.

The "more than" theme is used again by our Lord in this parable. If the sons of this age are resourceful in the use of unrighteous mammon, what about the saints who belong, along with their possessions, to the Lord? Jesus' purpose in the parable of prudence and energetic enactment of their high calling was to show them an example of how quickly and cleverly the dishonest steward devised methods to secure his earthly and temporal status. In substance, the Lord was saying, "Listen, why is it that the children of darkness scheme and plan and manipulate, and you hardly give a flippant thought to God and His strategy for the world?"

The first thing we need to consider is that Jesus admired a shrewdness that could come to grips with a crisis of a real situation. The steward saw things as they really were and dealt with them. He was about to lose his job, the books had to be turned in, and he had to find a way to save his neck. Jesus wants us to come to grips with the crises of life. Where will we spend eternity? What will our books show about how we handled the Lord's resources? How are we spending the years of our life in order to live forever with Him? Can we see not only the problem, but the potential?

Note the ways people look at a crisis. Some say, "The jig is up! There's no hope. It's all over now. What's the use of trying." Others react, "It's the greatest opportunity I've ever had to make something out of an impossible situation." Still others react to problems by saying, "You can't stand still. To do nothing is to go backward. This is the very time to expand." Jesus would like this last kind of wholeheartedness.

The second observation from the parable is that shrewdness produces an energetic, sagacious plan to solve life's problems. Jesus affirms the willingness in us to dare to believe that there is nothing too big for God. He wants people who see difficulties as a dynamic prelude to new advancement. We are not to throw up our hands in consternation, but fall on our knees in consecration. "Lord, what is it you want me to do? What is your wisdom for my situation that is beyond my capacity?"

203

Often the Lord allows us to drift into complexities which to us seem to be unsolvable, so that He can be the source of the solution. He wants to use our intellect, emotion and will to devise a plan that will astound us and the people around us.

In the secular world of business and planning there are people who delight in finding a way through an impossible marketing or product-development challenge. Others stand by wondering why they did not think of that.

A friend of mine developed the original planning for instant breakfast food for the busy American. He anticipated the need and provided a nutritious, healthy breakfast at a time when the breakfast food companies were confronting a dangerous low in sales. I am pleased that the man uses the same shrewdness in living his Christian life.

I meet frequently with a financier who is a member of my congregation. His eyes sparkle and his voice is excited when he tells me about a new deal he's working on. He has an uncanny sense of trends in thought and what will sell. He is one of the most forward-thinking people in our church. He's constantly strategizing new ways of setting creative goals and plans for our urban church to do more than solve problems. He sees potential. The source of his visionary thinking is none other than the Holy Spirit. Every pastor needs a band of courageous adventurers like this man.

Look at what's happened in television. The media, not the church, is shaping the mind of America. The best minds are constantly planning, testing, developing in order to stay ahead. We've all watched the skyrocketing career of Fred Silverman. We may not agree with either his methods or life-style, but are forced to admire the way he can analyze potential and grasp opportunities others have overlooked. He's moved from network to network, taking depleted ratings and devising new strategies to do what others never dared to think or do. We feel the pulse of the parable when we say, "Why isn't there someone like that at the head of the Christian enterprise in America?" We need there-must-be-a-new-way leaders in the church today. If media attracts them, why not the church? We have the same power available that raised Jesus from the dead!

It's often impossible to evaluate the effectiveness of programs in the church. Familiar procedures come to have the same authority as Scripture. We hang on to old methods long after they are worn out and no longer work effectively. I know a church where it would take a new Incarnation and Calvary to move the Apostle's Creed to another place in the order of worship! Even then it would rattle the staid members for whom familiarity has become a false god.

Now let's press on to the next thing our Lord is saying in this challenging parable. Jesus says that we are to use unrighteous mammon to make friends. What does that mean? The Lord is saying that if an unjust steward could use money to gain friends, why can't the children of light use it to make friends.

Our purpose is to use material resources as an expression of our friendship with God to make others His friends. That's the purpose of tithing and giving to Christian causes. Our money is used to support activities and programs that introduce people to the Saviour and care for their needs, in His name and for His glory. That is the standard we should apply when we give our money. I use this standard in my own distribution of my tithes and offerings beyond the tithe. I must be assured that as a result of my giving, people will become friends of the Lord through an experience of His love and forgiveness. Giving for ministries to human suffering must also include a concern for people's eternal salvation.

This often becomes very personal in helping individuals. When I give money, the Lord calls me to become involved with the person as a friend and care for his or her spiritual and physical needs. God entrusts us with resources to use for people. The more blessed we become, the more responsible we must be in our giving. We never know when we will be in need. Often the friends we make in the use of money become the source of God's help to us. Wesley was right: "Earn all you can, save all you can and give all you can."

A man confided in me an experience he had while going through his checks at income tax time. He's facing an excruciating divorce. He and his wife drifted away from the Lord and each other. His analysis of his checks over the past year unsettled him. He said, "I've just gone through what we spent last year. If I would have done that six months ago, I could have predicted the dilemma I'm in right now. So much money was spent on our own pleasure and luxury, and a pittance to the needs of others. Our self-indulgence has distorted our values. No wonder we lost our purpose and direction."

Jesus was not opposed to money. But He did know that it had the power to displace God in our lives. It's the first of the false gods. That's why He insisted that we use money to become friends with God and others. Some questions demand answering: Has our spending brought us closer or further from God? Has our use of our material resources accounted for the salvation and alleviation of suffering for any person this past year?

The Lord wants shrewdness in the earning and distribution of our money. Heaven should be full of people who will cheer us when we enter. There should be hundreds who are there to cheer us saying, "Welcome home. We are here because of you! You gave of yourself and your resources so that we could know the Saviour and live eternally. Thanks for being you." Then we will remember Jesus saying, "And I say to you, make friends for yourselves by means of the Mammon of unrighteousness; that when it fails, they may receive you into eternal dwellings" (Luke 16:9).

The last point of the parable is incisive. How we use what we have now will be the test for how much more the Lord will entrust to us: "He who is faithful in a very little things is faithful also in much; and he who is unrighteous in a very little thing is unrighteous also in much. If therefore you have not been faithful in the use of unrighteous Mammon, who will entrust the true riches to you? And if you have not been faithful in the use of that which is another's, who will give you that which is your own?" (vv. 10-12). The thrust of the message is that our preparation for greater blessings is to use what we have more completely for God's glory. This includes our gifts, talents, influence and opportunities, as well as our money.

The best way to grasp what Jesus is saying is to project ourselves into God's position of oversight of the world and the distribution of His immense resources of spiritual and material power. From His point of view, would we consider ourselves worthy of further investment?

When we go to a bank for the financing of some venture, the banker has every right to evaluate our effectiveness and faithfulness in the use of previous investment. Are we good risks? Will there be a return? How are we doing with what we have?

The aspect of Jesus' question in the parable that startles me is, "If you have not been faithful in the use of what is another's, who will give you what is your own?" For me that means there are blessings that are ours because we are the called, chosen, loved people of God. Salvation, the indwelling Spirit, and the assurance of eternal life are ours because we belong to Christ. How we use these gifts will determine the added outpouring of spiritual power we will be able to receive. But it's also true that if we do not grow in our faith, we are in danger of losing its dynamic potential for daily life. We will become ineffective in the most elementary aspects of our relationship to the Lord.

The place for us to start is clarified by the final admonition: "No servant can serve two masters; for either he will hate the one, and love the other, or else he will hold to one, and despise the other. You cannot serve God and Mammon" (v. 13). Jesus wants decisive, ardent disciples who are willing to go all out in their commitment. Now look at verse 16 for the secret to serving the Lord as Master of our lives: "The Law and the Prophets were proclaimed until John; since then the gospel of the kingdom of God is preached, and every one is forcing his way into it." Some translations render it, "are taking it with violence." The Greek word for forcing means determined, decisive appropriation. The Lord wants an enthusiastic response to Him and His reign in our lives. Then we will be able to grasp the exciting possibilities He is able to send our way.

The parable confronts us with the shrewdness of God. He's ardently on the move in history and in our lives. His timing is perfect and His innovative new directions are amazing. And He's ready to use you and me in His strategy. What has been does not need to determine what can be. The Lord's persistent challenge is, "Behold, I am doing a new thing! And you can be at the center of the adventure if I am the center of your life" (see Isa. 43:19). Nothing but a keen, ardent, wholehearted response will do. Everything's possible now!

20

How to Be a Lover

Luke 7:40-49: Parable of the Two Debtors

We are there—the banquet hall in Simon the Pharisee's house. A permissive Palestinian custom makes our presence a tolerated possibility. Uninvited strangers are permitted to come and go during a feast. A place with cushions to sit on, a safe distance from the festivities, is provided around the wall.

We have arrived before the host or the invited guests have appeared. It gives us an opportunity to survey the magnificent dining hall. We are not surprised. It bespeaks the Pharisee's position and power. The furnishings and banquet appointments are in keeping with the religious leader's station and dignity.

We watch the chief steward and servants carefully preparing the low table at the center of the room. Expensive settings are arranged at each place with a cushion for each guest to recline on while eating. The diners will lean on one elbow, and eat with the other hand, while their legs and feet protrude out from the table.

Just before the guests arrive, Simon enters the hall. There's no doubt in our minds that this is the host. An impressive man. He strides with decisive self-assurance. His pharisaic robes add to his bearing. We study his face. His eyes are penetrating, reflecting the confidence of years of study. The set of his jaw indicates the determination of a leader. Years of training and discipline make his movements incisive and calculated. He is in charge. Everything will go as planned; he will make sure!

A conversation between Simon and an underling reveals the purpose of the banquet. Jesus of Nazareth has been invited. A confrontation with the itinerant preacher is now unavoidable. The Pharisee speaks with measured words: "We must investigate the claim people are making about Him and the mounting charges the other Pharisees are pressing. The man is healing the sick, giving sight to the blind, exorcising evil spirits. Is the man a prophet? We shall see. Why honor such claims with a banquet? Quite simple. Some say this man is the Messiah. Of course, false messiahs come and go. But this one could be dangerous. He usurps the authority to forgive sinners. That will not do! We will watch Him carefully during the banquet and decide for ourselves."

The invited guests are now arriving: scribes and Pharisees, community notables. They are all talking about Jesus as they enter. All seem to know the purpose of the banquet.

Simon greets each one with the customary kiss of welcome. Servants wash their feet. As they recline at the table each is anointed with oil. The customs of hospitality are observed with impeccable perfection. Simon is carefully overseeing each detail to be sure nothing is omitted.

Other uninvited strangers slip in among us. We are

astounded by one of them. The murmuring gossip around us along the wall informs us that she is a woman of the streets whom Jesus had forgiven the day before. We watch her carefully as she huddles unobtrusively against the wall, fearing discovery and exposure. Surely a woman like that would never be permitted in Simon the Pharisee's house! Her demeanor shows the brokenness of the years. But there is a radiance that shines on her face. An unmistakable evidence of forgiveness. Even more than that, we observe a fulfilled look about her, as if the years of longing for true love had finally been satisfied.

There is a great stir around the banquet hall as Jesus of Nazareth enters. His winsome joy startles us. He has come to a party with full intention to enjoy Himself. There is a quiet peace about Him. Relaxed, open, vulnerable. Does He know what He's getting into? Of course. But what was there to fear? He trusts God implicitly and loves people unreservedly.

We watch Simon move across the hall to meet his guest. Reserve and restraint are expressed in his greeting. A startling contrast to the way the other guests were welcomed. We are disturbed by the fact that Simon offers no kiss of welcome. It is a tense moment when Jesus leans forward, expecting the customary greeting, only to find Simon rigidly aloof. A servant who has brought a towel and basin to wash Jesus' feet is motioned off. Jesus obviously feels the rebuff. The guests smile and look at each other with a knowing exchange.

Jesus is shown to His place at the table and quickly introduced to the other diners. Then there is a breathless silence. No move is made to anoint Jesus' head. The only guest denied the historic blessing. All eyes are on Simon. What will he do? We are watching Jesus. How can He stand this ridicule? He looks at Simon now with compassion. Simon thinks he has staged an eloquent put-down of Jesus. But it's Simon, not Jesus, who seems uncomfortable. Finally the embarrassment is broken when Simon bids his guests to begin eating.

We are so taken by the drama of rejection played out before us that we do not notice that the woman whom Jesus forgave has slipped out of the banquet hall unnoticed. Good thing. Exposure would certainly have produced a scene and punishment.

Simon does not wait long into the meal to begin his questioning of Jesus. He is condescending with faint praise of what the Nazarene has done for people. The Pharisee wants to know about the people's claim that He is a prophet. Others raise questions about His breaking the Sabbath and His authority to forgive sins. The interrogation rises to a high pitch. Jesus remains calm and quiet as the Pharisees press Him for an explanation they neither expect nor want.

At the height of the disputation we are aghast at the return of the woman. This time she does not hide among us at the wall, but moves directly to the banquet table. Simon and his guests do not seem to notice. We watch her as she moves with deliberate, determined steps. She is holding an alabaster flask in her hand, like the ones that are filled with nard, for anointing. Our attention is riveted on her as we watch her kneel at Jesus' feet. What is she doing? Would she dare? Yes! The weeping woman is anointing Jesus' feet. Now all caution is thrown aside. She releases the tresses of her hair to wipe away the tears from Jesus' feet.

Jesus turns from the table and is looking at the woman with gratitude and compassion. He accepts her gift of love. There is affirmation and assurance in His face as His eyes meet hers.

Now the whole banquet is disrupted and all attention

is focused on Jesus and the woman. Simon is enraged. Hot anger leaps within him. He is so shocked that he cannot speak at first. His eyes bulge with anger. It is obvious what charge he is formulating in his mind: "If this man were a prophet He would know what kind of woman this is who is touching Him. Even to allow her to touch Him is implication in her sin!" (see Luke 7:39).

But Jesus' prophetic powers of discernment are focused not on the woman but on Simon: "Simon, I have something to say to you." The Pharisee responds with defensive deference: "Say it, Teacher" (v. 40). The use of the honored title rings with mockery.

We listen as Jesus tells a parable. He might well have blasted the Pharisee for his pious judgmentalism. The point of the parable is even more incisive and impaling.

"A certain money-lender had two debtors: one owed five hundred denarii, and the other fifty. When they were unable to repay, he graciously forgave them both. Which of them therefore will love him more?" (vv. 41, 42). A long pause. Simon seems to know that Jesus is cornering him in front of his friends. His response is supercilious; again a mocking tone: "I suppose the one whom he forgave more."

Jesus is now in command. His voice is clear and firm. "You have judged correctly," He says, and then turns to the woman. "Do you see this woman? I entered your house; you gave Me no water for My feet, but she has wet My feet with her tears, and wiped them with her hair. You gave Me no kiss; but she, since the time I came in, has not ceased to kiss My feet. You did not anoint My head with oil, but she anointed My feet with perfume. For this reason I say to you, her sins, which are many, have been forgiven, for she loved much, but he who is forgiven little, loves little" (vv. 44-48).

The Lord's voice has grown in intensity, and now

rings throughout the banquet hall. The guests are stunned and dumb. Simon looks like he will explode with rage. There is nothing to say. Except to ask Jesus' forgiveness for the inhospitality and contrived effort to demean Him. We wait, wondering if that kind of greatness will surface in Simon. He keeps a grim silence that speaks loudly his smarting defeat.

Jesus' final words before leaving are not to Simon, but to the woman. The tender love and unlimited grace of heaven saturate His words. We are amazed at the past tense the Lord employs: "Your sins have been forgiven" (v. 48). A reaffirmation of the previous absolution.

This brings an agitated consternation from the other guests. They should not have been surprised. Jesus has just enacted and spoken the very thing they have come to the banquet to question and accuse. "Who is this man," they ask among themselves, "who even forgives sins?" (v. 49). Exactly what Jesus wants them to ask.

A lovely benediction is given only to the woman. Jesus has the final word. He was shabbily treated when He came. The ancient Hebrew blessing would not be given to the host or his guests. The woman alone would be so honored. But Jesus gives more than the traditional "Shalom, Peace!" Jesus tenderly confirms her new life. "Your faith has saved you; go in peace" (v. 50).

We observe the new dignity in the woman's carriage as she leaves the banquet hall. She has experienced love from the Master once again. Her experience of His forgiveness the day before had brought her there to express her irrepressible thanksgiving; now her assurance of His acceptance in the presence of the official leaders of the village sends her away bursting with praise and joy.

Jesus takes one last look about the table. He tries to meet Simon eye to eye. Simon's eyes are now immovably fastened on the floor. He dares not look at Jesus or

214

his guests. The Master leaves the room as quietly and unobtrusively as He entered. No victory, this. Only another evidence of the malignancy of pride and indomitable resistance to acknowledge sin.

It's time for us to leave also, but our minds race with the implications of what we have just seen. Jesus has taught us something about the source of love which challenges us. We talk a lot about how to be a lover of people and their needs. Now we are confronted with the basic ingredient of His kind of love. The words tumble about in our minds. They won't go away: "He who is forgiven little, loves little" (v. 47).

The parable of the two debtors in the context of the story of Simon and the woman has three tributaries of thought which flow into one great river of truth. Get into the fast-moving currents of all three, so that we can be swept into the conclusion our Lord has for us.

The first is that gratitude is the true motivation of love. When we are aware of how much God has done for us we are truly grateful. Simon had much to be thankful for. All that he had and was able to accomplish was a gift of God. We wonder what had happened to his sense of thanksgiving. Could it be that he had witnessed the sacrifices of the Temple without a personal experience that it was for him personally? Why else would there be so little compassionate love in his life? After all he had received over the years, how could he be so inhospitable to a teacher like Jesus? Even though he may have disagreed with His presuppositions, how could he justify the lack of basic courtesy? Thanksgiving for life's blessings and opportunities enables a sense of indebtedness but may not make us sensitive to the needs and plight of people less fortunate. There is a level of gratitude that never gets beyond self-satisfaction.

Many of us can identify. We are grateful for all God

has done, but we never break out of the cycle of the idea that God has blessed us because we are good, and we try to be good because God blesses us.

Simon's basic problem was hypocrisy. His position demanded that he be superior in knowledge and practice. He could not honestly admit that was not always true, because of the necessity of maintaining an image. Hypocrisy is to play a part. If all of life's energy is spent keeping up a front, then God and His blessings become part of the props of refortification. Soon we feel little need for God in any personal way. Simon was not a bad person. His problem was that he could not love. That's always the dreadful result of hypocrisy. We become incapable of compassion and sensitivity. Human need swirls around us and we are impervious. We forget that we have been blessed to be a blessing.

The second tributary of thought is focused in the parable itself. Profound gratitude is the result of forgiveness. Simon loved little because he had been forgiven little. The broken woman loved profoundly because she had been forgiven immensely.

The twist of the parable is that Simon was the five hundred denarii debtor, and the woman the fifty. That's the point Jesus intended. The Pharisee's pride-festering hypocrisy was a far greater debt than the woman's adultery. If he had only acknowledged his need for forgiveness, he would have been the one expressing gratitude to the Lord.

The implication for us is that if our carefully constructed self-righteousness has led to self-sufficiency, we will begin to believe that God is privileged to have us among His chosen people. Pride always runs up a monstrous debt with God. The sign that we are overextended in debt is that we think someone else needs forgiveness more than we do.

The forgiven woman becomes our mentor. The warm and gracious people of the world are those who have been forgiven. The greater the depths of contrition, the higher the heights of compassion. When we know that we are sinners saved by grace, we become lovers communicating hope to others.

The woman could not do enough to express her gratitude. She had to find a sacrament to express her love. Nothing was too demanding. The danger of ridicule, the fear of judgment from Simon and his ilk, the shame of public exposure of her sordid past were of little concern in comparison to her dominant need to thank the Master. When she witnessed the preposterous lack of respect and consideration by Simon, she had to balance the scales. The whole world needed to share her adoration.

We are left to identify ourselves in the story. The woman or Simon? There are some of us who identify with the woman immediately. We may not be implicated in her particular sin, but our own brand is no less culpable. The result is the same. And God will not bless the mess we have made of the gift of life. The story flashes with the lightning of unmerited favor, followed quickly with the thunder of forgiving love. There is no depth to which we can fall that our Lord will not stoop to find us and reclaim us. Do you believe that? There is nothing we can do or say that will negate Christ's love— except the pride of Simon. Only a sinner needs a Saviour. If there is no realization of our need, no sensitivity of the distance between what we are and could be—then we have blocked all possibility of being a lover. Simon could do many things except one—he could not love. The purpose of his existence had been lost in the fury of his own self-justification.

But wait! Doesn't God want us to get to the place

where we sin less and therefore have little to confess? Does He want only people like this pitiful woman? Isn't there some affirmation needed here for a Simon who disciplined his life? Of course. But never without a momentary dependence on God's grace. We should never lose the awareness of what sin cost God on Calvary. Nor should we ever lose sight of our need of atonement for the subtle sins. The mystery of our nature is that the more we grow in moral strength and character development, the further we go from the Source. That's the danger of the Simon in all of us. Growing in grace means ever-increasing sensitivity to areas of our life that need forgiveness and reformation. The acid test of our closeness to God will be our praise. Gratitude will always be measured in our vulnerability and viability.

Actually, I find a bit of Simon and the woman in me. I am aware of my need and the desire to be adequate all at the same time. What would I have done if I had been at that banquet? How would I have treated the Saviour? Imagination may help to reflect on that retrospectively. But a deeper question sweeps all others away. The Lord asks, "Your life is like that banquet. I have come today as your guest. How will you respond?"

The only acceptable response is to identify with the five hundred denarii debtor. There's the real test! How do we react when Jesus recounts the parable? Do we immediately put ourselves in the place of the greater debtor? If we can immediately think of others who have a greater need for forgiveness than we, that in itself is the evidence of how we will receive the Lord today. Simon's plight was exposed by the fact that he assumed that the woman was in that category.

All of this has a frightening conclusion in the third tributary. Jesus could give His beatific benediction only to the woman. Her confession of need was rewarded by forgiveness and the promise of evolving peace: "Go into peace" is the accurate translation of His words. Go into an ever-increasing experience of God's unifying, healing wholeness. What that means for us is that peace grows with each new realization of our sin. Each day has its realization of failure and missed opportunities. We will never be free of the consciousness of our potential or of the ready availability of grace. Life can be separated into the tight compartments of daily adventure and freedom to fail. We need not carry any tension of unconfessed sin into our tomorrows. Peace is the gift of God that replaces the anxiety of guilt.

All the tributaries have led us into the mighty river of the basic challenge of our study. To be a lover is to let God forgive us! We hold the awesome power to refuse or receive. Our forgiveness has been settled once and for all on the cross. We do not confess in order to be forgiven, but because we have been already. If we allow God to forgive us, we will feel a burst of gratitude. How can we thank Him for forgiving us? Jesus told us. What we do and say to others we do and say to Him. The way the woman cared for Jesus, is the way we are to care for people. We will never be able to do enough. Costly involvement, listening with love, forgiveness as we have been forgiven, second chances when they are least deserved, sacrificial giving of our resources for practical help, sharing the hope we have discovered in the gospel —all are ways to anoint the feet of Jesus.

That's how to be a lover. The more our Lord forgives us, the more we will become sensitive, compassionate, open and forgiving lovers. Our world desperately needs people whose gratitude has made them communicators of grace.

21

The One Thing God Won't Do

Matthew 18:21-35: Parable of the Unmerciful Servant

What's the one thing God won't do? He has all power to do anything. Nothing is impossible for Him. Yet there is something He won't do. He has made that clear in His own autobiography through His Son. The parable of the unmerciful servant tells us that God's forgiveness is revoked if we do not forgive *after* we are forgiven.

The parable was given in response to a blush of magnanimity by Simon Peter. He thought he could impress the Master with his benevolent offer: "Lord, how often shall my brother sin against me and I forgive him?" Simon set himself up for his own answer: "Up to seven times?" (Matt. 18:21).

The Lord's response was like a dagger. It pierced Simon's puffed-up piety. We feel with him the smarting of the incision into his numerical calculation of his willingness to forgive. Jesus said to him, "I do not say to

you, up to seven times, but up to seventy times seven"
(v. 22). That's four hundred and ninety times! Quite a
comparison to Peter's seven times. But Jesus meant
more than that. "Seventy times seven" was a Hebraism,
a saying of the Rabbi's rooted in Old Testament Scripture. It really meant on and on into infinity. Without
limits. Jesus is telling us that there can be no limit to
forgiveness.

But to be sure we don't miss the point, the parable of
the unmerciful servant makes the challenge undeniably
clear. It tells us something about God that we may not
be prepared to hear. The pathos of the drama of the
parable eventually penetrates to our judgments and arrogant unwillingness to forgive. At the end we are left
defenseless. The shocking, startling truth is that we are
to be to others what God has been to us. If we refuse,
we lose. The continuing experience of His love and forgiveness is dependent on our love and forgiveness to
others.

We are unsettled by that! Disturbed. Good thing!
Familiarity with this aspect of the autobiography of God
has dulled our perception of the danger the parable proclaims. Frankly, I am stabbed awake by the truth. I hope
for nothing less for you.

The king of the parable is God. That's why we're
shocked! What Jesus tells us about the behavior of the
king He wants us to know about God. The parable can
be retold in a paragraph. It will take a lifetime to live out
its implications. Our eternal life is dependent on faithful
obedience to its admonition.

A king wanted to settle his accounts with his debtors.
One of them owed him ten thousand talents. A talent
was worth about one thousand dollars. Simple arithme-
tic captures our attention. Ten million dollars! Quite a
debt. We are amazed. The debtor could not pay. The

221

king followed the law of the land: the debtor, his wife and children were sentenced to be sold into slavery. Now we are surprised. When the man prostrated himself before the king, asking for time so that he could repay the debt, the king felt compassion, released him and forgave the debt. What kind of king is this? Jesus had a greater One than any human king in mind: God. The immensity of the debt is forgiven by the immutable love of the King of Creation.

We would expect the most gracious and forgiving spirit imaginable to pervade the released debtor. Not so! Instead, immediately he goes out to find one of his debtors. The obvious point is that he was unwilling to accept the unbelievable generosity of the king. He wanted to use his respite of judgment to get the money he owed and pay back the king. Linger on that! The debtor was not about to build his life on the grace he had experienced from the king. He would pay back at the cost of his own debtors.

He might have started with a better prospect. How absurd. He demanded the payment of one hundred denarii from one of his debtors. A denarii was a day-laborer's wage. About twenty cents. At best, the man owed the king's debtor $20.00. What a contrast! Don't miss the hyperbole. Twenty dollars in comparison to ten million! A piece of change when compared to the millions owed the king.

Our surprise turns to anger and then to rage over the debtor's attitude and action. After all the king had done for him, how could he have so little compassion for one who owed such a paltry amount? Surely the joy of his own forgiven debt would issue in unbounded generosity. Rather, he did exactly what the king had every right to do to him with so much more justification. It's difficult to imagine his pitiless attitude and actions. He took his debtor by the throat, throttling and choking him. This violent indignity was permitted in Roman law. The cruel twisting of a guilty person's neck was often inflicted before he was taken to court. The unmerciful servant of the king vent his frustration and anger. Then, he threw his twenty-dollar debtor into prison. It was his right! No one could question that. But how could he do it after all the mercy he had received? Everyone should question that—including the king. He received news of the dastardly deed with incredulity. How could this be after he had written off the ten million dollars of the ungrateful rogue's debts? It was not what the king's debtor had done before his forgiveness, but afterward that was so despicable.

Now the king has no choice. His forgiveness of the debt is revoked. The debtor is handed over not just to the prison keeper, but to the torturers. The Greek is *tois basanistais* from *basanizo*, to torture. The meaning is that of terrible punishment. Not just servitude, but inflicted wounds of retaliation for the debt. Before, his sentence was to be imprisonment for his debt; now he is to be tortured. What did Jesus mean by that extreme language? The sentence was more permanent than purgatorial. The unmerciful servant would never get out for he would never be able to pay back the debt. He had sealed his own destiny.

We are gripped by the message even before Jesus gives the concluding explanatory sentence of the parable. We wonder why He had to hammer it home. It's disturbing enough. But He knows us and how we can evade an arrow of truth. There's no ambiguity when He concludes, "So shall My heavenly Father also do to you, if each of you does not forgive his brother from your heart."

The word "heart" is like a burred hook. We can't slip

off. We may say we forgive. We may conceptually forgive. But it is the vocation of the heart not to forget. Many of us say we will forgive, but not forget. Or that we will forgive the person, but not the deed. All are ways of evading the reproduction of the awesome completeness of God's forgiveness of us.

Well! What can we do with this parable? It's in the Gospel record to stay. We can't wish it away. Nor can we change its demanding meaning. It must change us. That will happen only if we put ourselves in the drama of the parable. Which role shall we play? We know the answer before we open the orders from the casting department. The part which experience has prepared us to play is none other than the unmerciful servant himself. But note: the lighting of the scene casts an odd shadow on the stage. It's a cross! We must interpret the parable from this side of Calvary. "Paid in full" is written across all our sins and debts.

This is a new rendition of "The King and I." How shall we respond to the King when He calls us to account for our debt? We can have no other posture than on our knees begging for mercy. Amazing grace! It's given in spite of all we've said and done. We are free because the polluted waters of our soul have been purified with a red substance flowing freely. The blood of the Lamb! Can we ever deserve a love like that? No! Can we ever negate a love like that? Yes! That's the shocking realization that thunders through the parable.

Want to step out of the characterization or the role of the unmerciful servant? Is there an indignation which makes you want to shout, "I'd never react like that! If someone forgave ten million dollars of my debt, I'd forgive everyone who owed me anything. You can be sure that I'd be the most forgiving person alive for the rest of my days!"

A loud silence prevails following our pious testimony. The Lord will not fill it with some beatific accolade. The silence articulates a question: "Well, have you? Have you forgiven as you've been forgiven?" We could give a flippant yes, if it were not for the flood of faces that surge through our minds. Then we know. There are lots of people who need our forgiveness. Then there are those whom we have said we have forgiven but with whom we want nothing to do now. Cheap forgiveness! Verbalism without a vital, reconciled relationship.

Miller's *After the Fall* rubs our face in our plight after man's rebellion. Jesus' parable might be called "After the Rise." What has happened since we were born again and received new life? That's the aching question of the parable. Has it made any difference? Have we forgiven as we've been forgiven? Has our attitude to people around us been consistent with God's acceptance of us?

John Wesley once heard a man say, "I never forgive." His response was incisive: "Then I hope, Sir, that you never sin." Indeed! Our forgiveness from God is intertwined inseparably with our willingness to forgive.

This was so crucial to Jesus that He made it a central tenet of the Disciple's Prayer: "Forgive us our debts, as we also have forgiven our debtors" (Matt. 6:12). The meaning is, forgive us to the extent we have forgiven. This is the only aspect of the prayer Jesus explained. "For if you forgive men for their transgressions, your heavenly Father will also forgive you. But if you do not forgive men, then your Father will not forgive your transgressions" (Matt. 6:14,15). There's no way to finesse that radical, irreducible maximum! But there is a way to experience it—by owning up to our debt before God. A fresh experience of His grace enables graciousness to others.

We are in debt to God. Paul was right, "All have

sinned and fall short of the glory of God" (Rom. 3:23). Our sin is rebellion against God: the willful desire to run our own lives, to shape our own destiny, to live by our own strength and grit. Our sins flow from the headwaters of that separation. What we do to demean, destroy and debilitate ourselves and others is sin. How can we repay the debt we owe for the ravage we make of our lives and the creation entrusted to us? We can't. No more than the unmerciful servant could raise ten million dollars to pay the king. All we can do is ask for mercy and forgiveness. And that's why Jesus came: to save His people from their sins. The cost was high! Calvary. It was there that Psalm 130 was enacted: "If Thou, Lord, shouldst mark iniquities, O Lord, who could stand? But there is forgiveness with Thee, that Thou mayest be feared .... For with the Lord there is lovingkindness, and with Him is abundant redemption" (vv. 3,4,7). Or Psalm 103:12,13: "As far as the east is from the west, so far has He removed our transgressions from us. Just as a father has compassion on his children, so the Lord has compassion on those who fear Him." Isaiah peered into the future to the cross when he wrote the words of the Lord: "Though your sins are as scarlet, they will be as white as snow; though they are red like crimson, they will be like wool" (Isa. 1:18).

Forgiveness was Jesus' message and life, as well as the purpose of His death. In the Sermon on the Mount, He said, "Blessed are the merciful, for they shall receive mercy" (Matt. 5:7). He went way beyond the teaching of His time. Moses did not require forgiveness of enemies. Yet Jesus said, "If your brother sins, rebuke him; and if he repents, forgive him. And if he sins against you seven times a day, and returns to you seven times, saying 'I repent,' forgive him" (Luke 17:3,4). No wonder the disciples reacted urgently, saying, "Increase our faith" (v. 5). We know how they felt. Forgiving as we have been forgiven is not easy. And yet, the Lord makes no exception to His demanding command.

The other day, when I was teaching the parable of the unmerciful servant, a holy hush fell over the room. The Holy Spirit gave us a very special gift to hear what the Lord was saying to each of us. When my exposition reached the concluding statement about the absolute necessity of forgiveness, there was a breathless silence. Each of us was convicted, cut to the core by Jesus' unequivocal assertion that what happened to the merciless servant would happen to us if we did not forgive from our hearts.

After the class, a woman came up to me with tears streaming down her face. When she spoke, her body shook with sobs. "This morning I realized that I have to forgive my mother!" she said. Then followed a painful account of what her mother had done to her in her childhood. It was a grisly tale. The woman's resentment seemed more than justified on the human level. But hatred festered in her soul. She had wondered often why she could not grasp the joy of God's grace. That morning she discovered the reason: she had not forgiven her mother. The Holy Spirit had taken the words of the parable and pierced her unforgiving spirit.

On most Wednesdays, I spend the day listening to people. Seventy-five percent of the people are paralyzed by an inability or unwillingness to forgive to the degree they have been forgiven by God. This parable is an alarming prescription for their spiritual sickness. I am amazed at how few church members have ever heard the demanding necessity of forgiveness after we have been forgiven. Recently, I made a survey of Bible-believing Christians to ascertain how many remembered or understood Matthew 18:35, and only one out of ten even knew it was in the New Testament! No wonder we find Paul's word to the Ephesians so difficult: "Be kind to one another, tender-hearted, forgiving each other, just as God in Christ also has forgiven you" (Eph. 4:32).

We forget what God has done for us. But more than that, we miss what God offers us right now. Fresh forgiveness enables freedom to forgive. Remember what Jesus said to Simon the Pharisee: "He who is forgiven little, loves little" (Luke 7:47). Only a realization of our need to be forgiven will give us a forgiving attitude.

The other morning I was awakened with a deep feeling of hostility toward a friend who had plagiarized a whole segment of my delineation of the nature and mission of the local congregation. The previous day, I had read his book and there boldly printed on the page were not only my concepts, but my exact words. What hurt was that my close, trusted friend had not even given passing reference to his source. What could I do? Sue? Surely, but what would that prove? A phone call afforded nothing but defensive denials from my friend. The least he could have done was confess and say he was sorry. He did neither.

As I lay awake fuming, I had two choices: to refuse to forgive and internalize the poison of my anger, or forgive, realizing that I was the recipient of forgiveness in so many areas of my life. Then the Lord said to me, "Lloyd, what thoughts have you ever had which I did not give you? What your friend has taken is mine and not yours. Forgive so that I can forgive you more fully in the future." I went to sleep free of the anger.

The parable of the unmerciful servant will become part of our character and response if we will take time to think about all the times the Lord has forgiven us. Write them down in a list. Then consider the people whom you have not forgiven. Be sure to list all the ones you have cut off because you do not trust what they will do even if you forgive. Now what will it take to be sure you have forgiven as freely as the Lord forgives you? Begin with prayer. Settle the matter with the Lord. Tell Him all about the hurt. Then ask Him for the grace to forgive. The next step is to verbalize and enact the forgiveness. Go to the people. Tell them. Write letters to those too far away for a face-to-face encounter. But at all costs, clear the slate.

Costly discipleship? Yes, but the cost is negligible in comparison to what will happen if we refuse. Can you imagine what it would be like not to be able to ask for God's forgiveness ever again? Add to that the danger of negating our salvation and we have motive enough.

We are in the presence of the holy God right now. We shudder with awe and wonder. We can't manipulate Him. We limit His blessings and power unless we forgive. By our choice not His.

22

Spontaneous Love

Luke 10:25-39: Parable of the Good Samaritan

The man has been on the edge of the crowd for a long time. He listens to the Master with a mixture of response and inner rebuttal.

It's obvious that the man is a religious lawyer; a scribe of the Mosaic law. His official robes declare his position, and his bearing communicates the assurance of refined legalism.

We study his face carefully. Tradition and training are carved into his features. At the center of his forehead is a meticulously positioned phylactery, symbolizing his orthodoxy. A small, black, calfskin box is bound tightly with leather thongs. An ancient custom. God had told Moses that the Hebrews were to remember what He had done for them in bringing them out of Egypt, by keeping a sign on their foreheads (see Exod. 13:9). In

Deuteronomy 6, the summary of the law is followed by the admonition, "And these words, which I am commanding you today, shall be on your heart; and you shall teach them diligently to your sons and shall talk of them when you sit in your house and when you walk by the way and when you lie down and when you rise up. And you shall bind them as a sign on your hand and they shall be as frontals on your forehead" (vv. 6-8). The practice of the phylactery resulted. Sacred passages, such as Deuteronomy 6:4,5, were inscribed minutely on parchment and placed in the box: "Hear, O Israel! The Lord is our God, the Lord is one! And you shall love the Lord your God with all your heart and with all your soul and with all your might." Leviticus 19:18 called for love of neighbor as oneself. The two were repeated together as a capsuled summary of the law. We are sure these Scriptures are inside the phylactery box on the lawyer's forehead. We wonder what the symbolic adornment means to the man.

As we watch his expressions, we sense that he is waiting to break in during a pause in Jesus' message. The Lord seems to sense it too. He finishes what He is saying and looks at the scribe inquiringly, as if to say, "Now, what is it that you have been wanting to say?"

We are amazed at the question the lawyer asks. It sounds studied, rehearsed; as if the man had mulled it over in his mind a thousand times. His tone betrays the lofty quest of the inquiry. Calculated, challenging, biting. "Teacher, what shall I do to inherit eternal life?" (Luke 10:25). Quite a question! Does the man really want an answer or is he trying to trap Jesus?

The Master looks him in the eye. A smile curls on the corner of His lips. He knows what the man is up to. The question is basic, and the man knows the answer before he asks. A debater's ploy. Jesus is not unsettled. He carefully words His sagacious response: "What is written in the Law? How does it read to you?" (v. 26). The Lord seems to know that the man wants to answer his own question. What he quotes from the law is inscribed on the parchments in the phylactery box on his forehead!

"You shall love the Lord your God with all your heart, and with all your soul, and with all your strength, and with all your mind; and your neighbor as yourself" (v. 27).

Jesus replies quickly: "You have answered correctly." Then He quotes Leviticus 18:5: "Do this, and you will live" (Luke 10:28). But the man did not want a simple retort like that. He had waited too long for a disputation with the Master to be cut off so summarily. He feels a need to justify his original question: "Yes, the Scriptures say you shall love your neighbor as yourself, but what is implied by neighbor? Who is my neighbor?" (see v. 29).

We are deeply moved by Jesus' patience. The lawyer is trifling with Him, and yet He dignifies the debater's device with an incisive parable. As we listen we are astonished by the way the Lord recasts the question and answers the one the official should have asked: not "Who is my neighbor?" but "How should I act as a neighbor?"

We are all drawn into attentive involvement as Jesus tells the story of a man who is robbed, stripped, beaten, and left to die on the treacherous road from Jerusalem down to Jericho. Everyone in the crowd knows about the danger of the "Bloody Way," as the 22-mile road had come to be known. It was a precarious road because of robbers who hid among the rocks, crevices, and caves. No one was safe along the 3,500 foot descent to Jericho.

We listen intently as Jesus tells about the priest and

the Levite who happen along the way and find the man. We all share consternation as Jesus says that the religious leaders passed by on the other side. We watch the lawyer's expression in response to that! Jesus has made an impression with His illustration. The lawyer is not ready for the telling twist which follows as Jesus continues. A gasp, and then a murmur ripples through the crowd. The name Samaritan invoked that!

"A certain Samaritan, who was on a journey, came upon him [the beaten man]; and when he saw him, he felt compassion, and came to him, and bandaged up his wounds, pouring oil and wine on them; and he put him on his own beast, and brought him to an inn, and took care of him. And on the next day he gave two denarii to the innkeeper and said, 'Take care of him; and whatever more you spend, when I return, I will repay you'" (vv. 33-35).

No one in the crowd, least of all the lawyer, expected that turn in the parable. The words priest, Levite, and Israelite were frequently used with thoughtless repetition in delineating the Hebrew people. Everyone had been following the story, expecting an Israelite to be the third character on the road. Jesus had used an element of surprise no one had expected. And of all the substitutes for Israelite in His progression, He could not have startled the crowd and the lawyer more than with the use of a hated Samaritan.

These Jews abhorred the Samaritans. Years of conditioning had contributed to their prejudice. The animosity had been handed down for generations, ever since the defeat of the Northern Kingdom in 722 B.C., when many Jews were dragged off into exile in Babylonia. Those who remained, intermarried with the Assyrians who were brought in to populate and occupy the land. They became half-breeds, hated by the Jews. After the exile, the Samaritans offered to help Zerubbabel rebuild the Temple. When refused because of the antagonism felt by the Jews, the Samaritans built their own temple on Mount Gerizim. Hostility intensified through the years. It was at a high pitch in Jesus' day. No wonder there is consternation in the crowd of listeners when a Samaritan is made the surprise hero of a story. None is more disturbed than the lawyer. He asked, "Who is my neighbor?" and Jesus used a "half-breed" as an example of what it means to be a neighbor.

The parable of the Good Samaritan is a vital chapter in God's autobiography through His Son. Like the other parables, it has a single, central theme. It tells us one flaming truth about God and the quality of life He wants us to live. Jesus exposes an aspect of God's love that He came to reveal and then to reproduce in His followers. The spotlight of the drama is on the Samaritan, but what he exemplifies is more than human kindness in response to specific need.

The point of the parable is that God's love is spontaneous. It is unqualified, and never limited by the rules of religion. Jesus Himself was the spontaneous, incarnate love of God. He tells His own story in the parable. The world He came to save was a Jericho road, and His response to human suffering was marked by spontaneity.

In that context, we can watch the drama replayed with deeper understanding. This is a parable of contrasts. Jesus wants us to see and feel the spontaneous love of the Samaritan in contrast to the calculated neglect and qualified concern of religious people.

Once again we are challenged to put ourselves in the parable. It is the story of the wounded, the wounders, and the kind of wound-healers we are to be. The wounded of the world are all around us, on the Jericho road of our life. They are those who have been debilitated physically, psychologically, or socially by no fault of their own. We cannot read this parable without asking, "Who is the 'certain man' on the road for me?" He or she may be in our own family, among our friends, at work, in our church, and in our community. We can be wounders or wound-healers in our relationship with them. The parable may force us to see that we are among the robbers who strip people of their dignity and personhood. Or we may feel the alarming identification with the priest and the Levite through our benign neglect. Jesus will have accomplished His purpose in the parable if we identify the wounded in our lives and long to express the spontaneous love portrayed in the Samaritan's immediate and uncalculating response to suffering.

The key word in the description of the priest helps us to capture what Jesus was trying to communicate to us. "And *by chance* a certain priest was going down on that road . . ." (v. 31, italics added). The Greek word translated here as chance is *sugkurian*. It means coincidence. But our use of coincidence does not seem to get at what was implied. Actually, it means a confluence of circumstances which seem to happen by chance, but is really the interweaving of events by divine providence for the accomplishment of a greater purpose. The Lord's timing and staging of life are always perfect for the fulfillment of His plan for us and the people around us. He puts us in situations and with people because of what He wants to do and say through us. The priest was on the road when the beaten traveler needed him. Living with spontaneous love requires that we see the "coincidences" of life as part of His plan.

Life is filled with serendipities. We are constantly meeting people who need us and whom we need. Life becomes exciting when we are free to give ourselves away in each relationship the Lord provides. We should be amazed constantly by the miraculous way He weaves together the destiny of different individuals. He will send us the people we need when we are wounded, and will place us in the lives of those who are wounded when He wants to love through us. Suddenly, life takes on a new quality. People with needs are not a burden; they are gifts of God for us to give away what He has given us. In the same way, when we are troubled and anxious, we can be sure that someone under orders from the Lord will be deployed in our lives for just the right word of encouragement, correction, or practical help we need. Availability to God, to be an expression of His spontaneous love, is the purpose of our lives.

The priest who came along the road did not conceive of his calling as a person or religious leader in that exciting focus. He was on his way to Jerusalem to perform religious duties. The needs of a person were secondary to being on time to officiate over the rituals in the Temple. The priests of Israel were divided into 24 courses or orders. Each division served in the Temple a week at a time, twice a year.

But before we are too hard on his neglect of the beaten man, we need to consider that he may have assumed the man to be dead. To touch a dead body would have made him ceremonially unclean for 24 hours. Perhaps he was rushing to serve in the Temple in Jerusalem that day. And yet, did the beaten man make no groans of pain? Was there no plea for help that would have dispelled the assumption that the man was dead? Try as we will to be kind to the priest, the truth is that his religious propriety kept him from a spontaneous response to suffering.

There's a story of a man in India, rushing home to his family to tell of his conversion to Christ. He stumbled over a poor beggar in the streets who pleaded for help.

His own confession later was that he told the man he was sorry that he could not stop to help because he had to get home to share the joy of his new relationship with Christ. We are aghast and critical in response to that. Then it occurs to us that there have been times for all of us when our enthusiasm for our faith has precluded specific concern for people in need. The Lord is testing constantly the authenticity of our love for Him in our practical caring for others.

So often after a presentation of the love of God in a class or sermon, the Lord gives me a "coincidence" of a person who needs me to express to him or her the exact thing I have taught or preached with gusto. Often, after I have spent a long Sunday preaching in two services in the morning and one in the evening, some needy person is waiting at the door, or by my car in the parking lot. Everything within me longs to escape and go home for a leisurely time with my family. The only way I have been able to handle the limitless demands of people is to surrender my time and energy to the Lord, acknowledge that He knows how much I can take, and flow in unreserved response to anyone who is placed in my way for help. It takes more energy to calculate whom I will help than it does to just trust the Lord to show the way, to place people in my path who need Him and provide the wisdom and strength I need to help each person with his or her problem, that I may earn the right to introduce the person to Him. There is a tremendous release which comes from the prayer: "Lord, I belong to you. All that I am and have is a gift from you. I will pass through this way only once. Guide me to the people you have prepared for what I am to give in your name." That prayer releases the tension of reservation, and makes life an adventure of being used. All that the Lord has given us of His love, experience in knowing Him, and material resources, is entrusted to us so that we might minister to people. What we do for people in need we do for the Lord. He comes to us in the lost, lonely, frustrated, fearful, beaten, and battered people of the world. Our response to them is our response to Him.

The Levite did no better than the priest. The Levites were assistants to the priests (see 1 Chron. 23:24-32). Jesus underlines the message of religious neglect by having the Levite emulate the irrelevant piety of the priest. The Levite is not a new aspect of the teaching of the parable, but an exclamation point on the priest's fear of involvement because of ritual regulations. It was as if Jesus said to the lawyer who instigated the parable, "Just in case you missed what I was saying about the brash contradiction of God's love in the priest, the Levite did no better. Now what would you have done? You are an official of Israel. Would you have lived out the mandate of the Scripture etched on the cowhide of the phylactery that you wear so proudly on your forehead?"

The contrast of the priest and the Levite with the Samaritan could not have been more pointed and startling. The Lord depicts the Samaritan as a hero in every way. We feel the empathy and tenderness of the man as he gives of himself for the wounded traveler. Nothing is left out of the vivid detail. "He came to him." Personal contact, not aloof benevolence. He personally bandaged his wounds. All concern that the same robbers may be lurking nearby to do the same to him is dismissed in the urgency of the need. He took his provisions of wine and oil and administered the first aid that was needed so badly. The bloody man was put on his own beast. He did not worry about how to explain the blood that was smeared on his own clothing.

The fact that the Samaritan brought the beaten man to the inn is loaded with meaning. The "half-breed" must have been known at the inn; a trusted tenant there himself on frequent visits. But even at the inn, the Samaritan "took care of him." Perhaps all night. Tender dressing of wounds and comfort for anguished cries of pain. The next day his instructions to the innkeeper are very significant. He paid two denarii for the beaten man's care. About 40¢ in our money. Two days' stipend for a laborer. A lot of money then. More than that, he offered to return and pay whatever else was spent for the man's care. Rehabilitation and rest would take a long time. Jesus nails home His contrast and example in the Samaritan's final words. Note the double use of the pronoun: "When I return, I will repay you" (v. 35). Like saying, "I, I, when I come back." The repetition of the pronoun implies: "You know me; I'll be faithful to my promise!" Had he done similar deeds of kindness before? Could it be that this Samaritan, whom any Jew would hate just because of his national heritage, was well-known for his spontaneous self-giving to distressed travelers along the treacherous road?

Now let's go deeper. The Samaritan fulfilled the Leviticus 19:18 portion of the summary of the law which the lawyer had so glibly repeated. He loved his neighbor as himself. Healthy self-love enabled him to care about a man in need. There's a subtle twist in the implication about the priest and the Levite. They did not love themselves sufficiently to help the beaten survivor. Their relationship with God was based on the fulfillment of the rules and regulations of their religion, more than on the deeper meaning of the great commandment. Insufficient love for oneself as loved by God will always result in stingy, niggardly response to the needs of others. The religion of the priest and the Levite excluded certain people and conditions of propriety. They probably could have repeated the requirement to love God with heart,

239

soul, strength, and mind, but exclusivism kept them from being channels of that devotion to a person who needed the Lord's care through them. The two impeccably ritualistic leaders were really more wounded than the man they passed by on the other side. The traditions and formalisms had taken a terrible toll on their capacity to care personally for others. They were beaten spiritually by the system, more than the man had been beaten physically by the robbers.

Meanwhile, back to the lawyer. Now Jesus is asking the questions. The lawyer tried to interrogate Jesus; now he is the one being interrogated. The roles are reversed. Jesus has won the disputation.

"Which of these three do you think proved to be a neighbor to the man who fell into the robbers' hands?" (v. 36), Jesus asked pointedly. What could the crestfallen advocate say? There was only one obvious answer. "The one who showed mercy toward him." Jesus completely shifted the emphasis of the conversation to discerning who acted like a neighbor, rather than who was the neighbor. Now He could press the point with undeniable force: "Go and do the same" (v. 37).

Suddenly we feel what the lawyer must have felt. The admonition is for us. Once we say we believe in Him as our Lord and Saviour, we are immediately called into a demanding, challenging, but very exciting, "go and do likewise" adventure of unstudied, spontaneous love. The wounded of the world are now our agenda. Wounding people with neglect is no longer acceptable. Are we willing to put aside our judgments, exclusivism, fear of involvement, privacy, schedules and time, to be available for the coincidences that will happen constantly if we are willing? The joy of Christianity is experienced when constraint is replaced by the inner motivation of instinctive love. When we accept the Lord's love for us and love ourselves deeply as we are loved by Him, love for our neighbor will flow freely.

As I was preparing to write this chapter, I was given a practical opportunity to live out what I had studied. One Sunday noon, after preaching on the spontaneous love of God, I took my family and some friends to a restaurant near our church. Outside the door to the restaurant I met a young man who had just heard my bold affirmation of the joy of giving ourselves away to people in need. He shared a problem he was facing. He needed money for rent. I had some bills folded in my pocket which I had gotten in preparation for a speaking trip I had to go on that evening. I asked the man how much he needed. The amount was exactly how much I had in my pocket—to the penny! "Go and do likewise" echoed in my soul. The man was able to pay his rent and I had to find a place to cash another check before leaving on my trip. Wouldn't it have been a travesty of authenticity if I had contradicted the message of the morning or the lectures on love I planned to give on the speaking tour? Only the about-to-be-evicted man and I would have known. But the Lord also would have known. And He had arranged for the young man and me to meet on a Jericho road in Hollywood, California.

Be sure of this: If you have taken this parable seriously and have grappled with the implications the Lord seemed to put on my heart to write in this chapter, you will surely meet your personified gift of a person in need. The question you will have to answer is not whether he or she is a qualified neighbor, but what kind of Christ-filled neighbor you will be. My prayer is that you have allowed Christ to love you deeply and richly, because, if you have, there'll be no limit to what you will want to do for that person in your expression of love.

23

The One Test
of a Great Church

Luke 13:1-9; Mark 11:12-14,19-22: Parable of the Fig Tree

What measurements would you use to evaluate the effectiveness of a church? What would you say distinguishes a great congregation?

Many of us think of the local church as an end in itself. Therefore, our answers about the success of a church would be to judge what happens within the building and program of the congregation. The size of the membership, the quality of the preaching, the vitality of the educational program or the warmth of the fellowship would be our measuring lines. We think of the church as something we go to for inspiration, enrichment and encouragement. These are all crucial elements of a dynamic church, but are not the ultimate test of greatness. The church is not only a place we go; it is what we are between Sundays. It is the equipping center for the ministry of the laity in the world. The effectiveness of worship, education and fellowship has a bottom-line accountability in the quality of people the congregation produces for discipleship in daily living.

The one test of a great church is the fruitfulness of its people. The congregation exists to produce fruitful followers of Christ. What does that mean? We must look to the Lord of the church, Christ Himself, for the answer. And there's no confusion or ambiguity about His expectation. The parable of the fig tree makes it painfully clear. It is one of Jesus' more difficult parables, not because it is obscure, but because it is so incisively direct. In order to comprehend and appropriate the full impact, we need to look at the parable itself in Luke 13:1-9, the corollary enacted parable in Mark 11:12-14,19-22, for the account of Jesus' last week in Jerusalem, and the illuminating passages of both the Old and New Testaments, which open windows of understanding on the text. Our purpose in this chapter is to consider fruitfulness as the final test of the greatness of the people of God. We will try to understand what Jesus means by fruitfulness for the church and for each of us as individuals.

A certain man planted a fig tree in his vineyard. When the tree grew to maturity, the owner came, expecting to find the one thing a fig tree should produce—figs. But he was disappointed repeatedly. There were leaves but no figs. Finally, he told the keeper of the vineyard to cut down the unproductive tree. "I've waited three years and there has not been a single fig!" he complained. "Why wait any longer? This unfruitful tree is taking up space and drawing precious resources from the soil. Get rid of it!"

The keeper of the vineyard interceded with an imploring appeal for a stay of execution. "Give the tree one more chance!" he begged. "Leave it one more year, and I'll give it special attention and more fertilizer. If that does not produce figs, then I will cut it down" (see Luke 13:6-9).

The parable ends abruptly. We are left to wonder about the fate of the unfruitful tree.

Jesus has used the strongest Hebrew metaphors imaginable in the parable. They are mixed for emphasis. Israel thought of herself as the vineyard of God. The psalmist and many of the prophets had etched the image into the Hebrew consciousness. Psalm 80 is an apt summary:

> Thou didst remove a vine from Egypt;
> Thou didst drive out the nations, and didst plant it.
> Thou didst clear the ground before it,
> And it took deep root and filled the land.
> The mountains were covered with its shadow;
> And the cedars of God with its boughs.
> It was sending out its branches to the sea,
> And its shoots to the River.
> O God of hosts, turn again now, we beseech Thee;
> Look down from heaven and see, and take care of
>   this vine,
> Even the shoot which Thy right hand has planted,
> And on the son whom Thou hast strengthened for
>   Thyself.
> It is burned with fire, it is cut down (Ps. 80:8-11,
>   14-16).

Isaiah focused the symbol even more sharply: "For the vineyard of the Lord of hosts is the house of Israel, and the men of Judah His delightful plant" (Isa. 5:7).

The people of God held the dual image for their identity. They were God's vineyard and also His special planting in the vineyard of the Promised Land. Both are mingled in the parable of the fig tree.

Our task is to discern what Jesus meant. Clearly the owner of the vineyard is God. Israel is the fig tree. Who then is the vineyard keeper? Jesus Himself. We are permitted to overhear the divine dialogue between the Father and the Son. Finally, the owner and keeper of the vineyard are one. Creator and Immanuel speak with one voice. The planter, expectant owner, and imploring advocate for one year more are all aspects of the One to whom we are accountable. Another phase of the autobiography of God.

The parable is both corporate and personal. The fig tree is both Israel and each individual who heard the warning. For us, its message is for the church and for each of us. The church is the new Israel, the tree of God. And yet, each of us will feel the impact of the parable only if we identify with that leafy, fruitless tree.

Mark's account of the same basic content is set in Jesus' final days in Jerusalem. Here it is a dramatized parable. Jesus noticed a fig tree with leaves. He expected to find fruit. To His surprise, He found none. In a focused moment of divine impatience, He cursed the fig tree: "May no one ever eat fruit from you again!" (Mark 11:14). The disciples were astonished.

No wonder. Why the great consternation over a fig tree that had no figs? We need some background on fig trees. Two things must be kept in mind. Mark says, "He found nothing but leaves" (v. 13). That's more than a horticultural observation. Leaves on a fig tree never precede the fruitage of figs. They sometimes accompany, but usually follow the fruit. Jesus, seeing the leaves, would expect to find figs. The other unusual circumstance was that the time of the year for figs was late in May or early June—Passover week was sometime between the last of March and the middle of April. It was most unusual for a fig tree to be in the leaf stage at that time of the year. Perhaps the tree had a favored position out of the wind and in the sun which caused premature foliage. But the issue for us is that the tree had leaves but no fruit. All of the life of the fig tree had run to the leaf. That's why Jesus cursed the fig tree: it was like Israel, the tree of God.

When the disciples and Jesus passed by the fig tree the next morning, they saw it withered to the roots. Peter expressed the astonishment of the disciples, "Master, look! The fig tree you cursed has withered!" (see v. 21).

Jesus' response startles us. No explanation! Just an admonition, "Have faith in God!" (v. 22). We wonder what that has to do with the withered fig tree. Then it dawns on us that this is the key for understanding both Mark and Luke's versions of the fig tree. The lacking quality of Israel was faith in God.

Now we can appreciate the alarm over a leafy fig tree with no figs. The outward forms of Israel's religion signified the knowledge and experience of God, but Jesus found only the leaves of pretension. Rites, rules, regulations, and restrictions had become more important than the fruit of personal faith. Jesus was concerned about the "weightier matters of the law— righteousness, justice, and love" (see Matt. 23:23). These could not be accomplished without a dependent trust in God.

Jesus talked a lot about fruitfulness throughout His ministry. At the end of the Sermon on the Mount He said, "Beware of the false prophets, who come to you in sheep's clothing, but inwardly are ravenous wolves. You will know them by their fruits. Grapes are not gathered from thornbushes, nor figs from thistles, are they? Even so every good tree bears good fruit; but the rotten tree bears bad fruit. A good tree cannot produce bad fruit, nor can a rotten tree produce good fruit. Every tree that does not bear good fruit is cut down, and thrown into the fire. So then, you will know them by their fruits. Not every one who says to Me, 'Lord, Lord,' will enter the kingdom of heaven; but he who does the will of My Father, who is in heaven" (Matt. 7:15-21). The Lord called His disciples to fruitfulness. His judgment on Israel was that the tree of God produced leaves of religion but not the fruit of righteousness in individuals and the nation as a whole.

That last week in Jerusalem precipitated a direct confrontation with the Hebrew officialdom. When Jesus raised Lazarus from the dead, rode triumphantly into Jerusalem, and cleansed the Temple, the battle lines were drawn. The fig tree focused the issue for Jesus. His response to the fruitless, unproductive tree enacted the divine indignation and impatience with irrelevant, entrenched religion. The people of God had prided themselves on their heritage as chosen of God, had substituted daily trust in God for ritualism and had lost personal relationship with Him in formalism. The outward forms of religion were not bad in themselves, but they were to be a result of faith, not a replacement of it. The leaves became more important than the fruit.

It would be fine if we could end our exposition with historical reflection about Israel. But the message is timeless. It speaks to the church in every age. The danger of leaf without fruit is ever-present. Today our buildings, massed choirs, magnificent educational programs, and religious organizations mean little if there is no real fruit as a result. But the parable is also personal, as it raises a question about each of us. Unless our prayers, churchmanship, and activity produce fruit, we are in danger of being cut off. The intercession of the vineyard keeper gives both comfort and urgency. "Give the tree one more year!" We have another chance. Now we can ask, "What is true fruitfulness for us?"

The answer to that is in what Christ wants to do in us and what He wants to do through us. Fruitfulness is never one without the other. One is experienced in our relationship with Him, the other is for our responsibility with others. Both are the challenge of Jesus' message on fruitfulness in John 15. It is impossible to catch the full thrust of the parable of the fig tree without a thorough understanding of what the Lord taught the disciples on the night before He was crucified. What He said to them is our guide to a fruitful life. The motive and method of fruitfulness is expressed in a powerful little word: abide!

We are to abide in Christ and invite Him to abide in us. "Abide in Me, and I in you. As the branch cannot bear fruit of itself, unless it abides in the vine, so neither can you, unless you abide in Me. I am the vine, you are the branches; he who abides in Me, and I in him, he bears much fruit; for apart from Me you can do nothing" (John 15:4,5).

When we abide in Christ, we appropriate all He has done for us. That means unreserved acceptance of His death for our sins and His resurrection for the defeat of all the enemies of the abundant life. The Greek word for abide is *meno*. It is drenched with meaning. To abide means to dwell, remain, and rest. The word also implies to continue in a relationship, faithful and unchanging. Sojourn, tarry and wait are synonymous for abide. Most of all, it means to remain continuously. We abide in Christ when we accept His love as our assurance, His forgiveness as our freedom, and His presence as our power. Fruitfulness has no beginning if it does not begin by abiding—trusting completely in Christ for our salvation and our eternal life.

But that's only the beginning. We were created for Christ to abide in us. He is the indwelling Lord in the contemporary power of the Holy Spirit. When we com-

248

mit our lives to Him, we become the post-Pentecost abiding, dwelling place of the Lord. That's the secret of fruitfulness. From within, He begins His transforming work.

The apostle John clarifies that in his first epistle to the churches. He writes to assure the Christians that they have been born of God because God's seed abides in them (see 1 John 3:9). We are the begotten of God, chosen to be reformed in the image of Christ. Through the seed of Christ in us, God's nature, revealed in Jesus, is reproduced in us. That means that our thought, temperament, and disposition are being remolded in Christ-likeness. The progression is exciting: we are born of God, chosen and called. We abide in His love for us in Christ, and then He abides in us for the transformation of our character. The fruit of Christ indwelling is the new you and I, recreated as new creatures in Christ.

Fruitfulness also is expressed through our personality. That's what Paul meant when he talked about the fruit of the Spirit. Christ's Spirit, abiding in us, manifests the character of Christ through us. Here then is personal fruitfulness as the result of Christ making us like Himself: love, joy, peace, patience, kindness, goodness, faithfulness, gentleness, and self-control (see Gal. 5:22). These are the figs the Lord wants to grow on the tree of our lives. None is available apart from Him. We can inventory our fruitfulness by evaluating the evidence of the fruit of His Spirit. But catch the wonder of it all: the fruit our Lord demands He imputes as His gift.

That presses us on to the fruit He wants to produce through us with others. It's all summarized in the Lord's commandment, "This is My commandment, that you love one another, just as I have loved you" (John 15:12). How has He loved us? The next verse answers our question. "Greater love has no one than this, that one lay down his life for his friends" (v. 13). There it is! Fruitfulness is loving people as we have been loved with giving, forgiving, sacrificial love. The test of fruitfulness is laying down our lives for others.

It meant Calvary for Christ. For us it means vulnerability, openness, and involvement with people. If we love people, we will want them to know the joy we have found. Fruitfulness is the sharing of our faith with others and introducing them to the love of Christ. Unwillingness to help others find Christ is not shyness, it is lack of love. It is as if we had discovered a cure for a form of cancer we are suffering and being unwilling to share our gift of healing. Can you imagine refusing to communicate our healing if it could help other sufferers? And yet, one of the greatest problems in the local church today is to liberate the dumbness of contemporary Christians about what Christ has done for them. There are church members who have occupied pews for years and can account for no one person whom they have helped live forever!

The apostle John knew no such reticence. "Again I say, we are telling you about what we ourselves have actually seen and heard, so that you may share the fellowship and the joys we have with the Father and with Jesus Christ his Son" (1 John 1:3, *TLB*).

Reproduction of our faith in others is the test of fruitfulness. We are productive trees in the Lord's vineyard if we have the figs of hope for people. We lay down our lives when we crucify our privation, separateness, and lack of concern. The Lord constantly sends us people to look for life through us. Many of them are as disappointed as He was when He went to the fig tree looking for fruit.

That was not true for a new-members class that joined our church in Hollywood recently. I can still feel the thrill I had when I looked over the faces of the 45 candidates for baptism and membership in the Body of Christ. The exciting thing about this class was that most of the people had been introduced to Christ and the church by members of the congregation. They had been loved, listened to, cared for and witnessed to by fruitful contemporary disciples. Joy filled the sanctuary as those members saw the tangible fruit of their ministry. There were people in the class from all walks of life. Each had been alerted to what was missing in his or her life by members whose character and personality radiated with Christ's indwelling power. Executives, professors, movie personalities, students, housewives, singles, couples, youth and adults all had been initiated to the abundant life by people in whom the fruit of the Spirit abounded.

As I received the class into membership and commissioned them to be fruitful disciples in their ministry, I was very aware that the new Christians would be able to grow in what they had discovered only as they too became fruitful. Christ's abiding presence would enable that. He will transform their natures to be like His own. Then He will expect reproduction of new life in others.

One of our deacons confessed, "I sat in this church for 20 years before I took seriously what I heard and began to be a fruitful Christian. I hate to think about all I missed during those years!" He is a part of a breed of articulate, contagious Christians who now measure their spiritual life on their effectiveness at multiplying the new life in others.

The only hope for our church or any church being great will be in the extent of the fruitfulness of the members. It's the one test of a great church.

24

How to Know
the Will of God

Matthew 21:28-32: Parable of the Two Sons

Discovering and doing the will of God is the only way to have a consistent experience of the abundant life Jesus came to reveal and enable in us.

I want to reach out to you as I write and you read this chapter. Empathy pulses within me. We all have decisions to make. The future looms with uncertainty. All of us are on the edge of some crucial evaluation of the next steps for our lives. What shall we do about the alternatives before us? How about the relationships that are demanding? How shall we act and what shall we do? In what way can we be maximum for God with the people we love? What does God want us to do in the complex problems that seem to defy solution?

Often we pray our prayers urgently seeking the Lord's

direction. We say, "Lord, show me your will!" Why is it so few people get a clear answer?

There is no question asked of me more often than this: "How can I know the will of God?" The question is a symptom of something much deeper.

Our family is blessed by the care of a very astute internist. He has a delightful way of asking incisive questions to get at the real reason causing the problem. When one goes to him with a headache, instead of giving a simple pain remedy, he plumbs the depths to find out the physical or emotional cause. He never deals with the symptomatic surface problem until he understands the reason.

In the same way, when someone says to me that he or she wants to know the will of God, I feel led by the Spirit of God to penetrate the inner reasons motivating the question.

Two basic assumptions guide my conversations with people about the will of God. The first is: If we are seeking to know the will of God, it's a sure sign that we are out of it. The second is: We cannot know the will of God unless we are willing to do the obvious, primary thing God has told us to do.

So often we thrash about asking people for advice about what to do in some situation. It's good that people have insights and experiences to share, but ultimately we have to go to God. Friends can help, but their perspective is limited by the boundaries of their own experience. They can't know all that's going on inside us or when the very thing we're going through is being used to make us stronger people. Only God knows us absolutely and only He is able to see the beginning from the end.

A man once said he needed two alarm clocks: One to wake him up, and the other to tell him why he is up.

Knowing the ultimate and specific will of God will do both. Wake us up to life, and help us to know what we are to do.

I agree with little that Nietzsche said except this: "If you know your why, you'll understand your how." That's the point of this chapter. It's dramatized in the parable of the two sons. To understand what Jesus has to say about both our why and how in this parable we must be careful to follow the line of investigation we have utilized in our study of the parables as the autobiography of God. We must consider the context, seek for the one salient point, ask what that tells us about the nature of God, and then discern what it means for our daily lives.

It's the last week of Jesus' life. He has triumphantly entered Jerusalem, purged the Temple, has taught with clarity about the judgment of God and has pointed to His death as the hope for the sins of the world. The chief priests and the elders of the people came to Him as He was teaching and said, "By what authority are You doing these things, and who gave You this authority?" (Matt. 21:23).

The Lord's reply was very direct. "I will ask you one thing too, which if you tell Me, I will also tell you by what authority I do these things" (v. 24).

Then He reminded them of the ministry of John the Baptist. "The baptism of John was from what source, from heaven or from men?" (v. 25).

He had them. If they said it was from heaven, Jesus would have every right to ask why they had not believed in John as a prophet. Conversely, if they said that John's ministry was not divinely inspired, they would incite the rage of John's disciples in the crowd. There was no safe answer to give. Their response was an evasive, "We do not know" (v. 27).

But some of them did. They knew all too well. Jesus was leading them on to the point He wanted to make: How could they deal with His authority as Messiah if they had not been willing to accept the authority of the one who prepared the way for His messianic ministry? We are prepared for the parable. How can we seek to know more of the will of God when we have not responded to whatever revelations of His plan for us He has unmistakably made known to us previously? The leaders of Israel had not been listening. Jesus had told them plainly who He was and that His authority was from God. He had not hidden His messiahship. Their question about His authority was like our question about the will of God. We already know more than we have done. Our question, like that of the leaders, is an exposure of our disobedience! We have not acted on the knowledge we have. Action is the nerve center of the spiritual life. Obedience is the opening of the thermostatic valve for spiritual power. Luther said, "I believe in order to obey; I obey in order to believe."

In that light, we are ready to consider what Jesus taught in the parable about obedience. Remember He was talking to religious people who were not doing what they believed, who were refusing to follow the guidance they had.

" 'But what do you think? A man had two sons, and he came to the first and said, "Son, go work today in the vineyard." And he answered and said, "I will, sir"; and he did not go. And he came to the second and said the same thing. But he answered and said, "I will not"; yet he afterward regretted it and went. Which of the two did the will of his father?' They said, 'The latter.' Jesus said to them, 'Truly I say to you that the tax-gatherers and harlots will get into the kingdom of God before you. For John came to you in the way of righteousness and you did not believe him; but the tax-gatherers and harlots did believe him; and you, seeing this, did not even feel remorse afterward so as to believe him' " (Matt. 21:28-32).

Catch the symbolism. In all the parables of the autobiography of God, the father represents God. The vineyard had been used repeatedly to represent the nation Israel, as we have seen in other parables. It also means the Promised Land and the realm of the Kingdom of God. Working in the vineyard is to cooperate with God in His plans and purposes for His people. Yahweh's persistent command was, "Go into the vineyard and work. Depend on my sovereign power and do my will in all your affairs. Trust me and I will bless my people." The two responses of the sons of the parable capture the attitude of God's people through the ages. One says piously, "I will, sir!" but never gets around to going. The other says resistantly, "I will not!" but then repents with regret for his disobedience and goes into the vineyard to do his father's will. Which does the will of God?

Let's keep this personal for you and me. Which son would we find exemplifies our attitude and follow-through?

Many of us find ourselves in the skin of the son who says he will go but never gets to work in the vineyard.

The oft-repeated words of the Lord's Prayer mock us. How many times in the last month have we repeated the phrase, "Thy will be done, on earth as it is in heaven"? We say it ritually without knowing what we are praying. What would it be like to do His will as it's done in heaven? I picture heaven as the realm of complete response to the glory of God. It's an eternal existence with the Father, completely free of all reservations or equivocations. All of our human devices to evade obedience will be gone. Unfettered, we will be able to praise God and do His will with no impediments. But heaven can begin now for us in this life. And it means unrestrained response to however much we know of what God wants us to be and do.

And yet, in our prayers we promise more than we do. You can count on the Lord! But we refuse to take the first steps to implement the vision. We are like the facile son who said, "I'll go!" but never went.

In worship we sing, pray and preach way beyond where we are willing to live. We talk a good game. Awesome truths are proclaimed and we respond with emotional excitement. What we do between Sundays is the test. "Observe the weekday and keep it holy" might well be the eleventh commandment. Have you ever found that before the Sunday is over, you have contradicted the promises you made during the morning worship?

A friend of mine sits down at his desk each Monday morning and says, "This is the week! In everything I do this week, I am going to do the will of God." Then, he says, often before Monday morning is over he realizes that he has slipped back into self-dependence, cultural values and company policies which cannot stand the test of the Kingdom of God.

Before we are too critical of my friend, we need to consider the ways we deny what we believe and what God has guided us to do. We see the issues and make bold protestations, but too often when we look back over a day we realize that we talked way beyond our action.

Have you ever had the feeling that God wanted you to do something and you avoided it? Ever feel the gnawing uneasiness that there are things He has made clear as action-steps and you resisted the guidance persistently? Not petulance; just neglect. I can identify with that first son. Religiously, I constantly promise God more than I produce. What about you? I suspect that we stand together under the impact of this parable. Most of us are great verbalizers who have the words without responsible obedience.

I remember a man in a congregation I served some years ago who was determined never to say or sing more than he was willing to do. Often, I would observe him in the worshiping congregation not singing certain hymns. When I asked him about his dumbness his response was, "I'm not able to sing that yet because I'm not ready to do what the words promise." And yet he was a man I could depend on. He would always do what he said he would do. When he pledged money, it was faithfully paid. If I asked him to follow up on a potential Christian, he would never let me down. The implications of costly obedience were lived out in his business and in his community. Each time he was challenged to do or give something for the cause of Christ, he would ask for a few days to pray about it. When he felt guided by God and said he would do what was asked, I could be confident that he would not come up with excuses later on. He was trustworthy. Any pastor would have to admit that most congregations have only a handful of people like that. Why is that?

In the parable of the two sons, neither son was commendable. Both categories are inadequate. What Jesus wants to do is to lead us beyond the dualism to a third possibility.

There should be no accolade given to a person who says "I will" and doesn't, or to a person who says "I won't" and finally does. Jesus wants us to know God so intimately and personally that as a result of that friendship we know what He wants us to do before the crises of life hit us. The most natural result of companionship with God is to work the vineyard. Daily obedience alone can prepare for drastic eventualities or spectacular opportunities.

The twist of the parable is: Why should we have to be asked to go into the vineyard to work? If the two sons knew and loved the father they would have known that by now the vineyard was theirs by inheritance. Those grapes and vines belonged to them and someday would be entrusted to their management. It was a family affair. Why did the father have to go recruit them like day laborers at the beginning of each day? What a demeaning insult to the father! He should have been able to visit them working in the vineyard without a daily negotiation for their labor. That's what Jesus implies in the parable. We are the sons of our heavenly Father. Why do we have to be reemployed in a calling that is ours by divine election?

The discovery of the will of God comes from habitual, consistent, repetitive communion with God. If we say, "I don't know what the will of God is for my life," it means that day by day we've not been listening to the elementary guidance which results from faithful prayer and communion. When we seek God, not just His will, we will be ready for life's crises. The Lord seeks open, receptive disciples who are obedient to what they have been told in order that God may give them immediate guidance for each new challenge where the reality of the problem intersects with the resources of His Spirit. The only way to know the will of God for life's big decisions is to be willing to start today to be obedient in the little things.

The psalmist's prayer in Psalm 119 is the basis for daily obedience which opens future guidance. We need to read it often as a chart for life's treacherous seas. "I shall run the way of Thy commandments, for Thou wilt enlarge my heart" (Ps. 119:32). All through the psalm the author asks for strength to do the basics so the Lord can prepare for him His blessings. Our enlarged heart is open to new vision. The psalmist had been like the first son who promised and did not obey and had been liberated to say he wanted to do the elementary commandments in order to know more of God's plan for him. In Psalm 86, David prayed the longing of all our hearts. "Teach me Thy way, O Lord; I will walk in Thy truth; unite my heart to fear Thy name. I will give thanks to Thee, O Lord my God, with all my heart, and will glorify Thy name forever" (Ps. 86:11,12).

A personal illustration may help to expose what I feel Jesus is saying to us in this parable. If you were to ask me what my wife thinks or wants in a certain situation, I should not have to go to ask her. Twenty-seven years of marriage should give me some knowledge of her convictions, wants and desires. If I had to say, "Just a moment, I will ask her to hear what she has to say about that," it would say something about our marriage. To be sure, most women want some mystery about them, but if your question dealt with the basics of life, I should be able to tell you without a lengthy consultation with my Mary Jane. I have lived, talked and prayed with her through the years. I know my wife. Should we be less sure of God and His will?

Charles Spurgeon often repeated his conviction that faith and obedience are bound up in the same bundle. Anyone who listened to the great preacher or read his works was confronted by the formula of his life. He who obeys God, trusts God; and he who trusts God, obeys God. Tennyson would have agreed. He said, "Our wills are ours, we know not how; our wills are ours, to make them thine." I am often reminded of James Jauncy's insight that God will never burglarize the human will.

He may long to come in and help, but He will never cross what Jauncy called the picket line of our unwillingness.

It would be fascinating to do a study of the teaching of Jesus centered on His message about our volitional capacity. A good title would be "The Theology of the Will—Or How to Know God Through Obedience." Jesus' constant demand was for the surrender of the will. His parables focus on the Kingdom of God—His rule in us and around us. Each one requires a decision to allow God to run our lives.

In this parable the inner meaning is that God is saying to us, "Go work in the vineyard. You will not know the specifics of what you are to do in each day until you actually start to work." He does not unfold His complete strategy for any of us. The next step is revealed if we take the first step. The rudimentary precedes the remarkable. Doing the basics daily prepares us for the beatific vision in the momentous pressures life deals out.

To be willing to go to work in the vineyard means three things. First, it means that we care about people and their needs. We are surrounded by people who need to know about God's love, to have us incarnate His grace in our attitudes, actions and words. The Lord has chosen us to be communicators of His gift of salvation and eternal life. We pass through the narrow gate one by one helped by some person who has been obedient to God to share His forgiveness and the promise of a new beginning. Unless our lives are being poured out for people who do not know the Lord, we have not begun our work in the vineyard. How can we plea for further knowledge of His will?

Secondly, work in the vineyard is following the obvious implications of the gospel in our relationship, responsibilities and the needs of our communities. Our

261

families, homes, churches, places of work are the realms in which we learn how to cooperate with the Lord to get His work done. We will be confused about our decisions in some strategic crossroad in our personal life if we have resisted being faithful to however much the Lord has clarified for us. We already know enough from the Scriptures for a lifetime of implementation.

Thirdly, unless we have praised God for what He has shown us in our personal needs in the past, He will not give us fresh guidance. Someone has said that the present is the past rolled up for action; the past is the present unrolled for understanding. As we work in the vineyard we must constantly affirm that the vineyard is the Lord's, He has made us recipients of the privilege of working by His strength and wisdom, and that consistent thanksgiving opens us up to be ready for greater responsibility. Again David articulates our prayer, "I delight to do Thy will, O my God" (Ps. 40:8).

Laurence J. Peter in his famous *The Peter Plan* said, "The hardest thing in life is to learn which bridge to cross and which to burn." What I've discovered from the parable of the two sons is that the uncertainty need not trouble a person who is at work in the vineyard. God is faithful; He will tell us what we need to do if we have been in consistent communion with Him long before the decision deadline.

On the night before Jesus was crucified He revealed to us what He had taught in the parable. In the garden of Gethsemane He did not pray to know the will of God but for the power to do it. The mandate of Calvary had been revealed long before that anguishing night of prayer. Because of what He was faithful to do on our behalf, we can face our difficulties with confidence. God will be with us. He never guides us to do more than He will grant us strength to endure.

Paul discovered that secret of knowing the will of God. "I urge you therefore, brethren, by the mercies of God [what He's done in Christ and has done repeatedly through Him in our needs], to present your bodies a living and holy sacrifice, acceptable to God, which is your spiritual service of worship. And do not be conformed to this world, but be transformed by the renewing of your mind [consistent, habitual prayer], that you may prove [test through experience] what the will of God is, that which is good and acceptable and perfect" (Rom. 12:1,2). The Apostle had experienced what he wrote. He was a man under orders. Because he obeyed, the Lord unfolded more and more of His strategy to him. He challenged the church at Ephesus to do all things "as to the Lord." The Thessalonians were reminded of the basics. "This is the will of God, your sanctification" (1 Thess. 4:3). Growth in holiness as called, chosen saints would take place in following what the Lord had already made clear. Fresh direction would be given as a result of essential ethics for daily living. We cannot expect to know the will of God if our lives are a rebellious contradiction to the message and life of the Master.

When our wills are obedient, the Lord will use all the faculties of our minds and emotions to impress on us what He wants us to do. He will use insight from others, confirmed in us by His Spirit, to point the way. But the final assurance will come in communion with Him. At the right moment, never too early or too late, we will know what to do or say. The answer will come from the voice of God within. But be sure of this: it will come while we are working in the vineyard!

25

Unmerited Favor

Matthew 20:1-16: Parable of the Laborers in the Vineyard

The sirocco woke the man from a deep sleep. He could hear the desert winds relentlessly blowing the trees outside and whistle through the cracks and crevices of the walls of his house. Years of experience as a day laborer in the vineyards had taught him what that wind meant. It was the time of scorching heat. The grapes would have to be harvested! The winds and heat would be followed by heavy rains and destructive high winds. The grapes would be whipped by the wind unless they were garnered quickly.

Good thing. At least there would be work. Bread to feed the hungry mouths of his family. The endless cycle of poverty would be broken for a time. There would be a good chance of being hired if he got to the marketplace early. With a surge of hope the man dressed quietly, so as not to wake his family.

The crimson sun was just protruding on the horizon when he arrived at the marketplace where day laborers gathered each day to expectantly wait for work. He was among the first to arrive. The owner of the vineyard had preceded them. He was obviously feeling the urgency of harvest, and wanted to hire all the hands he could before the sirocco subsided and the rains came.

The negotiations for the day's wage went quickly: a denarius was offered and the laborers agreed. About twenty cents, the going rate for sunup to sundown labor in the vineyard. It was six o'clock when the first crew began its work.

The early morning hours in the vineyard were usually cool, and motivated energetic work. Not that day. Even the early sun was blisteringly hot, and the winds felt as if they had been blown off a furnace. The laborer began his garnering with skilled hands trained by years of hard labor. But as he looked over the vineyard and all the grapes to be harvested, he knew that the early morning crew the owner had hired would not be able to finish before sundown.

At nine in the morning the owner left to return to the marketplace, to see if any more laborers could be hired. The man continued to work, but in his mind he speculated what the owner would offer the new laborers. Surely it would be a portion of a denarius. It would be good to have help. The day of labor was about 12 hours, and it would take many hands to finish the task.

The nine o'clock crew was not enough. The owner was working against time; the winds and the rains could come all too soon. He could not hide his concern and impatience.

The laborer was not surprised when the owner returned repeatedly to hire more help. Men from other villages seeking work were in the village waiting. New crews were hired at noon and three in the afternoon. Still the rows of unharvested vines stretched out before the laborers. They were all surprised when the owner went back to the village at five to see if he could hire still more men. There would be little more than an hour for them to work.

As each new crew was added, the early morning laborer calculated what he thought each would earn for the different durations of labor. He mused over the possibility of making more than the owner had agreed upon, almost able to feel the coins in his hands.

An excitement mounts in him as the day grows to a close. Six in the evening is welcomed as the end of an arduous day of intense labor. "It's all worth it!" the man says to himself. "I have been here all day and my wage will be greater than the latecomers."

The laborers line up for their pay. Everyone is absolutely amazed when the five o'clock laborers are called forth to be paid first. All eyes are fixed on the owner of the vineyard as he hands out the wages. What will these one-hour laborers be paid for their hour's work? A wave of consternation and unbelieving surprise sweeps over the line of workers. The owner of the vineyard paid the one-hour worker a denarius! How can this be? It meant one of two things: either the others would be paid more or—No one could abide the thought that they might all be paid the same. The early morning laborer felt a surge of greed. He thinks the best of the owner and is already multiplying what he could earn for a full day. Twelve denarii! But then fear grips his heart as the three o'clock laborers are also given a denarius. Anxiety grows as the noon-hour workers receive the same; but white-hot anger surges within him as the nine o'clock workers are given no more than the others.

When the owner places the denarius in the man's

hand, it's more than he can take. His emotions burst with a blast of indignation. "It's not fair! I've been working here all day. Is there no justice; no reward for hard work? What's the use of working twelve hours if one hour's work in the cool of the afternoon earns the same amount?" With that he throws the coin at the owner's feet. "You keep your dirty denarius!"

We look into the face of the owner. What is it we read? Imperiousness? Unquestionable authority? Dictatorial autocracy? He speaks deliberately. "Friend, I am doing you no wrong; did you not agree with me for a denarius? Take what is yours and go your way, but I wish to give to this last man the same as to you. Is it not lawful for me to do what I wish with what is my own? Or is your eye envious because I am generous?" (Matt. 20:13-15).

The parable of the laborers in the vineyard stuns us. What did Jesus imply by this dimension of the autobiography of God? In keeping with Scripture's identification of Yahweh as the owner of the vineyard of Israel, there is no question that Jesus wants to communicate truth about God's providence which stirs our thinking and demands careful reflection. What does this mean for us? Can we accept this seeming inequality about God's administration of the world? What ever happened to the idea that long, hard labor and faithfulness have some rewards? While we ruminate on that, Jesus finishes the parable with a statement that only intensifies our intellectual problem: "Thus the last shall be first, and the first last" (v. 16).

The parable had been motivated by the Lord's discussion with the disciples about the rewards of following Him. Peter, like the full-day laborer, wanted to negotiate for some assurance that the cost of following the Master would be worth it all. "Behold, we have left everything and followed You; what then will there be for us?" (Matt. 19:27). Jesus' response is very direct: "Truly I say to you, that you who have followed Me, in the regeneration when the Son of Man will sit on His glorious throne, you also shall sit upon twelve thrones, judging the twelve tribes of Israel. And everyone who has left houses or brothers or sisters or father or mother or children or farms for My name's sake, shall receive many times as much, and shall inherit eternal life" (vv. 28,29).

We are sure Peter liked that answer! But then the thunder struck when the Lord added, "But many who are first will be last; and the last, first" (v. 30). What did that mean, the disciples wondered? Did the Lord mean to imply that others who had not paid the price they had would also be rewarded equally? The first last? They had been first. Jesus had assured them of their reward. But when He suggested that others would be equally recognized with the inheritance of eternal life, they were alarmed. They did not understand that what the Master would accomplish in His death and resurrection would be for all who believed. Who's first or last should be irrelevant. When we put ourselves in the disciples' skin we can imagine how they felt. Most of us are willing to work hard and endure great deprivation if we are sure we will be recognized and rewarded more than those who have been less diligent.

Now we can understand why Jesus had to teach this mind-stretching parable and why it is so crucial for our understanding.

Two questions must be asked and answered by each of us. One is very personal, and the other may seem presumptuous at first. How old are you? What time of the day is it for your life?

I am indebted to Leslie Weatherhead for his tabulation of our age and the hours of a day. For some it's early in the day of life; for others we are close to midnight. Find yourself in this chart. Weatherhead says, "Take the measure of the years by reducing a lifetime of seventy years to the compass of the waking hours of a single day from, say, seven in the morning till eleven at night. Then if you are:

15	years	of	age,	the	time	is	10:25 A.M.
20	"	"	"	"	"	"	11:34 A.M.
25	"	"	"	"	"	"	12:42 A.M.
30	"	"	"	"	"	"	1:51 P.M.
35	"	"	"	"	"	"	3:00 P.M.
40	"	"	"	"	"	"	4:08 P.M.
45	"	"	"	"	"	"	5:16 P.M.
50	"	"	"	"	"	"	6:25 P.M.
55	"	"	"	"	"	"	7:34 P.M.
60	"	"	"	"	"	"	8:42 P.M.
65	"	"	"	"	"	"	9:51 P.M.
70	"	"	"	"	"	"	11:00 P.M."[1]

This helps us identify where we are in the adventure of living. If we have committed our lives to Christ and have been Christians early in the day, we have enjoyed years of the joy of fellowship with the Lord. But how do you feel about the person who is given equal rights and status with you if he or she becomes a Christian at the 11:00 P.M. hour? What if that person has been a high-living, irresponsible rounder? How do you react to the fact that there's no regard or reward for your whole life of faithfulness, obedience, and responsibility? We can empathize with the feelings of the whole-day laborer. Suddenly the parable is very personal.

Now we can wrestle with the truths about God that this parable illuminates like bolts of lightning.

The first is that we are called into the Lord's vineyard by election. The only basis of our hope is that God has elected us to know Him, receive His love, experience salvation through Christ's death and resurrection, and enjoy the delight of His indwelling Spirit. We did nothing to deserve it or earn it. Our calling is a gift. Paul captured the magnificent truth. "And we know that God causes all things to work together for good to those who love God, to those who are called according to His purpose. For whom He foreknew, He also predestined to become conformed to the image of His Son, that He might be the first-born among many brethren; and whom He predestined, these He also called; and whom He called, these He also justified; and whom He justified, those He also glorified" (Rom. 8:28-30). We did not choose Christ; He chose us Long before our desire to respond to His love, He was at work in us creating in us the longing for Him to fill our emptiness. So there is absolutely no credit to us that we are at work in the Lord's vineyard. We are there, early or late, by sheer grace.

This past week I had the privilege of introducing an old man and a teenage woman to Christ. A 16-year-old woman by the name of Beth is now filled with the joy and peace of Christ. She is excited about a full life ahead of growing in the Saviour. She entered the vineyard very early. The elderly man was close to the end of his life. His energies are spent; all he had to bring to the Lord was a long life of regrets. His whole life had been spent on himself and his own desires. The plow of self-concern had cut deep furrows on his brow and lines in his face. Now sickness had brought him to the realization of his desperate need for God. He was not ready to die. He feared the judgment of God. Then, as he repeated the sinner's prayer after me, I sensed the presence of the loving Lord. Afterward he said, "How I wish I hadn't waited so long. There's not much time left to enjoy my

270

new life." I assured him he had all of eternity.

Neither the young woman nor the old man was called and chosen because of what he or she they had or had not done. The reward was the same for both.

We put so much emphasis on when people respond to God. In evangelism we spend a great deal of time and effort trying to create the right atmosphere, have the best music, and set the most inviting mood. We forget that faith is a gift, and no one can respond to his or her election without the gift from the Spirit of God. Our only concern is to make the love of God clear, explain the gospel impellingly, and invite people to respond winsomely. If we care for them personally and God has worked in their hearts, they will respond. The glory will not be given to our effective methods, but to God.

Secondly, the parable of the laborers in the vineyard proclaims the unmerited love of God. That's a source of amazement for some and alarm for others. There are people who find it difficult to believe that God loves them in spite of what they have been or done. Others find it an affront that God does not love them *because* of what they've been or done. But Jesus is very clear in the parable: the wage is the same for all. But what a wage! Life now and forever, abundant and glorious through eternity. The important thing is not *when* but *that* we come into the vineyard.

That draws us on to the final flashing truth. Companionship is our only compensation. To labor with the Lord, long or short, is the blessing which is ours by grace. There's a sixteenth-century prayer which articulates the joy of that. "Teach us to labor and not to ask for any reward save that of knowing that we do Thy will." Thomas Aquinas knew the essence of that. One time he heard the Lord say to him in a dream, "Thomas, thou hast written much and well concerning me. What

271

reward shall I give thee for thy work?" Thomas' reply was, "Nothing but Thyself, Lord!" Companionship with the Lord is the ultimate reward. We are free to love God for God, not because of what He will do for us or we have done for Him.

I heard one of the elders of our church pray, "Thank You, Lord, that You called me on my mother's knee and helped me to know You as a child so that I could enjoy You all through the years." If you can say that, praise God. But if it's the noon hour of your life, the invitation is open. And if it's the last hour, it's not too late. A companionship that death cannot end can begin right now.

Note

1. Leslie D. Weatherhead: *In Quest of a Kingdom* (New York-Nashville: Abingdon-Cokesbury Press), p. 138.

26

God's Love Knows No Limits

Matthew 21:33-41: Parable of the Cruel Vinedresser

Come with me to the tower. There is a special parapet, a perch of observation on which we can stand. It gives us a vantage point to survey the vineyard. It is a magnificent vineyard, isn't it? We've had it for five years now. Look at the strong healthy vines; the fruit ready for harvest; row upon row, neatly cultivated and cared for. The hedge protecting the vineyard is a mason's masterpiece, stone upon stone. Notice the carefully excavated wine vat for the pressing of the grapes. One part is a bit higher than the other for the tramping out of the grapes and the other lower portion to receive the flow of the new wine.

We've done an excellent job managing the vineyard, haven't we? Remember the arduous labor under the sweltering sun? The trimming, pruning, fertilizing. It's all worth it now as we look at the fruit of our labors. We've done well, haven't we? We enjoy just standing there surveying what we've accomplished. The vineyard really belongs to us, though it's owned by the landowner. He rented it out to us, but we've done the work. There'd be no harvest without us. This is our vineyard!

We remember the laws of ownership and shared profits with the owner clearly delineated in the law of the land. Indignation surges through us when we reflect on the fact that we were obligated to pay one-third of the profits to the owner after the first five years of production. It's not fair! Will he forget? Perhaps his absentee landownership will be neglected and all the proceeds will be ours. It's our due, if not our right. Don't you agree?

Our place on the parapet of the tower allows us to watch for any approaching intruders—thieves, robbers, freeloaders, merchants who have come to buy the wine —or the emissaries of the owner who might come to claim his portion of the profits. We keep a careful eye on the pass through the mountain.

A solitary figure is approaching. Who is it? When he has come close enough for identification, we are alarmed. We knew the time would come sooner or later. It's one of the landowner's slaves! We know what he wants. Anger and greed capture our emotions. Defensive, protective. What right does the landowner have to get his profit? We've done all the work. This is our vineyard!

What shall we do? Beat him to an inch of his life. Some of us are appointed to do the deed. When we are finished with him we are shocked to learn that another slave of the landowner is coming through the pass. Crafty owner! He knows us. Kill this one. That will finish it. Not so. Another one comes. Stone him. Now we are told that a whole band of slaves is coming through the pass. We have gone too far to stop now.

Finish them all off and the vineyard will be ours.

When the day of treachery is finished, we return to the tower to savor the delicious feeling of commanding *our* vineyard. We laugh and joke with grisly glee.

Our giddy celebration is interrupted when we notice another person walking through the pass with deliberate measured steps. His determination is obvious even at a distance. Who can this be? We did away with all the slaves of the owner. When the approaching figure reaches the hedge we remark with fright that he looks like the owner, only younger. It's the owner's son! As he enters the vineyard, we exchange looks of mingled hate and acquisitiveness that knows no reason. Do you realize what we can do? The ownership must have been transferred as a legacy to the son. If we do away with the son, the vineyard will be ours forever! Why not? Who will ever know. Kill him. A last, final act of claiming the vineyard as our own (see Matt. 21:33-39).

Our experience inside the greedy hearts of the vine-dressers helps us to feel the impact of Jesus' parable delivered during the last week of His ministry in Jerusalem. Here is the story line of the autobiography of God portrayed with vivid and unmistakable clarity. There's no mistake about Jesus' intention. As we have noted before, Israel was the vineyard of the Lord. The prophets had come to claim the Lord's ownership and the fruit of righteousness. We know what happened to them. And the leaders of Israel were now the vine growers of the parable. With the same imperious defensiveness, they wanted no one to threaten their authority over the vineyard they controlled. Not even a rabbi from Nazareth. When He rode into *their* Jerusalem, it was like the landowner's son approaching the vineyard. Jesus' parable was a frightening introduction to themselves, if they could have heard and understood. When their maleficent manipulation was completed that week, the dastardly scheme was accomplished. The mob cried, "Crucify Him, crucify Him!" Golgotha was the place. The closed tomb sealed the end of the Galilean's persistent claim upon the vineyard. Or so the leaders of Israel hoped!

Now return with me to the tower. The time and place change. The images shift but the message is the same. What is the vineyard for us? Our life, plans, future? Or perhaps it's a loved one, our family, anyone whom we force to be an extension of our own ego. Then, too, it may be our image, our career, our church. What is it for you? Investments, trophies of success, properties, the accumulation of our hard work?

When did the transition from His to ours to mine take place for you? It happens before we know it. Then suddenly we begin to act as if the vineyard is ours. We earned it. Our arduous labor gives us the right of ownership. We want no one, not even God, to menace our self-management. We are willing to acknowledge that the landowner should be given credit for creating the vineyard of our lives, but we have made our lives what they are by effort and tireless striving. We recoil at the brash statement. The words rattle us because they match our life-style and attitudes more than we dare to admit to ourselves—or to God.

Suddenly the parable is alive with existential intensity. We are at center stage in the tower of our vineyard. What have we done to the repeated overtures of God's ownership of our lives? How have we done away with those who have tried to remind us that we belong to God? We leaf through our checkbooks and our investment of time and energy. A third? We fuss over the tithe! Prayers for instruction as to how to run our vineyard to the honor and glory of God? We think of Him only in the crises when vines yield no grapes.

I cannot read this parable honestly without thinking about the ways we act like the vine growers—as individuals, and as the church. As the people of God we are responsible to the Lord for what we do with what He has entrusted to us. How often has the Son come to claim us and been rejected, stoned and beaten in our ecclesiastical structures, neglected in our culturalized religion, and domesticated in our irrelevant piety?

In that context, we reread the parable. Five truths break through and invade our thinking.

First, the parable tells us about the preeminent privilege which is ours. Breathe your next breath with awe and wonder. Feel your pulse. Our hearts faithfully beat and send blood through our system. Think with your mind. What a magnificent capacity of intellect God has given us. Sense the emotions you can express. We have been wondrously made to express the love of God. Capture the freedom and power of your will. Our volitional ability enables us to decide and do. God has not left anything out. Just as the owner of the vineyard left all the resources to the vinedressers, so God has equipped us to live fully and joyously.

Second, think about the abundant allocation. The Lord has woven all our challenges and opportunities to create the person He has meant us to be. He is the playwright of our experiences, the director of our affairs, the stage manager of our circumstances. All that we might praise Him and live our lives to His glory.

Third, the parable forces us to evaluate the tragic transition when we claimed our vineyard as our own. When did the word "my" take on dangerous proportions? It's happened to all of us. We start out working for the Lord, and then we want the Lord to work for us, and soon the Lord is dealt out of any kind of daily

277

partnership in the development of our values or passions for life. It happens so subtly that many of us never realize it. We work hard, live "good" lives, try to be responsible, develop fine reputations and are recognized as examples of industrious management of life. But for all intent, and most of our purposes, we have taken charge of the vineyard as if it belonged to us.

There is nothing the Lord will withhold if we tell the world around us it belongs to Him. Praise and adoration are all He desires. The more we adore Him, the more He will entrust to us. In every family, church, company and community, He is in search of people who will humbly acknowledge Him as the source of the blessings He longs to pour out. Sin is nothing other than the rebellion that wants to get the glory which should be given to God. That leads us to the next point.

Fourth, the parable resounds with the justice of the judgment of God. There is a time in every believer's life when the issue must be settled about who owns our vineyard or it may be taken from us.

A clergyman in the midwest lost his church as the result of a tragic moral indiscretion. I will never forget what he said to me. "I ran my life and my church as if they belonged to me. I felt above checking and accountability. Then it happened. I did something I never thought I would do. Now I've lost everything."

A father told me about the breakdown of his relationship with his son who is no longer living at home and avoids all contacts. The father had made the son his private possession and demanded performance and perfection he had never been able to accomplish with his own life. The son became a thing and not a person. Just before he left home the boy said, "Get your hands off me. I'm not your private possession. You are going to run my life no longer!" Though the father was a Christian, he had forgotten that his lad belonged to God. Praise to the Lord had been replaced by pressure on his son. It was a pitiful look on the parent's face when he said, "I've lost my boy!"

A young wife came in to tell me that her husband was filing for divorce. As a Christian, she said she didn't believe in divorce, but all efforts to dissuade her husband had no success. The Spirit had given her great insight into what she had done to cause the fracture. "There was a moment when I could have changed," she said, "but I couldn't, or I guess I mean that I wouldn't. My husband needed warmth and all he got was control and stiff-armed rejection from me. Now it's too late."

We've all had to face the tragic results of our autocratic rule of our vineyard in some relationship or situation. There were repeated overtures from God to help us, but we refused. We've had to live with the shambles we caused. A realistic appraisal of life results in our acceptance of the mess we have made of portions of our vineyard. Each one of us knows. And so does God.

Jesus' words at the conclusion of the parable sound a warning. "Therefore I say to you, the kingdom of God will be taken away from you, and be given to a nation producing the fruit of it" (Matt. 21:43). We are amazed that the chief priests and the Pharisees were able to identify themselves as the vine growers of the parable. "And when the chief priests and the Pharisees heard His parables, they understood that He was speaking about them" (v. 45). But it did not lead to repentance. Instead of accepting Him as the Son of the vineyard, they sought to seize Him.

If we end the chapter here we would be realistic but not very remedial. There's more to the parable if we look once more at its meaning from the perspective of Easter and Pentecost.

We must go back to the tower for that. Look! There's another figure coming through the pass. As he gets close enough to distinguish his features, we recognize that he looks just like the Son. We go down to meet him. What can we do to him? When we stand face to face we realize who He is. Notice the nail prints in His hands, the spear wound in His side. He came back!

The final point of the parable then is that God's love knows no limits. The same God who judges us righteously, will not let us go. There is no failure, sin or arrogant demand to run the vineyard that He will not forgive if we ask Him. The indefatigable love of God keeps on persisting. The Resurrection tells us that. The power of Pentecost reassures us that nothing can defeat the love of God. The living Lord returns to the vineyard of our lives. Now the grace of Calvary is His warrant of possession. God's love never gives up. As long as we live and can breathe a breath, there's a new chance to invite Him into the vineyard and say, "Lord, this is your vineyard. It's never belonged to me even though I've acted as if it did. Forgive me. Thank you for your persistence and all of the overtures of love I've rejected." And His response is gracious, but firm. "You belong to me. Let us enjoy the vineyard together!"

Now we know the incomprehensible love He has for us and the lengths He will go to reach us. His faithfulness is the only sure thing we know and can build our lives on with any confidence.

What can we say? The psalmist has given wings to our grateful hearts.

> "Praise the Lord, all nations;
>   Laud Him, all peoples!
> For His lovingkindness is great toward us,
> And the truth of the Lord is everlasting.
> Praise the Lord!" (Ps. 117).

27

Ready, Aye, Ready!

Matthew 25:1-13:
Parable of the Wise and Foolish Bridesmaids

There's a chicory coffee concentrate from Scotland that provides a delightful bit of memory of my student days in Edinburgh. On the label is a picture of a kilted Scots regiment guard. The motto of the regiment is printed above the imposing, armed, prepared-for-battle highlander. "Ready, Aye, Ready!"

Not a bad motto for the beginning of a day. It usually sparks some interesting breakfast conversation at our house about the challenges of the day ahead. Often, when my wife asks me how I am and what's anticipated in the day before me, I put on a thick, studied Scottish burr and chant with gusto, "Ready, aye, ready!"

I would really like to mean that for every day and all of life. I'd love to be the kind of person who's ready for anything. Each day brings its unanticipated opportunities, serendipities and problems. I want to live to the hilt in each of them.

That's not possible unless we expect and hopefully anticipate meeting the Lord in each new day. He gives the day and He will show the way. Disappointments become appointments for Him to give new direction. Difficult people are gifts for new dependence on the Lord for what He will give to meet the trying relationships of life. Perplexities are the prelude to receiving new power from the resourceful Lord. He comes each day with the gift of joy.

Robert Louis Stevenson was right: "To miss the joy is to miss all." Joy is so much more than happiness. It is the result of the experience of grace—God's unmerited favor and changeless love. I am convinced that there's reason for joy in all the delights and difficulties of life. Joy springs forth whenever we experience the intervention of the Lord, maximizing the triumphs and tragedies of life. He brings good out of difficulties and multiplies our pleasures into blessings. He wants us to look for Him to invade the events of each day; to put joy in the joyless drudgery of life. We don't know what any day will bring. To be "ready, aye, ready" for life's surprises is demanding. It means being in good spiritual condition, with our prayer muscles well exercised.

I have a friend who precedes any significant statement she makes with, "Are you ready for this?" The question is a good one. How ready are we for what will happen to us and around us? So often I have heard people say, "I just was not ready for that! I was all set for the worst that could happen. I was caught off guard. I never expected something good to happen!" The lack of preparedness can minimize the truly creative experiences of life. We can become so negative that we expect the worst and are almost disappointed if it doesn't happen.

Our Lord wants a prepared and expectant people.

Ready to be "surprised by joy" as C.S. Lewis expressed it. Christ has called us to be adventurers who have trusted the future to Him and anticipate His interventions in the most unexpected places and situations.

The parable of the wise and foolish bridesmaids is the parable of preparedness for joy. It focuses the quality of unreserved, willing, hopeful anticipation Jesus wanted in His disciples, and now in us.

Here is another dimension of Jesus' autobiography of God. He is a God who breaks into life. He came in the Messiah, He will return in the Second Coming, and He comes daily, hourly, momentarily.

The Bridegroom had become a symbolic image of God Himself, and Israel the bride. It was in this context that Jesus told this very dramatic parable. The twist at the end was for those who were not prepared for the establishment of the Kingdom of God. They longed for the Messiah to come. When He came they were not ready. Nor would they be receptive when He would come again. Our calling is to be ready to receive Him. Preparedness to experience joy is the vocation of the Christian.

I interpret this to be one of Jesus' most positive parables. He taught it at the end of His ministry in response to the disciples' frightened questions about the future. Would the Lord return? How soon? What would be the signs? What was going to happen to them? Preparation for His ultimate return meant that they were also prepared for His penultimate, repeated returns as the reigning Lord of history. "Lo, I will be with you always" (see Matt. 28:20), in *all* ways! Concern for the last days was not to preclude readiness for each day. "Be on the alert then, for you do not know the day nor the hour" (Matt. 25:13).

Most interpretations of this parable are grim and

283

focused on judgment. There is fear in the Lord's return and a threat of accountability only if we have put off becoming prepared with honest confession, commitment to Him, and willingness to expose all facets of life to Him. If we have nothing to hide, we will want Him and long for His coming. There is joy in judgment for those who spend each day in preparation for the midnight hour.

The parable of the bridemaids is a parable of sheer joy. Weddings were a time of joyous celebration. Background is always helpful. The festivities lasted a whole week. Regular duties and religious obligations were dispensed with by law so that the wedding party and all guests could relish the full delight of the occasion. The high point of the week of wedding celebration was when the bridegroom came to the bride's home to take her to their new home. Great pageantry and drama had become a part of the tradition surrounding this event. The bride would ask 10 of her friends to be bridesmaids. Their special task was to be part of the processional from her house to her new marriage home. Usually this took place at night, so the major responsibility of the bridesmaids was to carry lamps to light the joyous way of the wedding party. The time when the bridegroom would come was kept a secret. It was to be a surprise, and the bride and her bridesmaids were to be waiting expectantly.

Jesus built His story with dramatic skill. The bridesmaids waited patiently for the bridegroom. Soon the exhaustion of the exciting festivities, coupled with the long wait, made them sleepy. One of the things a bridegroom would try to do was to catch the bridal party napping. The bridegroom was required by custom to send a courier ahead of him shouting, "Behold, the bridegroom! Come out to meet him" (v. 6). The bridesmaids were to be alert and out in the street, ready to meet him. Because the time of his arrival was uncertain, a great deal of humor and fun surrounded the time of his advent.

The parable has a gripping conclusion. The ten bridesmaids had fallen asleep, their lamps burning brightly. They all look alike as we observe them. They all slept, and they all had their lamps aflame. But as the hours went by, five of the lamps began to flicker and went out. Five of the bridesmaids had not prepared for the long wait. When the bridegroom's crier announced his coming, and all bridesmaids were awakened, five were not prepared to meet him. What to do? How tragic to miss the one thing for which they had planned and hoped for so long!

The wisdom of the wise and the folly of the foolish bridesmaids was that some were prepared for the joy of the coming of the bridegroom and the others were not. Five had not brought extra oil for their lamps. Frustrated frenzy ensued. They tried to borrow oil from the five who were prepared. They refused. Their supply was just enough for themselves. There was nothing for the unprepared bridesmaids to do but rush off to purchase more oil. They missed the wedding procession. If that were not disappointing enough, when they returned with their lamps replenished, the door of the bridal house was shut. They could not enter the joy of the wedding celebration. It was a custom to close the door of a wedding banquet after the invited guests had entered and not reopen it to strangers or drifters looking for a free meal. No amount of frantic rapping at the door would admit the late but now prepared bridesmaids. They had missed the joy!

Jesus clearly identified Himself as the Bridegroom. Israel, the bride, had not been prepared for His first advent, nor would many be ready for the second. But added to that, after the Resurrection, and through the gift of Pentecost, the Lord would constantly visit His people. Would the disciples, followers, and the chosen people of God be alert? That's the startling question the parable sets before us. Today, tomorrow, and on the ultimate Day of the Lord, will we be prepared? We become prepared for the final joy by being ready to receive the joy of daily interventions.

In the previous chapter we asked: If we were to die today, would we have accomplished our ultimate and unique purpose? The thrust of this chapter, based on the parable of the bridesmaids, is: Are we prepared to live today as if it were our last? If the end purpose of our life is accomplished, we need not fear the end of life; neither the end of the world nor the end of our physical existence. In that liberating assurance, we can be prepared for His surprises today. That's the context in which I want to consider three powerful truths this parable has to teach us.

Consider first the one who prepares us for the coming of the Bridegroom Himself. It may sound redundant, but it's true: preparation to receive the Bridegroom is to have a relationship with the Bridegroom. We look at the message of this parable through the dilating lens of Easter and Pentecost. The Lord who taught this startling parable rose from the dead and returned in the power of the Holy Spirit. Jesus was the portrait of the Father. He is also our portrait of the Holy Spirit. The Holy Spirit is no other than the Spirit manifested in the life of Jesus. The eternal Spirit who created all things, blessed and called Israel to be His people, dwelt bodily in fullness in Jesus Christ. The Holy Spirit unleashed at Pentecost is none other than the living, holy God whom we know through what He revealed Himself to be in Jesus of

Nazareth. His ministry is to teach us all that Jesus said and did. To make the gospel real and unresistible. From within us, in our hearts, the Holy Spirit gives the gift of faith to accept what God has done for us in Christ, and then to make us expectant of the Lord's interventions in our daily lives.

St. Bernard explains this vividly in his description of the monks. "However early they would wake and rise for prayer in their chapels on a cold midwinter morning, or even in the dead of night, they would always find God awake before them, waiting for them—nay, it was He who had awakened them to seek His face."

That's it! The Lord prepares us for what He's prepared for us.

The unprepared bridesmaids had not utilized previous experience of the custom of the coming of the bridegroom. They should have known they needed extra oil as much as a bridesmaid knows what her duties are at a wedding today. Only knowledge of the bridegroom could have prepared the foolish maids to be ready to acknowledge his coming, however late.

The oil of the Holy Spirit, the indwelling Christ, prepares us with expectancy and anticipation for the breakthrough of the Lord in each day's experiences. The old folk tune articulates the appropriate prayer in the light of that. "Give me oil in my lamp, keep me burning. Give me oil in my lamp, I pray. Keep me burning till the break of day." The song then goes on to joyously anticipate the Lord's coming: "Come Hosanna, Come Hosanna!" To desire oil in our lamps results in the expectant desire of Hosanna, the Lord.

The Christians I know who have been filled with the oil of the Holy Spirit are bright and radiant Christians. They want the Lord, long for His interventions, expect them and are ready for them in the complexities and confusion of life. They are constantly on the lookout. What is the Lord saying to me in this? What is He trying to teach me in this problem? How will He come into this opportunity and enable me to grasp its full potential?

Being filled with the Holy Spirit makes us ready-for-anything Christians. We can say, "Let life happen! Let it come with winter winds and its disappointments; its springtime of unanticipated delight; its arduous days and restless nights. We are ready! We are open to grow, agile to regroup, free to fail, willing to cut our losses and able to surge ahead."

John Arthur Gossip put it this way: "The life in God is rich and ample beyond all description. For anything and everything there is in Christ is ours for the taking and the using; it is indeed pressed eagerly upon us. And God's generosity is inexhaustible and never tires; keeps heaping grace on grace upon us, far beyond our reckoning."

How is it then, that some miss what God wants to give? They go through the drabness of daily duties unimpressed and uninspired by the repeated invitation of the Lord. He comes to us in people, speaks to us in uncertainties and reveals His power in our inadequacies. Yet many are unaware. Life moves aimlessly toward an uncertain end.

But then a crisis stabs us awake! Thank God for life's crises which focus reality. The tragedy, however, is that we can't get ready for a crisis in the midst of the crisis.

That's the second great truth Jesus teaches us in the parable of the bridesmaids. We cannot borrow preparedness. When the startling announcement of the bridegroom's coming awakened the bridesmaids, five were unprepared and tried to borrow oil for their lamps from the five wise bridesmaids. "Give us some of your oil, for our lamps are going out" (v. 8). The lamps were wooden staffs with a dish on top in which was placed a piece of rope or wick dipped in oil. Extra oil was usually carried to replenish the oil in the dish.

It's the lack of that extra supply that exposes the folly of the foolish. Their urgent request was for a portion of the supply brought along by the wise, prudent bridesmaids. The crisis was that there was not enough oil for all 10 to complete the procession to the bridal home. If the prudent maids gave some of their reserve to the foolish, imprudent maids, all 10 lamps would go out before the night's task was complete. That's the reason for the decisive reply: "No, there will not be enough for us and you too; go instead to the dealers and buy some for yourselves" (v. 9). That sounds cruel and insensitive, but in reality it's an honest statement about life's crises.

We were all alarmed when New York City's power system failed recently. There was a profound message in the tragic event. On the night of the blackout the New York metropolitan area was sweltering under a blanket of hot, humid air. With air conditioners running everywhere, the electricity load was exceptionally high. A severe thunderstorm knocked out main lines which fed electricity to the city. The computers failed to react quickly enough to make up for the loss. But the real problem was that New York City could not "borrow" enough power from other parts of the country and Canada. *Time* magazine, the following week, tried to explain the malady in an article entitled, "Why the Lights Went Out." That could be an apt title for this parable of unpreparedness.

Jesus wanted His listeners to grapple with the same question. Why did the lights of the foolish maids go out? Why do we run out of power today? We can't borrow the power of the Holy Spirit from others; we must be filled for ourselves. Without Him, the lights will go out at the midnight hour of opportunity and challenge. The time to get ready is before, not during the demanding moment. If we are ready, we can take it!

Shakespeare expressed this clearly:

There is a tide in the affairs of men
Which, taken at the flood, leads on to fortune.
Omitted, all the voyage of their life
Is bound in shallows and in miseries
On such a full sea are we now afloat
And we must take the current when it serves
Or lose our ventures.[1]

So many of us lose our ventures, miss our God-appointed opportunity, because we are unprepared to see and grasp the moment. The Holy Spirit helps us discern what is primary and crucial. He gives us the gift of wisdom to see the Lord's approach and open ourselves to be participants in His strategy.

We wonder why some Christians are more effective and useful than others. We try to explain it that they have unusual talents and have been given spectacular gifts. Not so! God is constantly looking for willing, cooperative, daring people who will believe that there is nothing which is impossible for Him. Most of us live with second, third or fourth best, because we are unprepared for the propitious moment when the Lord calls. The life of the saint is not marked by great deeds performed by human skill, but by miracles which result from the Lord's intervention.

The parable ends with a sad reality. The foolish bridesmaids scurry off to buy oil for their lamps, and return to the bridal celebration, only to find that the doors are closed. The moment of opportunity is past. It will never come again. That's the third urgent truth Jesus taught in the parable.

There is no more pathetic, poignant picture in Scripture than the five foolish maids standing at the door, rapping with importunity, lights now blazing brightly. They can hear the joy of the wedding banquet, the laughter, the music and dancing. But the door is closed.

Tennyson caught the pathos of the closed door:

Late, late, so late! And dark the night and chill!
Late, late, so late! But we can enter still.
Too late, too late! Ye cannot enter now.
No light had we: for this we do repent;
And learning this, the bridegroom will relent.
Too late, too late! Ye cannot enter now.
No light: So late! And dark and chill the night!
O let us in that we may find the light!
Too late, too late! Ye cannot enter now.
Have we not heard the bridegroom is so sweet?
O let us in, tho' late, to kiss his feet!
No, no, too late! Ye cannot enter now.[2]

Jesus was saying much more about human nature than about God's graciousness. There is a time when it's too late. Not for God, but for us. The abundant life is offered to us. We can miss the overtures of God each day. But the issue is that repeated resistance results in a life which cannot appropriate the invitation to live forever with God after death. If we constantly say no to Him in our daily lives, it will be impossible to say yes when the midnight hour of our physical demise occurs.

But in another perspective, it's never too late, not as long as we can breathe a breath and listen to the warning of this parable. It sounds the alarm. Here is God's personal word. Are we ready? Why not settle that once and for all! The tragic unpreparedness of the bridesmaids need not be our condition.

I have often lingered on the portion of the parable which stresses the late arrival of the bridegroom. Could it be a sign of grace? What if the foolish bridesmaids had awakened before the bridegroom came, and found that they didn't have enough oil for the long night or the procession? They could have realized their folly and hurried off to get extra oil before the bridegroom's arrival. That may not be intended in the parable, but it's certainly implied for us.

I am very aware of the times God has waited in order for me to get ready to receive His joy in either a tragedy or a triumph of life. Repeatedly I have had to confess, "Lord, if that had happened any sooner, I would not have been prepared. Thanks for waiting until I was ready to wait on you!"

Isaiah 30:18 is more than a memory verse now. It is an affirmation of the Lord's perfectly timed drama of my life. "Therefore the Lord waits to be gracious to you; therefore he exalts himself to show mercy to you. For the Lord is a God of justice; blessed are all those who wait for him" *(RSV)*. I pray that I will never presume on His graciousness. He gives me so many chances to get ready for what He has to give!

The question we must answer is, Are we sharing the joy of the Bridegroom right now? Or are we standing outside, feeling excluded and unacceptable?

That need not be our condition. The parable zeros in on us, not at the door seeking entrance, but at the time of our invitation to join the wedding party. It is the hour of preparation right now. Perhaps it's not as late as we thought. We can receive the oil of preparedness in full measure right now. The Holy Spirit is infringing on our consciousness. We can be filled, in fact, Paul commanded us to "be filled with the Spirit" (Eph. 5:18). The result will be a new preparedness for life—now and forever.

Once we have received the limitless power of the Lord within we will be ready for His approach around us. Right at this moment the good news is being sounded, "Behold, the Bridegroom is coming!" It's an exciting delight to be able to say, "Lord, I'm ready! Ready for anything and anyone! Lead on!"

And what we do with the gift of joy where He leads us will determine how long we will keep it. That's the demanding issue of the next chapter.

Notes

1. Julius Caesar, Act IV, scene iii.
2. The novice's song to Guinevere in "The Idylls of the King."

28

The Secret Source of Joy

Matthew 25:14-30: Parable of the Talents

The man across the lunch table didn't need to tell me. It was written on his face and expressed in his body language.

He went on to explain: "I used to be a joyous Christian. When I committed my life to Christ, I was flooded with a tremendous feeling of joy. But it didn't last. Now my faith is bland, my prayers are routine, and life is flat again. What's wrong? I wish you could help me find the joy I used to have."

The man's plea is one I hear a lot as I talk personally with Christians. How would you have answered him?

I responded with some questions. "What did you do to share your joy when you had it? What risks did you take in following the Master? What evidence of reproductivity is there? Were you involved in the adventure of sharing your faith? Can you identify anyone who is going to live forever because of you? Were you involved with people who were hurting? Did you ever feel the satisfaction of being a reconciler in broken relationships? Did your faith make a difference where you live —at home, at work, or in the aching problems of our community?"

My friend was shocked. He had not realized that joy is one thing you can keep only as you give it away by multiplying it in others, and in specific situations.

Jesus is concerned not only that we might be ready for joy in His interventions, as we considered in the previous parable, but also that we become adventuresome investors of His gift of joy. He follows His parable of the wise and foolish bridesmaids with the parable of the talents. The Lord was deeply concerned about what the disciples would do with the abundant life He had taught, modeled and entrusted to them. The parable unlocks the secret source of lasting joy.

Another aspect of the autobiography of God awaits our thoughtful discovery. The parable of the talents tells us about the creative God who calls us to be co-creators with Him in His evolving strategy in history. He expects a return on His investment in us. Our continuing experience of joy is dependent on that. It will be renewed constantly as we share His ongoing work in the world. That's what my joyless friend needed to learn. And so do we.

The parable of the talents was based on a familiar custom in Jesus' day. Local provincial leaders of the far-flung Roman empire often journeyed to Rome to lobby for continued power or when a new emperor took the reins of the empire. While they were away they entrusted their responsibilities to subordinates.

Once again, Jesus builds a parable on a known to

teach an unknown and unexpected truth. The end of His earthly ministry was on His mind. Several of His last parables are focused in the dramatic illustration of persons who go away leaving their investments, vineyard or kingdom in the care of trusted servants.

In the parable of the talents, it is a "man" who set out on a journey. Before he departed he entrusted to his servants his property. It's important from the onset that we clearly identify that *Man*. He is God. The Lord who owns the world. He reclaimed it in the Saviour Himself. The disciples are the servants. They expected Jesus to announce the imminent beginning of the Kingdom of God on earth. When He announced that He was going up to Jerusalem, they were sure the time had come for Jesus to take over with triumph and victory. The disciples had not been listening. Now the Lord had to prepare them for Calvary and His departure—and return. The Kingdom would come indeed, but in and through the disciples in a way they had not yet grasped. The creator God who had come to redeem the world would come again.

Jesus knew He was going away. The cross was ahead, and after that His resurrection, ascension and the anxious wait for Pentecost. But He would be back! From our perspective we know that. The parable was a needed message for the disciples. No less for us. It is our story too. As before in the other parables, Jesus has us entwined in the characters, and we are moved to find ourselves in the parable.

"For it will be as when a man going on a journey called his servants and entrusted to them his property" (Matt. 25:14, *RSV*). Three of the servants are singled out. One is given five talents, another two talents, and still another one talent. A talent is worth about $1,000 in our money. Quite a trust! We are tempted to focus too long on the diversity and seeming inequality of the trust. It is important to keep in mind that a talent was a very significant amount of money. Whether $5,000, $2,000 or $1,000, all three servants had a lot to work with while the master was gone. They were expected to invest and multiply what each was given.

Jesus has drawn us into the story with an unspoken but inherent question. What would you have done with your legacy? The first two went out with industrious verve and traded with the money. They bought and sold until they had doubled their investment. One man now had $10,000; the other $4,000.

Our eyes turn to the one-talent man. The parable was told to expose him. Everything else is stage setting; everyone else supporting characters. He was cautious, frugal and afraid. He took his talent and hid it in the ground. There were no banks at this time, as we learned in the parable of the treasure hidden in the field. The ground was the only place one could hide money and jewels. But even if there had been a bank, this servant would have put his talent in a safety deposit box and not in a savings account or a fast-return investment plan. He would take no chances with his master's money. The possibility of failure was like an icy fist about his heart. He could not risk!

"Now after a long time the master of those servants came and settled accounts with them" (v. 19, *RSV*). The five- and two-talent men offer him the results of their hard work. The master now has $14,000 from their adventuresome, daring investments and trading. Notice the money never belonged to the servants. The whole amount is returned to the master. The pleasure of their accomplishment came from the excitement of serving him and for his approbation: "Well done, good and faithful servant; you have been faithful over a little, I will set you over much; enter into the joy of your master" (v. 21, *RSV*).

The one-talent man hangs back with customary reticence. He is not eager like the other two. Smarting under the affirmation given them, he is quickly formulating his defensive explanation of what he had not done with his talent. We are astonished at his ready projection when he's called to report. "Master, I knew you to be a hard man, reaping where you did not sow, and gathering where you did not winnow; *so I was afraid*, and I went and hid your talent in the ground. Here you have what is yours" (vv. 24,25, *RSV*, italics added).

The response of the master is severe. Or is it? The servant blamed his master for his own unproductivity. That always brings a sharp retort. "You wicked and slothful servant! You knew that I reap where I have not sowed, and gather where I have not winnowed? Then you ought to have invested my money with the bankers, and at my coming I should have received what was my own with interest. So take the talent from him, and give it to him who has ten talents" (vv. 26-28, *RSV*).

The servant had completely miscalculated his master, whose chief concern was multiplication of his investment. The servant had made the critical judgment of him about sowing and reaping where he had not planted and winnowed. Actually, just the opposite was true for the master in his relationship with the servants. He had sown generously with his investment in all three of the servants. As for winnowing, the master had graciously left the servants in charge of sorting the chaff from the wheat of alternative possibilities of developing his investment. The servant had projected his fear and pressed an image on the master to protect his own frightened self-image. The master dealt out punishment according to the servant's idea of what he was like. That makes us wonder about our projected ideas of God and His judgment of us.

The parable of the talents requires bifocal vision. A long look back to what it meant to the disciples and a magnified look at what the Lord is saying to us.

The word talent came into our language from this parable. It has come to mean natural endowments and special gifts. We must be careful not to interpret the parable on the evolved meaning of talent over the years. Instead, we must ask: What did Jesus mean by the talent? What liberating legacy did He entrust to the disciples? For our consideration here, our talent is whatever our Lord has entrusted to us in order to live our faith and duplicate its power in others. I want to suggest that for us the talent is the gift of the abundant life Jesus entrusts to us. Daring to live it and sharing it with others is the qualification of "entering the joy of the Master." The parable of the talents flows swiftly and naturally around the words adventure, ambition, accountability, approbation and abundance.

We have been called into a high adventure. The Christian life is not just the conservation of values, but a confrontation with opportunity. We have been loved, forgiven and healed in order to join with the Lord in the Kingdom business. We have all been talented for that. Far too much has been made of the inequality of endowment in expositions of the parable. To have the one talent of the abundant life is beyond our deserving or expectation.

Our natural endowments, plus the gift of the indwelling Spirit, make us the spiritually wealthy of the world. All that we have is a trust. It does not belong to us. It's all equipment for the adventure. Anyone who has been given the gift of faith to accept and appropriate the grace of God in Christ, His death for us and His living presence with us, is talented beyond measure.

Do you think of Christianity as an adventure? For many of us it is a set of creeds, rules and regulations, the institutional church and dreary obligations. No wonder we identify readily with the servant who hid his talent in the ground. We think of our faith as part of maintaining the sanity of the status quo. If we can just get through our lives without too many crises or stretching challenges, we will be satisfied. We want to do reasonably well at our profession, raise a decent family, keep out of trouble and retire comfortably. If we show neither gain nor loss on the ledger sheet, at least we have the talent with which we started.

But what shall we say to a God of risk? He risked all in the Incarnation and in entrusting the Kingdom advance to a few humanly undistinguished Galileans. He is always out ahead, calling us out of our safe security. There is no continuing joy without risk.

We inventory our hidden talent—our minds, emotions, personalities, relationships and unlimited opportunities. All provided for us to enjoy and share the abundant life. Milton talked about "fugitive and cloistered virtue." There is a great deal of energy spent worrying over our buried talent—all in the name of normalcy which becomes mediocrity. Many Christians in the church have buried their talent in beautifully carved boxes of religious activity. We place flowers over the place of the burial and devise rituals of beatification on our caution and conservation. The institutional church is too often the sacred burial ground of entrusted talents. We forget that the church exists to multiply the talent of the abundant life in the world.

The Lord wants ambitious disciples. The word has become tainted in our time. Preaching and teaching over the years have made ambition antithetical to authentic spirituality. The question is the focus of our ambition. If it is for Christ and His cause, it is baptized with His affirmation and power.

Our Lord wants to maximize the years of our life. It is exciting when we feel an urgent purpose which demands the best we believe and can give. Ambition to do God's will gives vitality and dynamics to life.

The word ambition comes from the Latin word *ambitio*—to go around. It means eager movement around the opportunities of life in order to achieve a desired goal. I believe it is a God-given verve to achieve and accomplish. It is distorted when it is used for self-aggrandizement or our own plans and purposes for popularity or power. But the Lord gave us the endowment to experience fellowship with Him in attacking the needs of people and society. We have our life to live. What do we want to accomplish with it? We are only one person, and cannot do all that needs to be done. The lethargy of others around us often gives us the wrong benchmark. What we cannot do dissuades us from doing what we can. Like the one-talent man in the parable, we do little or nothing because others seem so much more gifted. Because we cannot be spectacular, we refuse to be significant in our assigned realm. Soon we blame others, conditions or our circumstances. Eventually we blame God. It's a dangerous thing to stifle ambition. When we smother our urge to achieve, we suppress our creativity. God can guide a moving person. He can take a person like Paul, who had the wrong expression of his ambitious nature, and change his direction so he can say, "How changed are my ambitions. All I want to know is Christ!"

If you are an ambitious person, don't negate it. God can take that desire to achieve and accomplish and use

301

it to build the Kingdom. If ambition has enabled you to be a success, then surrender the opportunities your realm of responsibility gives you. The Lord knows that human positions of power and influence can be used for His glory if we will entrust them to Him. In every company, community, or structure of society, there are people in strategic positions who have an opportunity to affect the lives of millions. The church and society can be dramatically changed if we thank God for the ambition He has entrusted to us to spread the abundant life.

Kenneth Hahn is a powerful leader in Los Angeles. As a supervisor on the County Board of Supervisors, he has spectacular influence. The Lord has given ambition to succeed and lead. A committed Christian, Kenny knows that he is where he is by the grace of God. Not only does he carry on his continuing responsibilities with prayer and momentary dependence on God, but he is aggressively working to expand the work of the Kingdom in our area. He has earned the right to be heard and followed. His power is used for immense good.

Last year during the holidays, when clergy of all faiths are extremely busy, he was able to gather the Christian, Jewish, and Moslem leaders of our megalopolis on a few hours' notice for a prayer meeting on the Middle East crisis. The news media responded and covered the event. The meeting unified our city around a common concern. As we left the meeting, one leader was heard to remark, "Only Kenny Hahn could have pulled this off!"

But you may be tempted to exclaim, "That's fine for him in his position, but what about me? I have no power." And yet, the biblical record and the historical account of Christianity's amazing expansion indicates that God used ordinary people to do extraordinary things because they did not deny the motivating power of ambition to do God's work, on His power, and for His honor and glory. Each of us has an irreplaceable calling in God's plan. Two things are required: to ask God what He wants us to do, and do it whether anyone else does or not.

When we understand Jesus' use of talent as our abundant relationship with Him and the authority to communicate His love to others, then we are all talented. The five- and two-talent men of the parable are used only to set the stage for the one-talent man's refusal to use and invest his talent. The point of the parable is for those of us who may not consider ourselves especially endowed with human capacities. If we have met the Saviour and allowed Him to live His life through us, we have been talented beyond calculation. The authentic test that we know and love Him will be our unquenchable ambition to be sure that the people around us know about the possibility of an abundant life.

Christ-motivated ambition is always coupled with relational sensitivity. It does not press the faith on loved ones and acquaintances without a caring relationship for the whole person. We are not ambitious to earn the Lord's approval, but daring because we already have it.

The parable of the talents clearly teaches that we are accountable for the way we use the talent of the abundant life. The master of the servants returned for an accounting. Christ returned in the power of the Holy Spirit to not only enable the ministry of the infant early church, but to assure a return on the investment of the church's stewardship of the new life. We are accountable every day, and on the ultimate day when we leave this phase of eternal life to go on to the next. The daily and final question when we die physically is: What have we done with the talent entrusted to us? As was the case with the talent-burying servant, excuses and projected blame will not do. God has sown the gospel in us. He has winnowed the chaff from the grain in life's challenges to give us human illustrations from our own experience, so that we might share what Christ can mean for others. He does expect reproduction! There will be no lasting joy if we bury our talent in the ground of refusal.

Recently I was shocked to learn that 97 percent of the people in the Hollywood area have no church home and do not attend regularly. Eighty seven percent of the San Fernando Valley suffers from the same lack. The statistics for the Los Angeles basin are no better. This means that there are people who do not know Christ and the joy of Christian fellowship where the members of my congregation live and work.

This motivated us to start a program called "Operation Come and See." It's based on John 1:45. Philip shared his excitement about Christ with Nathanael and asked him to go with him to hear the Master. Nathanael's response was "Can any good come out of Nazareth?" Winsome Philip's simple answer was "Come and see" (v. 46).

We asked our people to identify seven people out of the staggering percentage to come to church with them; to "come and see," and to hear about the abundant life. Not a lot to ask of people who have enjoyed the gospel and a dynamic church for years.

The most gratifying thing to me is how many church members dug up their talent and used it. In many cases it had been dormant in the ground of respectable churchmanship for years. Relationships with friends, neighbors, and fellow workers were established on a deeper level. Conversations about what a faith in Christ means flowed naturally before and after the contemporary Nathanaels were brought to church. A point of

304

shared reference about deeper things had been established. Now people who had been afraid to witness in the more traditional ways became identified among their associates as people who could be counted on for spiritual help. Many of them have been instrumental in following up on the "come and see" visitors.

At the conclusion of our worship services, a group of elders joins me in the chancel to talk with people who want to meet Christ, unite with the church, or receive help with specific personal needs. I am always amazed by the number of people who confess that they needed a chance to talk about the abundant life. Though they knew Christians around them in life, they did not feel an open receptivity to talk with them about Christ. So often we think of evangelism as buttonholing people. I am convinced that if we have a vital faith to share, and care prayerfully for people, we will have more opportunities to communicate the reason for the hope in us than time will permit.

And if we don't, there will be an accounting. We have been given the keys of the Kingdom. We can bind people by hiding our talent, or unloose them by sharing it.

Approbation was given to the servants in the parable who multiplied the master's legacy. We feel the warmth of his affirmation. Those who doubled his investment were invited to enter into his joy. The joy of companionship and the delight of shared industry are implied. The master and the productive servants were cooperating in a great enterprise.

What the master said to the reproductive servants, the Lord wants to say to us. Well done. Excellent! You are a devoted, full-of-faith, persistent and venturesome steward of the life I lived and died to provide. In sharing what you have, you have allowed my joy-beat to be the pulse of your heart. You have been faithful in this; now I will give you greater opportunities.

I have been in the adventure of caring about people for nearly 30 years. Without reservation, I can say that the most joyous moments of my life are after I have been midwife to a spiritual birth of a person. Sometimes it happens after brief friendship with a person; other times it takes months—even years—of persistent caring, involvement, and sharing of burdens and opportunities before the sacred moment occurs. All the other things I do as preacher, teacher, writer and administrator of a large church program have their significance only as this central privilege is appropriated. Whatever else I do, and much of it is exciting and satisfying, unless it leads to transformed lives through personal encounters, I will have accomplished little.

Many people long for greater opportunities and gratifying assignments. The Lord cannot trust us with much if we have been unfaithful with little. The faithful servants of the parable were elevated because they had done the basic essential. The same is true for us.

That leads to the final but extremely disturbing conclusion of the parable. It's what I call the law of "accumulative abundance." The Lord's voice is clearly heard through the master of the servants. "For to everyone who has shall more be given, and he shall have an abundance; but from the one who does not have, even what he does have shall be taken away" (Matt. 25:29). A hard saying. And yet it is an undeniable spiritual law. Just as our minds diminish if we refuse to think, our muscles become flabby if we do not exercise them, and any endowment is lost if we do not practice it, so too we will lose our spiritual joy if we do not communicate it. What we have will be taken away.

That seems negative until we look at the positive aspect of Jesus' verity of "accumulative abundance." When we use what we have been given, it grows in power. The people I know who are joyous Christians are those who have never stopped growing. They can be trusted with fresh insight, wisdom and power. The Lord can replenish a Christian who has used what he has. He can flow through a channel which is not stopped up.

The secret source of joy isn't a secret at all. It's too clear to miss. Jesus is neither ambiguous nor ambivalent. As I finish writing this chapter, He seems to be invading my consciousness for an accountability time. I hope He does the same with you. I welcome the time for a spiritual checkup. If I have shared my joy, I know there will be more to come. But if not . . . .

29

A Voice from the Dead

Luke 16:19-31: Parable of the Rich Man and Lazarus

The funeral service of a good friend lingers in my mind. My grief was not only because I had lost a friend, but because he consistently resisted becoming a Christian. Nothing that I or countless others said or did was able to break the shell of his self-sufficiency. Success and wealth insulated him from the recognition of his need. He was impervious to any efforts to introduce him to Christ and an assurance of eternal life. My friend acted like he would live forever. I believe he did. My concern was where, with whom, and how.

As I sat in the funeral parlor, I looked around at the faces of his family, friends, and business associates. What did they believe about death and an afterlife? Did any of them wonder about his or her own death?

The service was benign. A combination of soothing

music, poetry, and a eulogy which recounted my friend's accomplishments, attainments, and contributions to benevolent causes. Nothing was said about life after death. What could be said?

I wondered what my friend would have said to the gathering of loved ones and acquaintances if he had been able to return and speak about life after death. Would he have warned them, alarmed them, about what it's like to walk through the valley of the shadow of death without a Saviour, and to spend eternity in the irrevocable separation from God? He had not chosen to have a companionship with the Lord in this life. I ached over the fact that now he no longer had a choice.

What if we could hear voices from the dead? What would they tell us? What difference would it make to us? Would some of us be assured and others alarmed? There is growing interest in death and dying today. Accounts of those who have died and come back to life after a few moments have had great fascination for people. We wonder if any of the people whom we have known have ever wanted to come back across the great divide to tell us what they experienced after death. What would they say? Would we listen?

The rich man of Jesus' parable wanted to send a message back to his five brothers. Tradition has named him Dives, the Latin name for rich man. He had died and found himself in the fires of Hades. How he got there is the impelling story called parable of Dives and Lazarus. It is a gripping drama in three acts.

Act One is a study in contrasts. A tableau of the extremities of the rich and the poor. In one sweeping sentence, Jesus characterizes Dives vividly by describing his purple and fine linen. Habitually. He is never seen in any other than the auspicious and ostentatious haberdashery. His linen undergarment coat with long sleeves was probably made of Egyptian flax, often as valuable as gold. The cloak worn over his coat was made of costly purple material. Purple was a sign of royalty or immense wealth. The dye was obtained from the purple fish, a species of mussel, at prohibitive cost to any but the most affluent and powerful.

The way Dives lived was consistent with his clothing. "Gaily living in splendor" (Luke 16:19) are Jesus' words. The Greek words *euphrainomenos lamprōs* mean faring sumptuously or making merry brilliantly and magnificently. The picture is one of limitless wealth and indulgent, luxuriant prosperity.

The most telling aspect of Jesus' description was that Dives fared sumptuously "every day." That means that his feasting and frolic knew no reverence for the Sabbath or special days of fasting and prayer. So much is revealed in these two words "every day." No day was holy for Dives in his secular search for pleasure and satisfaction through all that he could taste and touch.

Lazarus is a startling contrast. He was "covered with sores" of leprosy (v. 20). The pitiful creature seems to contradict his name, which means "God is my help." This parable is the only one in which a character is given a name. The reason will become evident as the drama unfolds. Each day Lazarus is laid, contemptuously dropped (the verb for "was laid," *ebebleto*, implies that he was flung there with contempt and roughness), at Dives' gate to beg for crumbs from the wealthy man's table. The word for gate, *pylōn* in Greek, intensifies the contrast between Dives' splendor and Lazarus' squalor. It means a gate full of magnificent artistry and exquisite beauty. From that we get a picture of what Dives' mansion must have been like. A startling backdrop for Lazarus' pitiful plight. The leper does not even have enough strength to fight off the pariah dogs that lick his puss-oozing sores. We flinch at the vividness of Jesus' portrait. Lazarus is a consistent contretemps to Dives. We can imagine that Dives looked the other way each time he rode through his gates in his magnificently appointed carriage. But soon he did not see Lazarus at all. The narcotic of affluence dulled his sensitivity and awareness. Dives was no longer in touch with the reality that was focused in the anguish about him.

Act One has put us on the edge of our seats. We feel the alarming distortion of life. Pity is the only emotion appropriate for Lazarus' indigence and Dives' insensitivity. Is there no justice? How can God allow this blasphemous inequality? The act comes to an excruciating close with our questions unanswered.

Both Lazarus and Dives die. The disposition of their bodies dramatizes the dreadful disparity of life. Lazarus' body is flung naked on the burning rubbish heap outside the city wall. Dives is buried in a tomb aboveground reserved for the wealthy and powerful. But both men are dead, nonetheless. Death, the grim reaper, is no respecter of persons or position. We feel a heaviness, an indignant anger, as the curtain drops on Act One.

We are astonished by the revolutionary reverses portrayed as Act Two begins. We are ushered into Hades, the realm of departed spirits, in the unseen world beyond the grave. Again the contrasts startle us. Insight from the Hebrew beliefs about the afterlife help us to understand. Paradise and Gehenna were both considered part of Hades. But a great gulf separated the comfort, serenity and peace of Paradise from the torturous, burning fires of Gehenna. Paradise was called Abraham's bosom, a realm of blessed assurance with the patriarch and all the people who were experiencing the reward of beatific bliss. Gehenna, like the burning refuse heap outside of Jerusalem, which burned but was never consumed, was a place of eternal torment in the flames of punishment.

We look closely. Jesus draws the veil and shows us Lazarus in Paradise and Dives in the fires of Gehenna. "Justice at last!" we say to ourselves. We watch Dives' anguish. Exactly what he had coming, we reflect. Our indignation over his blatant neglect of human need during his life subsides a bit as we watch Lazarus enjoying the peace and comfort that life never afforded him here. An uneasiness begins to grow in us, however, as we wonder what implications for us the Lord will draw from this pitiful picture. We are relieved when Act Two draws to a close.

The scenery has not changed, however, as the final act begins. Our attention is riveted on Dives. He realizes where he is and that his condition in the eternal fires is irrevocable. Now he has no power to order underlings to satisfy his every whim and desire. The plight of his condition is intensified by his being able to see beyond the wide, yawning gulf between the fires of Gehenna and the solemnity of Paradise. He sees Lazarus reclining in Abraham's bosom. There are no leprous sores on his body; his face no longer has the pallid, tortured look of hunger. Joy radiates about him like a jewel in the sunshine.

We hear the screech and wrench in Dives' voice as he calls across the great divide. "Father Abraham, have mercy on me, and send Lazarus, that he may dip the tip of his finger in water and cool off my tongue; for I am in agony in this flame" (Luke 16:24). Dives is still giving orders! Imperious and indulgent of self even in hell. Strange twist of destiny: He had thrown bread crumbs out of his window for Lazarus to fight for with the wild alley dogs; now he wanted the liberated leper to cool his fevered tongue!

312

There is tenderness and unwavering firmness in Abraham's response across the abyss. "Child, remember that during your life you received your good things, and likewise Lazarus bad things; but now he is being comforted here, and you are in agony" (v. 25).

Abraham's words flash like lightning in Dives' soul. The thunder which followed was even more devastating to him. The thought of relief from the burning fire drained from his hope that his condition of punishment was temporary. There is a holy righteousness and justice in Abraham's voice as he continues, "And besides all this, between us and you there is a great chasm fixed [the words in Greek mean a huge chasm that has been and remains fixed], in order that those who wish to come over from here to you may not be able, and that none may cross over from there to us" (v. 26).

There is a long silence as the words toll the doom in Dives' soul. That soul has never known love, save for a selfish brand of self-gratification. All expectation of release is gone. His anguish is sealed for eternity.

We wait in breathless anticipation for Dives' response. There is nothing for him to do but remember and regret. As the relentless flames leap about him, the corridors of his mind are occupied by the first selfless thought he has ever entertained. His five brothers! They must be warned about what happens after death; they must be alerted to the fate of those who do not believe, show compassion, or prepare for eternity beyond death's decisive door. There is anguish and alarm in Dives' voice as, once again, he shouts across the fault that divides him from Paradise. "Then I beg you, Father, that you send him to my father's house—for I have five brothers—that he may warn them, lest they also come to this place of torment" (v. 27,28).

Abraham's answer is incisive: "They have Moses and

the Prophets; let them hear them" (v. 29). The Law clearly delineated the ethical life and the prophets had sounded a clarion call for justice, faithfulness, and obedience.

Dives persists with pertinacity: "No, Father Abraham, but if someone goes to them from the dead, they will repent!" (v. 30). Our hearts respond to Dives' plea. We are pulled with pity, strangely siding with this one we observed with angry consternation two acts before. Yes, Abraham, send someone! Warn the people. The people? It is I. You and me. Shock us with the traumatic truth before it's too late!

Abraham's words in response echo with the authority of the majesty and awesomeness of God. "If they do not listen to Moses and the Prophets, neither will they be persuaded if someone rises from the dead."

The curtain closes slowly on the final act as Abraham speaks. We sit motionless. Catatonic. Stunned. What does it all mean? And what can we do about the alarming drama Jesus' parable has played out before our eyes of imagination? The Lord has drawn aside the thick mysterious veil that stands between the here-and-now, and the then-and-forever-after. It has forced us to see not only what is beyond this life, but the inseparable link between life as we live it now, and how we will spend eternity. As we meditate on the stirring parable, and understand it in the context of Jesus' life, message, death, and resurrection, we realize that we have been given a warning which can become the basis of a vibrant hope. We need to ask the Lord to penetrate our minds and hearts with the profound truth He wants to communicate to us. We stand together, writer and reader; the Lord has something to say to us. The truths mount in ascending power and resound in our souls.

The first is too good to be true, and yet too true to be

taken lightly. Jesus has clearly told us that we will all live forever. Immortality is not our choice. Death is not an ending, but a transition in immortal life. When our physical existence ends we will live on in spirit. As we noted earlier, our souls—the life composite of intellect, emotion, and will—are impervious to the power of death. That is both awesome and frightening, the basis of our hope and our deepest anxiety. All fears have their root in the ultimate fear of dying. The question lurks: Where will we spend eternity?

The second truth of the parable follows the first with disturbing clarity. There are two distinct realms of life after death. The Hebrews of Jesus' time had appropriate images which pervade the parable. We have Jesus' total message and the undeniable convictions of the New Testament. Jesus left no room for evasive equivocation about the reality of heaven or hell after death. In the Sermon on the Mount, He admonished, "But lay up for yourselves treasures in heaven, where neither moth nor rust destroys, and where thieves do not break in or steal; for where your treasure is, there will your heart be also" (Matt. 6:20,21). He came proclaiming the kingdom of heaven, and called people to begin a relationship with God which death could not end. His prayers were to "Our Father who art in heaven" (Matt. 6:9). Our ultimate reward was to be in heaven, and the Lord assured His disciples, "Let not your heart be troubled; believe in God, believe also in Me. In My Father's house are many dwelling places; if it were not so, I would have told you; for I go to prepare a place for you. And if I go and prepare a place for you, I will come again, and receive you to Myself; that where I am, there you may be also" (John 14:1-3). On the cross, our Lord asserted His authority and promised the penitent thief that he would be with Him in Paradise.

But Christ's teaching about hell was no less vivid. He spoke of the "hell of fire" (Matt. 5:22) and the danger of being "cast into hell" (Mark 9:45). People were stunned by His directness about Satan's beguiling power to distort their potential for heaven. "And do not fear those who kill the body, but are unable to kill the soul; but rather fear Him who is able to destroy both soul and body in hell" (Matt. 10:28). Jesus was deeply concerned about anything in our lives which keeps us from ultimate commitment to God. "And if your hand or your foot causes you to stumble, cut it off and throw it from you; it is better for you to enter life crippled or lame, than having two hands and two feet, to be cast into eternal fire" (Matt. 18:8). The Pharisees' resistance and hostility brought forth the undeniable reality of hell in Jesus' message. "You serpents, you brood of vipers, how shall you escape the sentence of hell?" (Matt. 23:33).

Clearly, Jesus Christ came to liberate people from the power of Satan and the punishment of hell. Hell is eternal separation from God and all the resources of His love and forgiveness. The Lord came into our fallen creation to save sinners. He put it incisively so there would be no doubt. "For God so loved the world, that He gave His only begotten Son, that whoever believes in Him should not perish, but have eternal life" (John 3:16). The abundant life He lived and offered to those who followed Him was not only for this side of the grave, but forever.

That moves us on to the third salient truth of the parable. What we believe, and what we do about what we believe, determines our eternal destiny. Lazarus did not go to Abraham's bosom because he had been poor, nor Dives to hell fires because he was rich. Dives' destiny was sealed by the gulf which existed in his soul long before he died. The parable teaches us that we will continue in eternity in the spiritual condition in which we have spent the years of our life on earth. The poverty of Dives' life in the midst of uncalculable wealth was that his existence was divided from reality. Long before he experienced the gulf in Hades, there was a gulf between him and an active implementation of however little he believed. We assume he was a Hebrew. As such, he not only neglected the rites and rituals of his religion, but the basic requirements of the Law and the Prophets about care for the poor and needy. He was so completely centered on himself and his possessions that he no longer even saw Lazarus at his gate.

We dare not press the parable too far or have it teach more than Jesus intended. We do not believe that caring for the poor will get us into heaven. But in the light of the other parables on the judgment of God, we are told that whatever we do to the lost, lonely, imprisoned, hungry, and sick, we do to Him.

There is a tragic insensitivity which engulfs us when we divide belief from caring about people. It's usually the result of an inadequate relationship with the Saviour. Belief in Jesus Christ as Lord and Saviour is the basis of an eternal life. But faith without works is dead. As dead as works without faith. We cannot escape the impact of Scripture: the acid test of our faith is in our relationships. Dives had a growing chasm in his inner being. The gulf was between him and God, and that manifested itself in a gulf between Dives and himself. He lost track of a basic morality. Right and wrong became relevant to what served his purposes. Finally, a leprous beggar was an obstruction at his gate—an intrusion on his private world of sumptuous satisfaction. He died out of relationship with God, himself, and people in need.

The pulse of Jesus' message quickens with the fourth

penetrating point of the parable. Our Lord exposes the impotence of death. It is absolutely incapable of destroying the inner person. Dives and Lazarus were alive in Gehenna and Paradise immediately after death. Death did not destroy consciousness, memory, or self-identity. Dives knew himself to be Dives devoid of all the accoutrements of his accumulation. He had the anguishing legacy of remembering what he had been and failed to do. There was no escape. He experienced regret, but could do nothing about it. That's the most disturbing description of the hell of fire imaginable: to spend eternity in the burning flames of remorse and self-incrimination. The only thing worse than that in the parable is Dives' capacity to see across the gulf to what might have been in the joy of fellowship with God.

We know the grief of life's might-have-beens or the if-onlys. But on this side of the grave there is always the hope that we can do or say something to change the regrets of life. Death dashes that hope forever. We will have to live with the person we have become. Dives is the pitiful portrait of the excruciation of the unchangeable, immortal condition. Frightening!

The rich man's sin was one of neglect. What he failed to do was caused by the person he had become. Now he would have to live with that person forever. A burning fire, indeed!

The final thing the parable teaches us is that the demarcation line of death is final, and there can be no communication with those on this side of the grave. The most dreadful experience of hell must be the desire to warn our loved ones about the gulf that is excavated in this life and irreparably set for eternity. We will be able to see what is happening to people we love on this side, but they will not be able to hear us. There have been claims of mysterious manifestations and communications from the dead in dreams and through mediums. These are not enabled by the Holy Spirit but, if at all, by the Evil One.

There is only one voice from the dead. His name is Jesus. He alone has come back. His voice is like "the sound of a trumpet" (Rev. 1:10), and like the "sound of many waters" (Rev. 1:15). He speaks with undeniable, irresistible clarity. "Do not be afraid; I am the first and the last, and the living One; and I was dead, and behold, I am alive forevermore, and I have the keys of death and of Hades" (Rev. 1:17,18).

Abraham's words to Dives, that the living would not listen or be persuaded if someone rises from the dead, are both true and false. Many did not respond to the resurrected Lord when He returned as the vanquisher of death. But many did. They became participants in what history called "the colony of the resurrection." Death had lost its sting because it had no power to destroy the eternal life of their souls; the grave had no victory because it interred only the frail body from which the living spirits of the saints rose at the moment of physical demise. The death rattle was but a portent of the rapture of a relationship among the company of heaven singing "Hallelujah and Amen!" The unconquerable charter of the church was written in the red blood of Calvary and sealed with an empty tomb: "I am the resurrection, and the life; he who believes in Me shall live even if he dies, and everyone who lives and believes in Me shall never die. Do you believe this?" (John 11:25,26).

The question must be answered. Do we believe? Everything, now and forever, depends on how we answer. Abraham was wrong, at least about us. Our basis of eternal hope is in our response to the Voice from the dead. We are persuaded *because* Someone, the Lord Himself, the Author of life, has risen from the dead.

This parable is a fitting climax to our studies of the parables as the autobiography of God. It tells us the ultimate truth about God. He is creator of heaven and earth; and He has given us life on earth so that we can share His life in heaven. Jesus stated it unequivocally: "God is not the God of the dead but of the living" (Matt. 22:32). And that includes you and me. He cannot abide the thought of eternity without us. That's why He came and comes. He lived among us as Immanuel, loved us with prodigal love, died for our sins out of limitless grace, opened the door of heaven, and offers us life without end. All so we could hear and believe the voice from the dead. "And this is eternal life, that they may know Thee the only true God, and Jesus Christ whom Thou hast sent" (John 17:3).